To Mi Dora

Spirit Large!

Juley xx
x
14/08/2021

Oladipo Agboluaje
PLAYS ONE

Introduction by Victor I. Ukaegbu

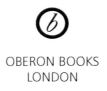

OBERON BOOKS
LONDON

WWW.OBERONBOOKS.COM

First published in this collection 2013 by Oberon Books Ltd
521 Caledonian Road, London N7 9RH
Tel: +44 (0) 20 7607 3637 / Fax: +44 (0) 20 7607 3629
e-mail: info@oberonbooks.com
www.oberonbooks.com

Contents

Introduction

Oladipo Agboluaje belongs arguably to the *third generation* or category of playwrights of African and British heritage[1] whose dramaturgies differ from the writings of first- and second-generation writers of African and Asian descents; the latter's subjects and dramatic styles were shaped and defined primarily by their experiences of colonialism. The works of first-generation writers (poets, novelists and playwrights of mixed African and British heritage in Britain from the late 1930s to the early 1960s were characterised by nostalgia and an interest in pre-colonial histories and cultures broken and fragmented by colonialism. Among these were Jamaican-born poet James Berry, Andrew Salkey and Stuart Hall, Edward Kamau Braithwaite, Wilson Harris, and Edgar Mettleholzer of Guyana, Samuel Selvon, CLR James, and VS Naipaul of Trinidad, and Chinua Achebe and Wole Soyinka of Nigeria. These writers were non-pretentious about their cultural agendas as they set about de-mystifying, explaining, re-interpreting and validating the cultural experiences of pre-colonial societies, their histories and myths. Some of their subjects and themes, although designed to provide readers with authentic representations of pre-colonised cultures, were overtly anti-colonial in sentiments and played on cultural binaries. Others, motivated by a sense of social responsibility and drawn by compulsion to explain the cultures of indigenous societies, produced writings that sought to contest the misrepresentations perpetrated and perpetuated in colonial histories written mostly from the viewpoints of colonial administrators and anthropologists.

Their successors, the second-generation writers among whom are Caryl Churchill, Linton Kwesi Johnson, Buchi Emecheta, Mustapha Mutura, Edgar White, Caryl Phillips, and Hanif Kureishi, set upon a different course, that of retrieving and re-writing pre-colonial, colonial, migrant, and dislocation experiences using the linguistic and narrative tropes of erstwhile colonisers as well as the hybridized languages they produced. Their works conveyed a radical and ideological fervour that was both essential in the development of post-colonialism as a literary and later subsequently as a multidisciplinary, multi-reading framework for analysing the political, social, economic, and literary developments of postcolonial societies. Second-generation writers of African and Asian descents include those born during colonialism and their countries' struggles for independence and those born in the immediate aftermaths of political independence. The Marxist radicalism espoused in some of the writings by second-generation authors of dual heritage is motivated by factors such as the ideological impetus and social activism of their predecessors, resisting cultural hegemonies and homogenisation of their experiences. Another important factor is their rejection of *other* and *marginal*[2] as critical categories for describing their historical experiences in relation to mainstream white society. Their impacts on the literary scene produced a polyglot of writings on new subjectivities and relationships and generated a distinctively British multi-narrative framed by Britain's former colonial enterprise.

Although Black British writing (I'm using the term here in a very broad sense) started with social awakening and occasional apologetics by first-generation writers, second-generation writers resented the second-class citizenship bestowed on non-white communities in Britain. Second-generation writers confronted their marginalisation with bold assertions of their rights of being and inclusion. Some of the changes in writing styles were accomplished through a combination of abrasive self-determinism and cultural radicalisms that Alex Sierz (2001) would describe later as 'in-yer-face'. These approaches and the contributions of social and sociological theorists such as Edward Said (1991) (on Orientalism) and James Stuart Hall (1993) (on Cultural Identity and Diaspora) to mention just a few, inevitably expanded the literary space and subjects of work by writers of African and Asian descents in Britain. Their writings went from them-us, centre-margin and dominant-other binaries to an exploration of postcolonial and postmodern conditions, from social tensions and sub-cultures to resisting racial hegemonies and essentialisms as well as interrogating gender, ideology, identity, sexuality, migration and diaspora, etc from several perspectives.

By the late 1990s postcolonialism and postmodernism changed and expanded the literary space in Britain and globally. Debates continue as to whether postmodernism has rendered postcolonialism 'posthistoric' in which case, the stage of human history it 'claimed to offer explanation and understanding' (Breisach, 2003:10) for has ended. Edward Said (1993) regards postmodernism's claims to a post-history era as another hegemonic instrument designed by the West for global dominance. Existentialism and human conditions, sociocultural relations between individuals and people groups, societal and inter- and intra-community tensions, diaspora concerns and geopolitics are some of the common subjects interrogated in postcolonialism and postmodernism. Whatever their relations both discourses, together, have expanded the space for new writings in prose, poetry, live art, and dramatic texts and have produced, in their wakes, what I consider to be a third generation of writers distinguishable from their first- and second-generation forebears in three important respects. Firstly, while the first generation accepted and lamented their sojourner second-class citizenship, the second generation rejected all that and asserted their rights of citizenship, of belonging and place (see Proctor, 2000 and McMillan, 2006). Secondly, third-generation writers are unequivocal and confident about their place in society; they celebrate their dual heritage with vigour and ideological radicalism, whilst abjuring the angst of their predecessors. Thirdly, third-generation writers and writings adopt different tropes, from indigenous African and Asian conventions as well as from postcolonialism and postmodernism, they draw their subjects and inspirations from both discourses and write specifically for heterogeneous audiences and multicultural societies with different layers of interdependencies. Their constituencies are polyphonic, simultaneously local and diasporic. Even when they historicise particular experiences or are set in *home* continents and societies in Africa, Asia and the Caribbean – as are two of the plays in this volume – their subjects and characters link cultural geographies in a literary space of incredibly diverse stylistic influences in which indigenous, postcolonial and postmodern conventions converge to create a literary topography that is simultaneously local and 'glocal', the term used by Giovanna Buonanno, Victoria Sams and Christane Schlote (2011: 1, 14) to describe British Asian theatre's capacity to mirror cultural peculiarities without losing its global frame.

In the online article 'Black British Literature since Windrush' written as part of the BBC Windrush season for the Summer of 1998, Onyekachi Wambu (1998) highlighted what I consider key characteristics of third-generation Black British writing: 'it announced a literature that would look back to its source, but would be far more self-confident about its own position in Britain. It wouldn't be marginalised as 'Black', 'Commonwealth' or any other kind of literature that put it at the edges. It would be a fully fledged member of the broad range of British writing.' [http://www.bbc.co.uk/history/british/modern/literature_01.shtml.] Their subjects derive directly and indirectly from the unfinished socio-political and cultural agendas started by first-generation but tackled more fully by second-generation writers; existential angsts, social deprivations, problems of agency, racism, identity crisis, racial tensions, diaspora and the politics of migration and dislocation and their off-shoots of family and group dynamics, social fragmentations, cultural radicalism, religious fundamentalism, sexualities and critical self-examination. Third-generation writers are neither segregationist and insular nor motivated by celebrating cultural monolithism and the past. Although rooted in the struggles and subjects of their predecessors, as we see in the works of Fred D'Aguiar, Tunde Ikoli, Paul Boakye, Ayub Khan-Din, Hanif Kureishi, Meera Syal and many more, these writers rewrite Britain (Proctor, 2000; Sierz, 2011) and destabilise hegemonies and geographies of place, time, history and location. In essence, contesting territorialities in what Michael McMillan (2006) describes with regards to Black British writers and performers, as 'reimagining of the self in a cultural and political context, where identities are continuously fragmented and hybridised' (McMillan, 2006: 60).

In this increasingly polyphonic and pluralistic theatrical landscape the number of theatre companies, such as Talawa, Tiata Fahodzi, Tara, and Tamasha that aim their works primarily at more than one of the many sections of Britain's multicultural society, has grown. The creative possibilities for writers and the abundance of materials thrown up by new spaces and historiographies are endless and not lost on Oladipo Agboluaje who, since his debut in 2003, has become one of the most prolific of the third generation of Black British playwrights referred to here. His plays, no less so the five in this volume, *Early Morning, The Estate, The Christ of Coldharbour Lane, The Hounding of David Oluwale,* and *Iyale (The First Wife)*, can be grouped under a distinct category of postcolonial, postmodern writings on Nigerian-British diaspora experiences. The plays reveal distinguishing characteristics that have come to define Agboluaje's dramaturgy. Among these are an over-arching concern for interrogating the impacts of macro conditions on individuals and sections of British society alike, in other words, using the microscopic as point and canvas from which to interrogate the forces and conditions that shape relations at all levels. His plays can be read and staged against many backdrops; they convey non-polemical, ideologically centrist but unmistakeably Nigerian-British perspectives on many subjects from twenty-first century postcolonial conditions to tensions surrounding dual heritages, cultural nationalism and radicalism, religious fundamentalism and diaspora concerns. His episodic storytelling style and plots derive from his dual cultural background and education in Nigeria and Britain. His characters and stage directions reveal anxieties about directors and performers misunderstanding his apolitical centrist stance or worse still, turning the spotlight from critical self-examination and individual responsibility to politics.

Since his first play, *Early Morning* (2003), Agboluaje has written over 30 literary pieces including stage and radio plays, short stories and films. His plays have been staged to full houses and with good reviews in Europe, Nigeria and the US. The plays in this volume vary in style and subject and reveal a stylistic development that started with experimentation in episodic structure in *Early Morning* to complex interplay of storytelling and presentational staging in *The Estate* and *The Hounding of David Oluwale*. Agboluaje's defining dramatic features include combining subtle comedy and loquacious humour, flashbacks, archetypal and symbolic characterization, and minimal staging. His dramaturgy emphasizes the dialogic interplay of character and setting as politicized sites. His narratives reveal both an attention to detail and emphasis on physical vocabulary for rendering his colourful, complex characters and the social forces that shaped them. His settings are more than mere physical constructs; they are best presented as part of the semiotic fabric of characters and narratives. One of his strongest dramaturgical tools is to combine short, pacey rhythmic dialogues into well-made storylines. The desire for a strong storyline drives, to some extent, his use of storytelling techniques such as flashbacks, dramatized narrations and dream sequences. Storyline is employed more overtly as a dramatic facility is *The Estate* and *The Hounding of David Oluwale* and in the prequel, *Iyale (The First Wife)*.

A FEW WORDS ON THE PLAYS IN THIS VOLUME

Early Morning is about three Nigeria-born office cleaners who question their decisions to leave better-paid jobs and lifestyles in Nigeria for menial jobs in the UK. The sudden realisation by the three office workers (Kola, Ojo, and Mama Paul) that their wild dreams about a Britain of unimaginable opportunities are wide of the mark generates a tense atmosphere of anger, bitter disappointment, bickering and uncomfortable self-examination. *Early Morning* satirises the seedy, underpaid underside of capitalism; it is unsympathetic with the characters' claim that every black person in the UK workplace is an innocent victim of racism and discrimination. Agboluaje focuses instead on the illogical expectations of the characters, black and white. Far from implying

11

that the conditions of modern-day migrants, the majority of whom live in Britain legally, are only marginally different from the experiences of seventeenth- and eighteenth-century slaves and indentured labourers as one of the characters claims, the playwright uses the workers' experiences to deconstruct cultural myopia and assumptions about the rights and wrongs of history. The simplest of his full-length plays, *Early Morning* is the start of Agboluaje's experimentation with dramatic features that would grow in sophistication in later works. These include minimal staging, symbolic characterisation, critical self-examination, rejection of polemics, and play on humour and slapstick and the physicality of language. Other dramatic features are the interests in diaspora subjects and settings, identity crisis, characters caught in shifting diaspora subjectivities and quest for a 'total' theatre dialectic that celebrates theatrical syncretism and hybridity as shown in the integration of indigenous African and western performance conventions, such as African episodic structures and European plot devices.

The Estate is a vibrant, colourful play set in modern Nigeria in which a family gathers to honour the memory of their late patriarch, Chief Adeyemi. In the play Helen, former house-girl and now young widow of Chief Adeyemi plans a lavish public celebration of her late husband's meritorious legacy. Despite the façade of civilised normality, the stage is set for shocking secrets as each turn of event reveals the sham beneath the actions and statements of the motley, disingenuous characters. As tensions grow and recriminations fly, Agboluaje unpeels layers of seedy dealings, greed, sibling rivalries, unexpected alliances and union between unlikely characters, betrayals and intrigues underneath the peaceful polygamous family set-up and the rise of a new socio-economic order as power shifts to the late chief's former servant, now Pastor and de-facto owner of the estate. The stage turns into a platform for characters to play out the dying throes of their fading dreams; old cores are dragged out for settling and once-secure alliances are exposed as shams. *The Estate* is a very dynamic play, the episodic structure, strong storyline and rich pickings of subjects and complex multi-dimensional characters such as Pakimi who gives religion and pastors a bad name and the domestic servants cast in the moulds of cunning conniving servants of old comedy will delight producers, directors and actors alike. Like good comedy of the serious and funny category in which events take unexpected turns and supposedly harmless statements lead to surprising revelations, the play handles characters and their shenanigans with theatrical dexterity.

Power relations and intrigue, marginalisation, corruption and manipulation are expounded in the tragic social satire, *The Christ of Coldharbour Lane*. Set in the seedy underworld of Brixton, England where it is difficult to separate religion and manipulation, and where social deprivation often dovetails into crime, the play is unusual in its combination of a complex plot and episodic structure. The result is a complicated, fairly difficult play in which Agboluaje communicates his satirical take on the connection between poverty and faith in the supernatural and people's reliance on charlatans and deluded schizophrenics like the main character, Omotunde, for answers to their problems. The playwright retains his interest in motley characters; this time they are not only hapless and trapped, their situation and setting are used as barometers for exploring how the damaging effects of government's policy on gentrification impacts the very marginal sections of society the policy was designed to help. In the play Agboluaje explores competing subjectivities, none clearly defined and none capable of surviving in the socio-economic chaos of a specifically postmodern setting. The tragic outcome plays out on all levels and there is neither hope nor redemption: Dona, convert to the Mission and trainee for leadership; hardened sex-worker, Maria; and Sarah, wheel-chair bound, unemployed dole collector, all surrender their capacities for action whilst creating the platform for religious hacks and con artists to thrive.

The Hounding of David Oluwale, a stage adaptation of Kester Aspden's novel of the same title is a documentary drama based on the discovery on May 4 1969, of the battered body of 38-year-old schizophrenic, David Oluwale in the river. The play follows the style of a forensic investigation and relies on official records and eyewitness accounts to unearth the official white-wash surrounding the verdict of death by misadventure reached by the police inquiry into the victim's death. In the style of a true documentary, the play returns to the scenes of incidents and uses witnesses' accounts and official records to reconstruct the facts, one of such witnesses being David Oluwale's ghost who guides DCS John Perkins and the audience on a public inquiry into the circumstances of his death. The play avoids the polemics and theatrics of head-on confrontation of racial discrimination, stereotyping and prejudice. Avoiding the distraction in such an approach Agboluaje uses the legal framework and setting of the court to probe the victim and his victimisers and in the process pieces together various raw evidences and compelling counter-arguments that expose the institutional racism and stereotyping reminiscent of the 1998 public inquiry into the racist killing of 18-year-old black teenager, Stephen Lawrence in

1993 in Eltham, south-east London. However, unlike Sir William Macpherson who came to the damning conclusion that the police in the Stephen Lawrence case was institutionally racist after examining the original Metropolitan Police Service investigation, the un-named Judge in *The Hounding of David Oluwale* goes through the same judicial process before coming to a slightly different conclusion; he avoids mentioning the role racism played in David's death and blamed the actions of a few police officers instead of the whole police force. As in his other plays in this volume, Agboluaje uses the microcosm or the actions of a small section of the population to expose the cultural tensions beneath the surface of society.

Similar to *The Estate*, the prequel *Iyale (The First Wife)* is a fast-moving play with many twists. It does not disappoint and reveals the shaky family foundations and social deprivations beneath the behaviours, cunning and graft exhibited by characters in *The Estate*. *Iyale* foregrounds the events and characters in *The Estate* by exposing the genesis of the self-serving selfishness, greed, betrayal and official corruption in *The Estate* as the surface symptoms of deep-rooted scars and problems on the nation's psyche. In effect, the muted fatuousness and excesses we see in *The Estate* are not mere aberrations, they can be traced to a historical pattern of abuses characterized by political high-handedness and excesses that the population turn a blind eye to and condone for personal and cultural reasons. In effect, the actions of the characters; Pastor Pakimi's betrayal of his religious vow and calling, the corruption of the ruling political and military elites, the sexual predation of Chief Adeyemi and the domestic abuse he inflicts on his stiff upper-lipped conscientious first wife, the shameless disloyalty and infidelity displayed by sexually voracious house-girl and lover to Pakimi, Chief Adeyemi and his son, Yinka, are all symptomatic of bigger problems at all levels of society. In the midst of such huge moral, ethical, and religious deficits and absence of cultural and political censures, religious quacks, corrupt politicians and soldiers, and social miscreants become the shocking role models to a citizenship that is driven only by its own mindless pursuit of excess. It is not surprising that the citizens including the socially disadvantaged servants like Helen and Pakimi will stop at nothing to achieve their nefarious personal goals, irrespective of the damage they cause on the way. A reading of *Iyale (The First Wife)* and *The Estate* together before performing either will offer directors and actors useful insights and workshop materials for characters and situations.

In conclusion, Agboluaje's plays can be described as episodic with a strong narrative thread. His writing style is framed by a subtly evocative exploration of subjects, themes and characters that is akin to a witnessing of facts than a debate. His characters and language are physical, his narrative or storylines reveal without the need for polemics or soapbox rhetoric. His images speak for themselves and require little embellishing; even when they are deployed as counter-narratives their purpose seems to be to witness and show. The plays in this volume strike a dialogic centrist note. The syncretic dramaturgy Agboluaje uses in them is not necessarily an act of postcolonial appropriation or postmodern posturing, his style and plays are his responses to the artistic and historical necessities to stage his readings of postcolonial, postmodern, and diaspora realities as he sees them.

Dr Victor I. Ukaegbu
Associate Professor, Theatre and Performance
Department of Media, English, Cultural Studies & Performance
School of The Arts, The University of Northampton
Associate Editor, *African Performance Review*
General Secretary, African Theatre Association

REFERENCES

- Ashcroft, Bill, Griffiths, Gareth, Tiffin, Helen (1989) *The Empire Writes Back: Theory and Practice in Post-colonial Literatures.* London and New York: Routledge.
- Breisach, Ernst (2003) *On the Future of History: The Postmodernist Challenge and its Aftermath.* Chicago and London: The University of Chicago Press.
- Buonanno, Giovanna, Sams, Victoria, Schlote, Christane (2011) 'Glocal Routes in British Asian Drama: Between Adaptation and Tradaptation' in *Postcolonial Text* Vol 6, No 2; pp. 1–18.
- Hall, Stuart (1993) 'Cultural Identity and Diaspora' in *Colonial Discourse and Post-colonial theory: A Reader.* Eds. Patrick Williams and Laura Williams. London: Harvester Wheatsheaf; pp. 392–403.
- McMillan, Michael (2006) 'Rebaptizing the World in Our Terms: Black Theatre and Live Arts in Britain' in *Staging New Britain: Aspects of Black and South Asian British Theatre practice*; pp. 47–64.
- Proctor, James (ed.) (2000) *Writing Black Britain 1948–1988: An Interdisciplinary Anthology.* Manchester: Manchester University Press.
- Said, Edward W (1991) *Orientalism: Western Conceptions of the Orient.* London: Penguin.
- Said, Edward W (1993) *Culture and Imperialism.* London: Chatto and Windus.

- Sierz, Alex (2001) *In-yer-face Theatre: British Drama Today*. London: Faber and Faber Ltd.
- Sierz, Alex (2011) *Rewriting the Nation: British Theatre Today*. London: Methuen.
- Stein, Mark (2004) *Black British Literature: Novels of Transformation*. Columbus: Ohio State University Press.
- Wambu, Onyekachi (1998) 'Black British Literature since Windrush' [online]. Available from: http://www.bbc.co.uk/history/british/modern/literature_01.shtml [Accessed 20 December 2012].

NOTES

1. I use *generation* in the broadest sense to describe literary history or when writers' work became available to the public. Classifying writers is a complex undertaking; any number of factors from whether writers were born in or migrated to Britain, their age on arrival and the age of their target audiences, whether they live in or pass through Britain occasionally, and the convergences in style and subject matter across authors of different reading and writing ages complicate such a task. Mark Stein proffers a more comprehensive problematization of the challenges inherent in classifying authors according to *generations* in *Black British Literature: Novels of Transformation* (2004).

2. I define *othering* on Theodore Shank's (1994) use of the term to describe cultural and socio-political settings in which there are 'people who are perceived as having political and economic power and there are other cultures existing alongside the dominant one' (Shank 1994: 3) and on Ashcroft et al's (1989: 8-9; 12) use of 'centre-periphery' to define relations between formerly colonised cultures and their erstwhile colonisers in postcolonial discourse in *The Empire Writes Back*.

EARLY MORNING

Early Morning was produced by Futuretense and was first performed at Oval House Theatre in March 2003, with the following cast:

OJO	Tunde Euba
MAMA PAUL	Golda John
KOLA	Ofo Uhiara
MIKE	Mark Leadbetter

Director, Emma Wolukau-Wanambwa
Dramaturg, Liz Ingrams
Set designer, Mamoru Iriguchi
Fight director, Terry King

Characters

OJO

Nigerian, middle-aged, a generous helping
of stomach. Always has a mischievous twinkle
in his eye.

MAMA PAUL[1]

Nigerian, middle-aged, well-proportioned,
a no-nonsense woman.

KOLA

Nigerian, early twenties,
student, from a well to do family.

MIKE

British, late thirties, working-class, jobsworth

---

1   Mother of Paul

Act One

The large office of a city bank, at 6 a.m. There is litter everywhere. KOLA, 20, plays snooker, using his broom as a cue to knock scrunched up papers from a desk into a bin. He hears footsteps approaching. He stops messing around and clears the rest of the waste paper on the desk into the bin. Enter MAMA PAUL. She is middle-aged and rotund. She observes KOLA with disdain. KOLA brings out a can of polish and sprays it too liberally over the desk. She marches up to KOLA and snatches the can away from him.

MAMA PAUL: (*Shakes the can.*) Are you fighting chemical warfare? You've finished the polish on just one desk!

KOLA: But you complained yesterday that I wasn't cleaning the desks properly.

MAMA PAUL: And this is how you do it properly? This is what you do when I'm not around.

KOLA: These office people, they manufacture waste. There's enough rubbish to build ten pyramids.

MAMA PAUL: Professor of useless knowledge that is not your problem. But I will give you problems if I catch you messing around again.

KOLA: I don't see why I should kill myself for the workers here. They never look us in the face. They never say hello to us when they meet us.

MAMA PAUL: That's how they show their appreciation for our hard work. By letting us get on with it.

KOLA: They see us as their slaves.

MAMA PAUL: It is not yet ten minutes into the shift, you've started with your nonsense. If you don't like it find another job. Nobody begged you to work here.

KOLA: (*Huffs.*) It's too early to start talking about these things.

MAMA PAUL: Shut up then!

KOLA: I know that…

MAMA PAUL: You don't know anything! In Nigeria you had servants to clean up after you. You expect the same here. Get the bin liner and pick up the papers. And do it properly.

They set about cleaning the office.

KOLA: *(Looks at the clock.)* Ah, how long does it take Mr Ojo to clean one little office?

MAMA PAUL: What is your own business? Do you know how long Mr Ojo has been here?

KOLA: That's what I'm asking.

MAMA PAUL: Don't be funny with me, idiot! Since you came here you've been a handicap to us. Why do you need this job, anyway? Doesn't your father steal enough money for your upkeep?…

KOLA: My father is not a thief…

MAMA PAUL: …It is not enough that you have ruined Nigeria for us, you want to come and spoil here too.

KOLA: So I've spoiled Nigeria because I used too much polish on a desk?

MAMA PAUL: Because you're an idiot that's why. *Oya,* quick! Before Mike arrives for inspection.

KOLA: Na wa for you, Mama Paul, you love doing this shitty work.

MAMA PAUL: You think they pick money from the streets? Now shut up and work before I slap you.

KOLA: You were not threatening to slap me when I loaned you £20.

MAMA PAUL: How much is £20? Chicken change.

KOLA extends his hand to MAMA PAUL.

I will pay you when we collect our wages this week.

KOLA: You said that two weeks ago. I didn't come here to fund your lottery addiction.

MAMA PAUL: To make money you must spend money. *Oya!* Stop talking. We have five more storeys to go.

Enter OJO, a fat middle-aged man. He is wearing an ill-fitting tracksuit with a sports cap that perches uneasily on his Laughing Buddha frame. In one hand is his cleaning stuff while in the other is a large, heavy bag wrapped in a bin liner.

MAMA PAUL: Mr Ojo, you took long this time, oh.

KOLA: But I said so before…

MAMA PAUL: Who is talking to you?

OJO: *(Panting.)* I had to collect this bag from downstairs. Yeh. *(Puts down the bin liner. Stretches his back.)*

KOLA: Mike is the only one authorised to sign for deliveries for the agency.

OJO: It's my private property.

KOLA: But Mike said no more bringing of personal items to the office.

OJO: I know what that buffoon said.

KOLA: Let's not start this week the way we ended last week, I beg.

OJO: Mike has no respect for my skills. Fred let me sign for all deliveries. He respected my experience in paperwork.

MAMA PAUL: *(Fondly.)* Freddie, Freddo. I wonder where he is now.

KOLA: Regimes change. We have to adapt.

OJO: Like how we've adapted from being men to being menial workers?

KOLA: You know what I mean. We have to move with the times.

OJO: *(To MAMA PAUL.)* Has Mike come down yet?

MAMA PAUL: He will soon be here for inspection. I beg oh, let's not have any *wahala¹* this week.

OJO: *(Hides the bag.)* There will be no *wahala*. *(Picks up a duster and cleans a desk nonchalantly. Ominously.)* It all depends…

MAMA PAUL: This is what we are saying. Between this lazy boy and your attitude we will soon be fired. Mike will make good on his threat to give us all written warning if we misbehave again.

OJO: Let him. He is a bastard.

MAMA PAUL: Mr Ojo, please don't start this morning.

OJO: *Bastard!*

---

1   trouble

KOLA sweeps around OJO's bag. He prods it with his brush and, seeing OJO is looking the other way, sneaks it open. He gets past the bin liner to see the sack. As he attempts to open the sack OJO sees him and bangs on the table next to KOLA with his fist.

KOLA: *(Jumps.)* I was trying to clean underneath!

OJO drags the bag to under another desk.

(Jokingly.) It must be something ominous for you to hide it in a bin liner. Are you helping the Iraqis to hide their weapons of mass destruction?

OJO: Mind your business.

KOLA: You want to overthrow our bosses? A coup against our bosses starting with Mike. *(Laughs at the thought.)* I hope you've not been sniffing glue from the desks.

OJO: Your father sniffs dogs' anuses, you animal! Because they say 'London na Leveller' that does not mean we've forgotten how we do things back home.

KOLA: I'm sorry, Mr Ojo. I've spent too long in this country. *(Prostrates.)* See me on my belly.

MAMA PAUL: *(Sniggers.)* See rich boy prostrating. Kola is asking for your forgiveness, Mr Ojo. Remember what our elders say. You beat a child with one hand and pet him with the other.

OJO: Then for fools like this one, you stamp on their heads with both feet. Because you see me here working beside you, you think you can disrespect me.

MAMA PAUL: Mister Ojo!

OJO: *(Grudgingly.)* Stand up.

MAMA PAUL: *(To KOLA.)* Make sure you go back and wipe the polish off that table… Waste of space…

KOLA: Mama Paul, what's your own, now? Leave me to do my work.

OJO: What work?

KOLA: Mr Ojo, you too?

MAMA PAUL: Do you think he is blind? Or because we don't talk?

KOLA: Don't talk! You have been abusive towards me since my first day here!

OJO: Whose fault is that? Ordinary cleaning you cannot do. Before you joined us we were the best team in the agency. *(To MAMA PAUL.)* You remember his first day?

MAMA PAUL: You spilled orange juice over a floor we'd spent ages buffing. Your carelessness stopped Mr Ojo from winning cleaner of the month for the fourth time in a row.

KOLA: This job is nothing to be proud of. Cleaning for three hours at this time of the morning and smelling of crap for the rest of the day? Our own brand of eau de toilette has made me woman repellent.

OJO: You were woman repellent from the day you were born.

KOLA: *(Uneasily.)* What makes you say that?

OJO: The mere sight of you. But show girls your money they will breathe in deeply, even if you smell like a sewer. The smell of money covers every odour.

KOLA: *(Recovers.)* Mr Ojo, you can spoil your life for money.

OJO: You are young.

KOLA: Uh-huh. And if you make money, what will you do?

OJO: I will take Mike fox-hunting. He will be the fox.

KOLA: *(Winking.)* Not a coup again?

MAMA PAUL: Kola, don't encourage him. Things are bad enough between them already. Mr Ojo, don't joke that kind of joke. The wrong person could be listening.

KOLA: Like someone we know. Not so Mama Paul?

MAMA PAUL: Mr Ojo, don't take your bitterness towards the agency to lie against me. You've been here long enough to know they prefer to hire management staff from outside.

OJO: I have done better jobs. Why should I be jealous just because they made a less qualified person supervisor? You are too friendly with Mike.

MAMA PAUL: I told you what happened. I had rheumatism.

OJO: In your bottom? Since when did you start liking white men?

KOLA: And since when did white men start liking big bottoms?

MAMA PAUL: We were in a tight spot. He could not get by to reach my leg.

KOLA: So he decided to rub the part nearest to him.

OJO: Shut up! Is Mama Paul your mate?

MAMA PAUL: Thank you, Mr Ojo. See how quickly he has forgotten his manners again. WC without toilet roll.

OJO: I have not finished with you yet, Mama. What have you been telling Mike about me?

MAMA PAUL: I don't talk to him even about Kola.

OJO: But when the two of you are doing love in Tokyo, you can let something slip.

MAMA PAUL: Even if we are doing love in Peckham, I could never do such a thing.

OJO: Anybody who has power is your best friend. You were the same with Fred, too. That is how you used to go out with an army general in Nigeria.

MAMA PAUL: *You* are the one telling my secret to the whole world!

KOLA: I thought Sanni Abacha only slept with Indians.

MAMA PAUL: Your mother slept with Sanni Abacha! Mr Ojo, you are the one giving Kola chance to insult me. *(To KOLA.)* You have no manners. I wonder what kind of university you attend.

KOLA: And what has university to do with manners?

OJO: Oxford?

KOLA: No.

OJO: Cambridge?

KOLA: No.

OJO: Then you are not in university.

KOLA: The University of East-West London has a fine reputation. Ask anyone. I will bring our prospectus for you to see.

OJO: My friend, our people are wiser about all things London and New York. I bet you did not tell your friends that Dalston is the nearest train station. If your grades were good enough, you would be at Ibadan or Nsukka.

MAMA PAUL: No, Mr Ojo, I don't agree. Students in Nigeria don't read anymore. The campuses are always closed. If it is not the lecturers going on strike it is the students rioting. If the students are not rioting they are engaging in cultish activities.

OJO: Now who is exaggerating?

MAMA PAUL: In my nephew's campus this boy wanted this girl to like him by force. When she did not agree for him, he poured acid over her head.

KOLA: *(Recoils with horror.)* Shit! What happened to the guy?

MAMA PAUL: He ran away and was never seen again. His father is a big politician, so he must be studying abroad. The poor girl went to the media, but they would not pick up her story. In the end she committed suicide.

KOLA: That guy will return home to a hero's welcome. Nobody will question him over his past, except the students even if it means taking to the streets. That's why our governments keep closing down our institutions. They fear our potential to overthrow them.

OJO: You want to copy your South Korean counterparts, *abi*?[2] Can you catch surface to air missiles between your toes? Pompous weaklings like you will stand in front of tanks blowing grammar.

KOLA: That does not mean we should not fight for change. Nigeria is for all of us. Why should only a few bastards and their spoilt children enjoy while the rest of us eat out of dustbins?

MAMA PAUL: Brent calling Bonny Light crude! You are one of the spoilt brats benefiting from the system! And you talk of change!

KOLA: Am I not a cleaner? I am one of you.

MAMA PAUL: Once your allowance arrives, you will disappear. People like us send money to our families. You collect money from yours. You males are all the same. Take, take, take.

KOLA: You don't know anything about me.

---

2   is that it?

MAMA PAUL: Deny it.

KOLA: You don't know anything about my family.

MAMA PAUL: *Deny it*!

OJO: *(To KOLA.)* So why are you here?

KOLA: You say?

OJO: Are you deaf? Why are you not fighting alongside your comrades?

MAMA PAUL: He is a part-time Mandela.

KOLA: It's like the army. Some of us are recruits, some are field marshals. Some of us must prepare to lead the revolution.

OJO: Others die, you reap the victory spoils. You are not that stupid after all. *(Pats KOLA approvingly on the cheek.)*

MAMA PAUL: You are a stupid hypocrite. You were talking like a warrior, next thing you don't mind for other people's children to sacrifice their lives for you. Idiot without leave to remain.

OJO: Sometimes it's good to be pragmatic.

KOLA: But you said that it's good that I'm studying here. Ah-ah! If not that you and Mike are knowing each other Old Testament style…

MAMA PAUL: *(Angrily.)* Eh? What did you say? What did you say just now?

MAMA PAUL chases KOLA around the office.

MIKE: *(Off.)* Yemi, haven't you finished with the buffer yet? I need to use it for…

Enter MIKE, the supervisor, aged 40. He is of average height and build. He exudes an air of authority. MAMA PAUL sees him first.

MAMA PAUL: Ahem, Mike, Mike. Do you need some tea?

MIKE: I don't believe this. You haven't done a thing.

MAMA PAUL: Oh, no. We have cleaned…

MIKE: Ojo, what are you doing here?

OJO: I work here, remember?

MIKE: Get up to 27th – now. Kola, get that buffer going. You should have brought it up to me ages ago. And when you do this time make sure it's switched off. Yemi, you're supposed to supervise him. Will you look at this place! I could hear you right down the hallway, for Christ's sake.

OJO: So you are spying on us now, is that it?

MIKE: Don't think I won't give you all that written warning 'cos I will. I meant what I said last week. The agency said you were the best team they had. All you've given me so far is grief.

OJO: Smart people don't believe everything they're told.

MAMA PAUL: Ah, we have been working. See this place is clean already and we've only just started.

MIKE: We can't be in the same room. What have you been doing since you left the stock room?

MAMA PAUL: You should have seen this office when we got here. Mountains of rubbish. It took us two hours before we realised that Mr Ojo was buried alive. We had declared him killed in action.

OJO: It took them an hour to dig me out. Another second more and it would have been goodbye for me. The judge at my inquest would have called it death by misadventure in the line of duty against impossible odds. Your Queen would have awarded me the Victoria Cross.

MIKE: You were assigned to 27th when you finished on the 18th.

OJO: I finished there before they finished in the stock room.

MIKE: Last week, you said you couldn't do 18th by yourself.

OJO: We are not slaves! You yourself, why did you have head office re-deploy our team members? You want them to think you're an efficient supervisor on our sweat. You left only three of us to clean this whole building, while all you do is sit around playing with yourself in the Executive Suite.

MIKE: I *clean* the Executive Suite.

OJO: Fred used to clean the Executive Suite and come down to help us finish up.

MIKE: I'm not Fred. Obviously he did all the work. Now he's gone, you can't handle it.

KOLA: The fact is that there used to be more than three people cleaning this building.

MIKE: You weren't even with us, then. What do you know about it?

OJO: We need more bodies. We cannot die just because we work for you.

MIKE: You have to stop yakking and get this place in order or else I'll give you the warning. The choice is yours.

OJO: You call that a choice.

MIKE: You either do the job or go. It's no skin off my nose. I'm sick of your petty lies and childish excuses.

OJO: I am not a child!

MIKE: You're not doing your job properly. Nothing gets done and the bank complains to the bosses.

KOLA: So, Mr Ojo, you aren't that good and you keep yabbing me all the time…

OJO: *(To KOLA.)* Shut up! *(To MIKE.)* Mister, I've done better jobs, you hear? You cannot talk to me anyhow.

MIKE: Here we go again. So what if you used to be a high ranking civil servant? This ain't Nigeria. You've come here to work, we've given you a job so do it! People like you don't get plum jobs. Get used to it! I don't have time to argue with you, you…

OJO: Nigger?

MIKE: *(Taken aback.)* What?

OJO: Great minds think alike, eh?

MIKE: So now you're a blooming mind reader. Just get up to 27th. *(Runs his finger across a table OJO has dusted.)* Who dusted round here?

OJO: Ah, is it still dirty? It was when you opened the door. Dust must have followed you in. I will clean it one more time before I go up to 27th.

MIKE: Let's just try and get through the day without getting on each other's nerves, okay? Go over this place again. *(More to himself.)* Bloody wanker. *(To MAMA PAUL.)* Yemi, I will have a cuppa. Bring it up to me in the Executive Suite.

MAMA PAUL: Sure, Mike.

MAMA PAUL brushes past MIKE as she exits. MIKE and OJO glare at each other.

MIKE exits.

OJO: *(Goes after MIKE and shouts.)* Bloody wanker yourself!

KOLA: Come on, Mr Ojo. That table doesn't look like you touched it.

OJO: So what?

KOLA: So Mike was right to tell you to go over it again.

OJO: Only because he has the authority vested in him by Her Majesty the Queen. He's only a backwater council estate, graffiti-scribbling, lift-shitting riffraff.

KOLA: Whoa, easy, Mr Ojo. Do you know him that well?

OJO: I know his type. Lowlife! If we were in Nigeria, he would be my house-boy.

KOLA: But we are not in Nigeria.

OJO: You think I don't know that, moron! I said *if, if* we were in Nigeria he would be washing my pants. I've seen him flashing his nyash[3] on 'Match of the Day'. He's used up his fifteen minutes of fame. I bet he doesn't even know how to keep a cricket score, the bushman.

KOLA: Because Mike doesn't know how to keep a cricket score doesn't make him a bushman.

OJO: So, Mike is from your village, eh? He is now your countryman. Your albino brother is a bushman! Just because an idiot can become a supervisor does not make him a civilised person. Why don't you just stand in line with Mama Paul and let him bugger you. Then I will know you are from the same family.

KOLA: You shouldn't cast aspersions on a man's sexuality.

OJO: I can say what I bloody like! Are you gay that you are offended? In fact, your arsehole looks like you've had a baton rammed up it. Did Mike shag you New York police style?

KOLA: Mr Ojo!

---

3   bottom

Enter MAMA PAUL, looking dishevelled. She looks around the office.

MAMA PAUL: Ah, what have you been doing?

OJO and KOLA eye her with disbelief.

Hey, before you accuse me, I only went to make tea for Mike. Don't look at me like that.

KOLA: When did making tea involve hard labour? Not so, Mr Ojo?

MAMA PAUL: Mr Ojo, remember your age. Don't join this stupid boy in bearing false witness against me. If you do, when I win the lottery you will not share inside the money.

OJO: How can you think that I will side with Kola on anything against you?

MAMA PAUL: You have sided with him before.

OJO: That was to make him feel like one of us.

KOLA: Mr Ojo! Money will make you disown your spirit. Everyone knows the lottery is fixed. I've never wasted any money on it.

MAMA PAUL: You are now Professor of Lottery Studies, not so? How many times did you play before you gave up? Come on, tell us. You see now. That is why black people do not progress. You do not persevere. You want everything immediately, without working for it. Why can't you be patient, pay your dues and reap the rewards when the time comes? And when something does not work, you begin to form stories, telling lies and spoiling it for others. It is always somebody else's fault. If you know how to pick the right numbers you will win, simple. There is no Underground delay in this one.

KOLA: Then tell me, how many black winners do you know of? Go down to Peckham on lottery day, you will see our people buying their tickets and wishing each other luck. Do they not all return the following week to go through the ceremony all over again? This whole lottery business is a conspiracy to prevent black people from buying newspapers. That way, we will never be informed of what's happening to us in the world.

OJO: God in heaven. What has the lottery got to do with buying newspapers?

KOLA: Quite simple, Mr Ojo. When you put your hand on the coupon it leaves a deposit that can be picked up by melanin-sensitive tracers, so that if a black person gets the winning numbers the ticket is destroyed. Opportunity cost won't let you buy a paper because you've blown the rest of your money on scratch cards, and there's no way you're going to sacrifice your cigarette money. No access to information means we cannot know what the government is plotting against us.

OJO: You have been standing outside Brixton Station for too long, my friend. But you will make a good spin doctor. You surprise me.

MAMA PAUL: The boy is talking nonsense. Don't go and write that down in your exam. You will be a cleaner forever and a useless one at that. Whether you like it or not I am going to be a millionaire. I spend fifty pounds a week on the lottery. And with the special prayer my Church pastor does for me, God is on my side. I know the Lord will not forget me when my time comes. And the Holy Spirit is telling me that time is soon. Just imagine, winning a quadruple rollover. Hey! I will buy a Lear jet to take me to Sainsbury's and an Airbus to go to Brixton market. I will employ Michael Schumacher as my personal driver for my custom made Rolls-Bentley-Cadillac-Benz-Lexus. Lennox Lewis will be my bodyguard. I will buy Buckingham Palace. I will buy New York and Paris. I will show people how to spend money. Everybody will be hailing me as the goddess of money.

OJO: All hail Mama Paul, the one and only goddess of money!

MAMA PAUL: *(Dances.)* Hail me!

KOLA: Prostrate to the Cash Madam! *(OJO and KOLA prostrate.)*

MAMA PAUL: I say, hail me!

OJO: The mama who sleeps on dollars and towels her body with pounds!

MAMA PAUL: I cannot hear you!

OJO: The madam who cleans her anus with naira!

MAMA PAUL: Wash me! *(OJO and KOLA shower her with rubbish.)* Oh yes! Oh no! Stop! This is used toilet paper!

OJO: *(Smells a piece.)* Gah! You see the savages that work here? I will put it in the Executive Suite when we close.

MAMA PAUL: Don't, Mr Ojo.

OJO: Mike will be held responsible.

OJO makes to head off to the executive suite. MAMA PAUL blocks him.

MAMA PAUL: Mr Ojo! I don't have time to look for another job.

OJO: You are the one in debt because of your lottery addiction.

KOLA: That is why you begged me to death for the £20.

OJO: I won't even remind you of how much you owe me.

MAMA PAUL: I've said I will repay both of you. I just need my luck to change. I've given my pastor two hundred pounds for the lottery numbers prayer. Very soon, it will happen, in Jesus' name. But for now, let's not jeopardise this job. This is a good agency. Their managers are all right if you know how to get along with them.

KOLA: I don't give a rat's arse. Once I graduate I'm shooting from this place.

MAMA PAUL: Find another job! Your mates work in the supermarkets. You can blow grammar. Do telesales. Those of us who have no choice, leave us to do our job.

OJO: I have a choice.

KOLA: *(Sniggers.)* Between the mop and the buffer? Or between 18th floor and 27th floor?

OJO: Watch your mouth! You are the reason Mike talks to us as if we are animals. When you cannot do ordinary cleaning.

MAMA PAUL: Tell him, Mr Ojo. Tell this phone card without pin number.

OJO: You don't realise our contribution to the shit-stained, graffiti-scarred, paper-strewn city of London. We are the revolutionary army of environmental sanitation at the forefront of biological and chemical warfare. The elite force of waste disposal sent in to destroy the axis of evil before they hatch their plans of world domination. All over the developed world, we are obliterating the terrorist network of litterbugs. We have built a coalition force from all over Africa to come here and make the world a cleaner place for other people's children in what will go down in history as the 'Dirty' War.

KOLA: I don't think that's the reason you came to London.

OJO: Why is everybody else here, apart from you, Mister 'My Father is a Millionaire'? To make money to carry back home. I would have done security but I don't have the legs.

KOLA: There are cleaners who live like big men back home.

OJO: After working how many shifts in a day? And then the things they get up to after work. I'm too old to run between ten jobs.

MAMA PAUL: Mr Ojo, are you not going up to 27th?

OJO: I'd better go now before that hyena returns to gnaw at the remnants of my dignity. *(Exits.)*

MAMA PAUL: Take the duster and start from there. I'll start from here.

KOLA: So you used to go out with an army general.

MAMA PAUL: Mind your business.

KOLA: If you gist me, you can keep the £20.

MAMA PAUL: *(Pause.)* He was a state governor at the time. He was very generous.

KOLA: He could afford to be generous with Nigeria's money…

MAMA PAUL gives KOLA a withering look.

Er, sorry, please go on…

MAMA PAUL: …I was very young then. But my parents did not want me to marry a Hausa. He became a minister in the last military government.

KOLA: Eh?

MAMA PAUL: I've been unlucky with men. There are so many useless ones around. The last agency I worked in was full of stupid white men. They spoke to us like we were

35

children. They were so crude. They thought God created black women for cleaning toilets and serving tea.

KOLA: No shit. At least here we share the toilet duties.

MAMA PAUL: Share? I have to go over everything you do! That is why I play the lottery, so that I can come out of this dirty work and be a cash madam like my mates back home.

KOLA: Some of your friends are cash madams?

MAMA PAUL: Because you see me as I am you think I don't know people? When they come to London for business they stay at my place. Seeing them handle bundles of cash, it makes me wonder where my life has gone. Most of them dumped their idiot husbands ages ago. I was the only one still playing the faithful wife. Look at them, look at me.

KOLA: Don't you ask them to help you out? You could be their agent here.

MAMA PAUL: Which Nigerian will share their secret of success with anybody? They show me their money, drop a dash and return home with their goods. I am struggling to build one house. Some are building their third. Something must happen soon. I'm too old for this work.

KOLA: What about your husband?

MAMA PAUL: My family life does not concern you.

KOLA: You've short-changed me for the £20.

MAMA PAUL: I'm the reason Mike didn't fire you when you flushed the office keys down the toilet.

Enter OJO.

OJO: My God. You people have not done a thing since I left.

KOLA: We were getting organised.

OJO: Have you used the buffer yet?

MAMA PAUL: Not all of us are drive-by cleaners.

OJO: Mike told us to hurry up. You too were shouting we should work. You want that buffoon to come and start haranguing us again?

MAMA PAUL: I will talk to him. *Oya*, Kola, get to work.

KOLA: *(Goes to the buffer.)* I'm not cleaning this office by myself.

OJO: *(To MAMA PAUL.)* Oh, you will give Mike one of your bottom power sessions again, eh? Either you are very strong, or it's true the white man's penis is small. Get proper servicing from a brother.

MAMA PAUL: Mr Ojo! Stop this dirty talk. I've told you I don't like these false accusations.

KOLA: *(Fiddling with the buffer.)* How do you put this thing on again?

OJO: How many times will I show you? Clear a space at the back for my bag.

KOLA: Mr Ojo, this bag of yours looks sinister.

OJO: It's just an ordinary bag.

KOLA: Hidden inside a bin liner. *(Can barely lift the bag.)* God, are you a scrap metal dealer in your spare time? *(Knocks over a container of cleaning fluid.)*

MAMA PAUL: Look at this idiot! How are we going to clean this mess?

OJO and MAMA PAUL rush over to inspect the spillage.

OJO: You see why we think so lowly of your intelligence.

Enter MIKE.

OJO, MAMA PAUL and KOLA line up to block the spillage from MIKE's view.

MIKE: Where is that buffer, Kola? *(Sees OJO.)* What are you still doing here? I told you to clean 27th.

OJO: I have.

MIKE: No you haven't. I've just been up there to check. What's your problem? Is it too insignificant for you to clean?

OJO: I don't know the meaning of insignificant.

MIKE: Yemi, you stay and get this place in order. Kola, you go to 27th. Ojo, you do the toilets.

OJO: I am not cleaning the toilets! That is Mama Paul's job.

MIKE: Don't do the toilets and you get a written warning. After that comes dismissal. Well, what are you still hanging about for?

OJO: You still haven't told me the meaning of insignificant. I'll use it when I write my appeal.

MIKE: You're on a short leash, Ojo. *(Notices the bag.)* This isn't one of the bags we use for refuse. Whose is this?

OJO: Mine.

MIKE: What's inside?

OJO: My personal belongings.

MIKE: So what's it doing here?

OJO: I still don't know the meaning of insignificant.

MIKE: 'I don't know the meaning of insignificant'! Oh, come on, Ojo, that doesn't even qualify for your top hundred bullshit excuses. You complicate security matters by bringing personal effects to work! Things go missing and the agency gets the blame for hiring dishonest people. That's how Fred got fired! The agency nearly lost the contract because of him.

KOLA: Eh? You mean Fred got fired? What did he do?

MIKE: There'll be a bag check before you clock off. And for the last time, get this place cleaned up! Or by the end of the shift, all of you will be looking for work. ALL OF YOU! *(Exit MIKE.)*

MAMA PAUL: Did you hear that? Oh God, what kind of nonsense is this? *(Starts cleaning rapidly.)*

OJO: See how I belittled him. You see, he doesn't know the meaning of 'insignificant'! He heard it while looking for porn on TV. His finger must have pressed '2' on the remote by accident.

KOLA: So, Fred got fired.

MAMA PAUL: Here what you two are talking about. We are going to lose our jobs!

OJO: See how small the life of a cleaner is, when a person like Mike can hire and fire.

KOLA: That's why the agency brought him in. You were on Fred's side so they made the way for Mike to take your job.

OJO: Exactly! Fred said he would recommend me for supervisor. You see the kind of devious person I am up against? You see?

KOLA: Yes but if Mama Paul was sucking up to Fred, he could have given her the job.

OJO: But Mama Paul did not become 'Cleaner of the Month' three times in a row. I laid a record in this agency, and they refuse to give me my due. And you can see the hand of Mike in it.

MAMA PAUL: Kola, come on, get going to 27th.

KOLA: This is a cappuccino company. Whites on top, blacks at the bottom. It doesn't matter how hard you stir you will never rise to the top.

OJO: Now you understand how an oaf like Mike can be made boss over me. You can see the threat he poses to our very existence.

MAMA PAUL: I'm not the only one who will be affected if Mike sacks us. Let us work, please!

KOLA: He was in the army, you know. He retired as a sergeant.

OJO: No doubt working in covert ops like Operation Asylum Seek and Destroy. We are his next victims.

KOLA: He might be suffering from Gulf War Syndrome. He fought in Iraq, you know. He won a medal.

OJO: The army don't give medals to catering staff. They are reserved for their greatest killers. Would our lives be in such peril if it were not so?

MAMA PAUL: Hey, let us finish here…

OJO: And for what? To be in bondage? People like us should be big men at home where others come and prostrate to you every morning as you shower them with money. You are the guest of honour at every party. They even hold dog-naming ceremonies if they know you'll be there to spray them with pounds and dollars. All the top musicians record songs for you. Praise-singers chant your name. Doors open without you being there to walk through them.

You sleep on a bed of women every night. Universities confer on you uncountable honorary degrees…

MAMA PAUL: Let's clean up this office before the workers arrive.

OJO: No.

MAMA PAUL/KOLA: What?

OJO: I said, NO.

MAMA PAUL: Mr Ojo, I know you and Mike are enemies, but can you not just…

OJO: *(Grabs the implements from MAMA PAUL's hands and casts them aside.)* Kola, put away that buffer. Are you not scared that we could be doing this forever?

MAMA PAUL: Yes, but…

OJO: That one day, your children will ask you 'Daddy, Mommy, what did you do in your life' and you will say, 'I was a cleaner'?

KOLA: Time is really against us, oh!

OJO: Or when in your old age, your grandchildren ask why do you smell of rotted cabbage? If you are not afraid, something is wrong with you. Do you think God said, *(Points to members of the audience.)* you, you and you, cleaners. You, you and you, supervisors. You, you and you, Prime Ministers? He said the earth is the Lord's and the fullness thereof. Do you want to be cleaning up after those whose fullness is here, thereof and thereafter?

MAMA PAUL: Well, I don't really, but…

OJO: It's not enough for people like me to make a stand against our oppressors. We must fight them. Together. Mama Paul, your constructive engagement with the enemy has landed you in a ditch. Don't you want to get out?

MAMA PAUL: Once Mike gets me more hours, I'll be able to cover my debts.

OJO: On the pittance that you earn? How many hours will you work to cover the amount you owe in rent and council tax? Your bills? Your cable TV? Your credit card? Me?

KOLA: And me!

OJO: What money will you have left to play the lottery?

MAMA PAUL: *(Sobs.)* It's a hopeless situation. If only I can get six numbers…

OJO: Tears will not solve your problem, believe me. And you, Kola. With people like Mike in your way, do you think you will ever amount to anything in this country? Not only are you in the wrong university, you are in the wrong skin.

KOLA: Well…

OJO: The agency took from me what was rightfully mine using Mike as their spearhead. They never liked me because I am their worst nightmare; I am an intelligent black man. And they will get you too.

KOLA: Yes!

OJO: But they are not the only ones. Oh no. The government is in on this. They are leading the anti-melanin conspiracy.

KOLA: Yes, my theory…

OJO: The Prime Minister has set aside ten billion pounds to ensure that we remain cleaners. It is part of a clandestine plan called 'Aid, not trade, for Africa'. That's why they can't fund their own railways, education and pensioners, but they have money for war. It is part of their ongoing plan to subvert the destiny of all black people.

MAMA PAUL: Was it reported on CNN?

OJO: Schools attended by black children – like your own, Kola – they are having their funding cut. How can they receive proper education? Youth centres in inner cities are shut down as soon as black children start to benefit. Do you know what that means?

MAMA PAUL: That they have realised that black children don't study?

OJO: For goodness sake, Mama Paul, keep up! Your children's future is at stake. We must fight for them and for ourselves!

KOLA: We can talk about it when we finish cleaning up. And… Oh God, I'm going to be late for my first lecture. Mike said there would be a bag inspection.

OJO: Then truly it is time.

KOLA: Not yet.

MAMA PAUL: Kola, take the broom.

OJO: *(The sound of martial music as OJO clambers laboriously onto a desk. He stands upright, with an imperial air.)* Events make man. The enemy has struck the first blow and we must respond accordingly.

MAMA PAUL: Mr Ojo, what are you talking about? Come down from the table.

OJO: Ladies and Gentlemen, today marks the era of change. Since I arrived here, the door of opportunity was not just slammed shut in my face, it was sealed with polyseal. This has been the lot of blacks in this useless country. Shall we continue to live as second-class citizens in a land our forefathers built?

KOLA: The Jamaicans say they built the Underground.

'Land of Hope and Glory' plays as OJO makes his speech.

OJO: The hour of change has come. I hereby declare that a new government has come to power. The office of Prime Minister and the Cabinet are hereby dissolved with immediate effect. The Houses of Parliament shall parley and party no more. The Queen and the Royal Family are to be sent to the Tower to await sentencing at my pleasure. My official residence will be Buckingham Palace and my office at Number 10 Downing Street. Today heralds the age of Blackocracy.

'Land of Hope and Glory', street beat version takes over.

Government of the blacks for the blacks by the blacks. Our time is here and now! Blackocracy is the Other Way. The Other Way is the only way. There is no going back, there is only going black.

KOLA: I think it will be easier if we just cleaned this place, or what do you think, Mama Paul?

MAMA PAUL: Maybe if we humour him a bit, he might return to his senses.

OJO: You are the ones who are not thinking right. Kola, my bag. Bring my bag, I say.

Grumbling, KOLA drags the bag and with MAMA PAUL's help, puts it on the desk.

You want to know what's inside. First: are you truly ready for change?

MAMA PAUL: *(Nonchalantly.)* Yes, we are ready.

KOLA: Er, yeah, yeah, whatever. I'm ready.

OJO: Then it has begun!

OJO whips out a pistol from the bag. MAMA PAUL and KOLA scream and dive under a desk.

You said you are ready!

MAMA PAUL: I am not ready to die. Please Mr Ojo!

KOLA: It's Mama Paul who owes you money!

MAMA PAUL: Ah, Kola you want Mr Ojo to kill me! Mr Ojo, I will pay you everything I owe you. I will pay you right now!

OJO: For God's sake! The Blackocracy has begun. Are you with me or not?

MAMA PAUL: *(Still under the desk.)* Mr Ojo, I am with you, just don't shoot me.

OJO: I said… Come out here.

MAMA PAUL and KOLA come out from under the desk with their hands raised.

Will you put your hands down, ah! Look, I have guns for you, too. Here.

OJO hands MAMA PAUL a pistol.

I will supply all the cleaners in the surrounding offices with guns. Let's get cracking. Our fellow cleaners are waiting.

MAMA PAUL: *(Fondles the gun with nostalgia.)* See me with a gun. I've not held one since General Moham – I mean since my army boyfriend took me to the firing range and I accidentally shot a Corporal. If my parents had allowed me to marry him, I would have been a minister's wife, or I would have staged my own coup. Mr Ojo, do not forget me on your day of glory.

OJO: The day of glory is here. Ask and you shall receive.

MAMA PAUL: Minister of Finance.

OJO: What do you know about economics?

MAMA PAUL: Nothing, but I know you.

OJO: Kneel. *(MAMA PAUL kneels.)* By the power vested in me by myself and by all black cleaners in Great Britain, I hereby appoint you Permanent Minister for Finance. Arise, Mama Paul.

MAMA PAUL: Thank you, Your Majesty.

KOLA: I think we can stop joking and get cracking with this mess here.

OJO: Infidel! I knew you for a closet reactionary. You think this is a joke?

KOLA: Yes, and I stopped laughing ages ago.

OJO: Stay where you are! Mama Paul, join me here. You see gun and still you don't believe. You cannot hold up the Blackocratic process. Are you with us or are you against us?

KOLA: I am with you if it means we will clean up this place before Mike returns.

OJO: Mama Paul, a hand. *(Clambers laboriously down from the table.)* Nostalgic for the days of slavery, eh? I have a present for you from the toilet of 27th floor. To absorb you into the Other Way, clean the menses that found its way under my royal shoe – with your tongue. *(Sits on a table and raises one of his shoes for KOLA to lick.)*

KOLA: What?

MAMA PAUL: You want our royal father to repeat himself? *Lick*!

KOLA: You people have gone mad.

OJO: You are mad for mentioning Mike's name. What will he do when he returns? Sing 'God Save the Queen' with my gun in his face? Order me to clean up and then go for another tea break?

MAMA PAUL: King Ojo, show this bastard of no fixed address the power of Blackocracy. *Lick*!

KOLA: No!

MAMA PAUL: Attention! Mutiny within the ranks! Take aim, fire!

MAMA PAUL grabs KOLA by the neck. He resists. She knocks him to the ground with the butt of her pistol, drags him on his knees and shoves his face into OJO's shoe.

OJO: That's it, Mama Paul. Roll his head round and round. Let that tongue clean off every foreign body. We have only just started the Blackocracy and already he wants to spoil it. You think kicking in the window of a MacDonald's is going to change the world? Conservative revolutionary! Where are your guns? Where are your martyrs? Your memorable slogans and speeches? All will be forgotten once Starbucks opens on Peckham high street.

KOLA: *(Still struggling under MAMA PAUL's grip.)* I am sorry, sir! I am sorry!

MAMA PAUL: *Shebi,[4]* you wanted to clean. Clean now. Clean!

KOLA: *(Crying.)* But I told you this morning how I was going to be a true revolutionary! I did!

OJO: A student riot is nothing to compare with the Blackocratic revolution.

KOLA: If you let me, I will prove myself to the Other Way.

OJO: Mama Paul.

MAMA PAUL stops rubbing KOLA's face in OJO's shoe. She does not let go of him.

Prove yourself. Say the Blackocratic Pledge.

KOLA: The Blackocratic Pledge?

OJO: Say it!

KOLA: Er, OK, OK. I, I pledge, I pledge allegiance to Blackocracy?

OJO: Go on.

KOLA: … To be faithful loyal and honest…

OJO: Uhuh.

KOLA: …to serve Blackocracy with all my strength, to defend its honour and glory, so help me God.

MAMA PAUL: You have spoken well, although it is bad manners to talk with your mouth full.

OJO: Mama Paul release him.

---

4   But

MAMA PAUL lets go of KOLA who runs off to one corner of the office to throw up.

Now do you believe this is serious?

KOLA: Y-y-e-s-s.

OJO: I did not hear you!

KOLA: *(Hastily.)* Yes, sir, Emperor, President, King Ojo.

MAMA PAUL: Now you will learn to respect your elders, you dog of unknown pedigree.

OJO: It's all right, Minister for Finance. He is yet to have a mortgage. We must accommodate nonentities, especially young renegades like this goat. The glorious future of Blackocracy rests on the hooded jackets of our youths. By hook or by crook we must make them realise that there is no other way but the Other Way.

KOLA: *(Under his breath.)* Emperor Jones.

OJO: What did you call me just now?

KOLA: I said, 'Emperor O'Jones', you know, just making it sound groovy.

OJO: I am not one of your mates, you animal. How dare you funkify my name? There is shit on my other shoe.

KOLA: I was only anglicising it, sir! I did not mean to offend you.

MAMA PAUL: He is your Royal Highness to you! Monkey of no fixed tax band.

KOLA: Your Royal Highness.

OJO: You are learning. If you make progress I might make you Minister for Education.

KOLA: Me? Minister for Education? Thank you, your Highness, your Royal Highest Highness.

MAMA PAUL: Bootlicker.

OJO: My people, the sun of black Africa shall rise over this country. But this land is infected by something worse than the bad breath of politicians. And in keeping with the tradition of revolutions – being a traditional man myself – blood must be shed as an act of purification. We must wipe out all our enemies who do not wish us to be rich like them. The white oppressors will be dealt with ruthlessly.

MAMA PAUL: How ruthlessly?

OJO: How ruthless can you be?

MAMA PAUL: Do we not breathe air? Do we not drink water? Ruthlessness, is it not human nature? Why be the slave when you can be the master? Blackocracy's flag shall fly above a mountain of bones, above the rubble of cities. We shall conquer all races. We shall take back what the Westerner and the Arab have taken from us. We shall pay them back in their own coins. We shall make them slaves of the revolution!

OJO: What of you, Mr Part-time Mandela?

KOLA: *(Cautiously.)* Your Highness, if I may… There is this philosophy called Negritude. It's a consciousness of blackness in which we are the opposite of the white man. Where he is violent, we are peace loving. We sing where he shouts. We dance where he does military drill…

OJO: And that is why the monkey has a long tale! That is how our forefathers danced their way into slavery and colonialism. You will break dance when the multi-nationals collude with our government and force our farmers to buy GM seeds.

MAMA PAUL: Are you blind to the slaughters of Africans because of our mineral resources? Which poor people benefit from it? You dare open your mouth to tell us about black philosophy of peace and love. When you are one of the bloody collaborators.

KOLA: I am not!

OJO: History tells us the only language oppressor and oppressed understand is force! To rule the roost, you do not have to be fair, you do not have to be honest, you do not have to be bright. God knows you do not even have to win an election to be a democratically elected president.

MAMA PAUL: He is young and stupid.

OJO: If you cannot be ruthless, you can be ruthlessly dealt with.

KOLA: But, your Highness, violence only leads to more violence. Let's use the Other Way to create a better world.

OJO: Don't blaspheme! There is no Third Way crap here. The sequel is never as good as the original. The Other Way *is* the Other Way. It is the only way. Nothing else can come after it.

KOLA: But we can usher in humane change – real change. That could be the Other Way's philosophy.

OJO: Do the math! Have Africans retaliated for all the plundering we've suffered? No. Does anyone take us seriously in world affairs? No! Aren't you fed up with seeing us portrayed in the news always as basket cases? Aren't you ashamed of seeing us being 'saved' by pop stars turned saints and gap year NGOs? I ask you for the last time. Are you with us or not?

KOLA: I have no choice but to say yes.

OJO: A wise choice. Now, we must secure this area. Take your positions!

KOLA: Mr Ojo, I don't have a gun.

OJO: You are Minister without Gun. Move!

MAMA PAUL and KOLA assume 'attack' positions.

Carry out the first phase of our programme, Operation Blackout.

MAMA PAUL: We have secured the area, sir! There is a total absence of white in this sector.

OJO: Well done. Return to base.

KOLA and MAMA PAUL come to stand by OJO.

Our first mission is a success. Next we shall move as an irresistible force from office block to office block, liberating our people. No one else can do it for us. Not Labour. Not the Tories. Don't even let us waste time on the LibDems. To spread the message we shall commandeer all telecommunications. BT will be a piece of cake. All the cleaners are our people. Some will be deployed to seize the radio and TV stations. Include the Sky Network, especially the sports channels. I think there's a match on tonight… Where was I?

MAMA PAUL: Professor Ojo! But we cannot have a dirty revolution. Let us tidy up this place a bit…

OJO: Mama Paul, there is shit on my other shoe.

MAMA PAUL: I am sorry, President Ojo. But if we are going to take a photograph of this our decisive victory, it should not be called 'The Battle of Dirty Office'.

OJO: Leave that for our spin-doctors to consider. Besides, did I not state this is a dirty war? Ethnic cleansing is on the table for when we deal with the enemy.

KOLA: She must eat shit! Mr Ojo, she is trying to play for both teams. Let her be cleansed too.

OJO: It is not your place to tell me what to do, you hear? Insubordination leads to mutiny.

MAMA PAUL: *(To KOLA.)* If someone forces your mother to eat a bowl of shit, you'll pass her a spoon? I pity her for having you as a son, I swear.

KOLA: Leave my mother out of this!

OJO: Enough, comrades. We must stay alert or we lose the advantage. Anything can happen at any time, especially when we show a disunited front. We must invest our energies wisely and beware of companies that use funny accountants. That way we can collect our dividends at the close of trading.

KOLA: Mr Ojo, this is serious MBA grammar. You are talking the talk!

OJO: I am talking big man talk. The economy is the lifeblood of any government. Do not underestimate the importance of unit trusts, stock options, leveraged buy-outs and numbered Swiss accounts. One must prepare ahead of time. *Forza* Roma, Football *Italia*.

MAMA PAUL: Pope Ojo is speaking in tongues! Oh, you are a complete leader. Every inch of you is spot on like a German penalty kick. I must emulate you! Pastamacaronispaghettinoodle-tandoori!

KOLA: Er, Mama, leave the spiritual semantics to our leader. King Ojo, what next?

OJO: We are in a bank, in a room full of computers, and we have a student – you, Kola. We need money to spray people with, so they will know this is a Nigerian revolution. Sit down and get to work. Wherever this bank's money is I want you to conjure it.

KOLA: The kind of information we need is safeguarded by passwords. We cannot access it just by turning on a PC.

OJO: Fiddle with the keys like they do in the movies, maybe by accident you will discover the password.

KOLA: It would be easier to rob the bank.

OJO: And how do we open the vault? What are you good for?

KOLA: Mr Ojo, I too like the smell of money. If I were a manager here I'd get you the financial records, no waste time. But we are the cleaners. We come before the staff arrives. We leave when the staff arrives. But now that we are revolutionaries – and some of us are still Minister without gun – we can spread our wings and fly to the apex of our dreams.

OJO: (*Dreamily.*) Big Man.

MAMA PAUL: *(Dreamily.)* Cash Madam.

KOLA: *(Gaining in confidence.)* Gone now the shackles of neocolonialism and capitalist captivity. Dead now the theories of postmodern otherness and decentring of the subject, for we are now the centre! No more the trawl of bus 133 early in the morning, ferrying our brothers and sisters to the City to do degrading work. Only to make ourselves scarce by the time the Northern Line – the black line – ferries the whites to their comfy jobs. Since we built the Underground, you should make public transport free for all black people. That way I won't have to dodge fares any more.

OJO: *(Disappointed.)* You know how to fare dodge but you don't know how to hack into a computer. Of what use is a fare dodger to the Revolution?

MAMA PAUL: This is not fair! This is not fair at all. You two cannot be making big speeches and not allow me to say my own on behalf of our sisters.

OJO: *(Disconsolate.)* Say something then.

KOLA: *(Urgently.)* Mr Ojo, you want her to disgrace our women? The blackocracy is on infant legs. We will lose all our female supporters if we present Mama Paul as the face of blackocracy.

OJO: Talk, Mama Paul.

MAMA PAUL: Thank you, President Ojo, don't mind that car of expired MOT. He has never slept with a woman.

KOLA: *(Shouts.)* I have!

OJO: *(Impatiently.)* Oya, Mama Paul, your speech.

MAMA PAUL: Sorry. In the name of Jesus…

Sound of footsteps approaching.

KOLA: Shhh… It must be Mike coming.

OJO: *(Whispers with malevolent glee.)* God answers prayers. Assume attack positions.

They assume attack positions. Blackout.

End of Act One.

Act Two

Enter MIKE. He does not notice them but sees the spill.

MIKE: My God! The floor's ruined! Where are these monkeys? Ojo! Yemi! Kola!

They jump out of their attack positions to catch MIKE by surprise. He is oblivious of their new disposition, and of their guns.

What the hell have you all been doing since I left? You've got less than an hour before the bank staff arrives! And what happened to the floor? You've stained it so badly there's no way we can cover it up. Kola, I told you to sort out 27th. The toilets, Ojo, what about the toilets? *(Riffles through his pocket, brings out a pen and pieces of paper and signs them.)* Here you go. Here's your written warning, and I've put insignificant in yours so you can spell it properly when you write your stupid appeal. *(Hands letter to OJO, then to MAMA PAUL and KOLA.)* And why haven't you cleaned this office, Yemi? It's worse than before!

MAMA PAUL: Oh, no. Look at that corner. I did it just before you walked in, you can ask… *(Her voice trails off in the glares of OJO and KOLA. She resumes her attack position.)*

OJO: *(To MIKE.)* Paper, scissors, gun. I win!

MIKE: *(Notices OJO and MAMA PAUL are holding pistols.)* What the hell is going on? What are you doing with those? Where did you get those guns?

OJO: *(Approaches MIKE and slaps him.)* From there! Does that answer your question? Who were you going to fire?

MIKE: *(Yells in pain.)* What's going on? What are you doing?

KOLA: Reading poetry! You are now the first captive of the Blackocratic Revolution.

MIKE: The what? Hey!

KOLA drags MIKE and pushes him down on to a chair. He takes a piece of rope and ties him up but does not secure him properly.

Let go of me! Hey! There's no way you can get out of here. Once the workers clock in, they'll discover what's happening and call the police. You can't blast your way out of here with two pistols.

OJO opens the bag and throws a pistol to KOLA who misses it and runs clumsily to pick it up.

OJO: Don't panic! *(To MIKE.)* You want to use your military psychology on us. We have our own counter-insurgency expert in Mama Paul.

MAMA PAUL: Kill and Go – that is my method. Dead soldiers can't use psychology on anyone.

OJO: I've enough arms for all black cleaners in this city. What do you think of that?

MIKE: You mean you have an army? You've taken over the country?

KOLA: *(Chuffed that he has his own gun.)* Not quite. We have only just… *(OJO casts him a withering look.)* I mean… So you are a spy sent by the agency to find out our plans, not so? Talk!

MIKE: I've just come down from cleaning the Executive Suite! Yemi brought me tea there, didn't you Yemi? That's where I've come from!

OJO: From making contact with the enemy!

MIKE: No! I had my tea while I was waiting for the buffer… Look, what do you want? I'll give you anything, pay increases, more hours in smaller offices. I'll even recommend you all for the supervisor vacancies that are coming up, yeah? I can't say fairer than that. I'll throw in a company car for you as well.

KOLA: You are nothing but a lowly supervisor. You have no say in staff promotion.

OJO: *(Thinking.)* But he can recommend people to management. Don't underestimate the power of a supervisor.

MAMA PAUL: You don't know, he might be friends with the personnel manager.

OJO: As one big person to another.

MIKE: Exactly! I'll tell Cherie to sort it all out for you once we get back to the office. If you just let me go…

MAMA PAUL: Has Sharon left? Since when?

OJO: Sharon has not left. This bastard is trying to play us!

MIKE attempts an explanation but is cut short by a slap from OJO.

MIKE: Ow! I can't think straight. You've a gun to my head!

OJO: It doesn't matter one jot who is the personnel manager. There is a new game in town that will sweep away everything that has come before it.

KOLA: Tell him, President Ojo!

MAMA PAUL: Tell him his life story!

OJO: What are you?

MIKE: What am I?

OJO: You are an oppressor. You were so stupid as to use the name Mike Bond, thinking that we could not put two and two together…

MIKE: But Mike Bond is my real name.

OJO: You should have kept your real name – *James* Bond. You're part of the government's plans to destroy black people. In *From Zimbabwe, With Tobacco*, you escaped from Mugabe. They reassigned you here! This is another day that you're going to die, spy!

MIKE: No, no. You've got it all wrong. I'm not a spy.

OJO: Management brought you from outside. They pushed me to the sidelines. I who have been working here for so long and know the ins and outs of this business. How could that happen if there is no ulterior motive behind it, a wider scheme of the New World Order?

MAMA PAUL: Tell him, King Ojo.

OJO: It must be that you are their paid assassin! Why else would they hire an ex-commando?

MIKE: I'm not an assassin! I was an infantryman.

OJO: It is a pity. I would have preferred our first captive to be Blair or Bush. We will make do with you. Be grateful. We have helped you reclaim the fifteen minutes of fame that you wasted on 'Match of the Day'.

MIKE: I've never been on 'Match of the Day'.

OJO: So you deny your bottom appeared on the highlights on Saturday night with the repeat broadcast on Sunday morning?

MIKE: I swear I've never been to a Premiership match! I can't afford it.

OJO: Mister Man, you should go out like a Gulf War hero telling the truth…

MIKE: But I am telling the truth. I don't get paid extra for being an ex-soldier, honest.

OJO: But Mr Bond, you get all expenses paid holidays with beautiful women thrown in. You get VIP tickets to watch Manchester United versus Arsenal.

MAMA PAUL: We see the brand new car that you drive to work every morning.

OJO: Bristling with gadgets a CIA agent would envy – to kill me, the Black Liberator.

MIKE: Jesus Christ, it's a company car. I drive an F-reg. I do.

OJO: And your yearly holidays? To Sangatte, to Dover, to Guantanamo Bay!

KOLA: To plot our downfall with the racist bastards!

MIKE: They're just holidays! Package tours. Cheap flights. I save up with the missus all year round. By the time we return, we're broke.

MAMA PAUL: *(Takes a cigarette lighter out of MIKE's chest pocket, lights it and circles it around his groin area.)* I've just remembered one method of torture my General boyfriend taught me.

OJO: I am still interrogating the prisoner.

KOLA: You are talking as if you and management are not one and the same thing. A hydra-headed axis of evil.

MIKE: I'm an employee just like you. How can I be part of them?

OJO: Very easily. The agency is a wing of MI5 and you work for them. You framed poor Fred so that you could get to us.

MIKE: Fred got fired for stealing loo rolls. He was nicking them from the store and from inside the toilets. The bank found out.

OJO: You think we cannot see through your deceit?

MIKE: The other team was in on it. The agency couldn't prove it so we had them transferred. That's why Fred's gone. That's why you're the only ones here. As soon as I get back to the office I'll make sure we get more staff in tomorrow. That's a promise.

MAMA PAUL: So Fred got fired.

KOLA: For stealing loo roll! Ha! How miserable is that?

OJO: Liar! Fred was a rare thing – a good white man. Have you ever bought us KFC?

MAMA PAUL: Ask him, Mr Ojo!

OJO: Fred didn't know about your plot. He thought the agency was a real cleaning company. He recommended your enemy for promotion and you got rid of him!

MIKE: It's in the report. He stole loo rolls.

OJO: We were going to make him an honorary black man, an assimilated African. We were… Wait, this is another delay tactic to stop us from meeting our historic appointment! You are a first-class spy.

MAMA PAUL: Ah, it's true, President Ojo. See how we got carried away. Let me handle him. He will not try it again. Moron without N.I. number.

MIKE: Look, the workers will soon arrive. The quicker we get back to work the better. Let's forget this whole thing ever happened, eh? What do you say? I promise I won't say a word to anyone. Not a word.

MAMA PAUL: It's too late. The fart is out of the anus.

OJO: We have all the proof that you are a government operative.

MAMA PAUL: All those long tea breaks…

KOLA: Staying put in the Executive Suite…

OJO: Feeling up Mama Paul…

MAMA PAUL: Mr Ojo!

OJO: We will deal with the agency and then the government. First things first.

MIKE: What are you going to do to me? Cut off my hands? Slice off my lips?

MAMA PAUL: What lips?

KOLA: What do you take us for, cannibals? What do you think these guns are for?

MIKE: But I've done nothing to you.

OJO: *(Laughs cynically.)* Still in denial. We are the plaintiff, prosecution, judge and jury. We are the chief and only witnesses to bear testimony against your skulduggery. Our sentence is final and this is just the preliminary proceeding. If Nigeria's economy had not collapsed, where would a monkey like you get the chance to command me? Where?

KOLA: What qualifications do you have?

MIKE: I left school without any.

OJO: You see? Yet you have become a supervisor just like that, over others that are better qualified. How did you become a spy?

MIKE: I worked my way up. I deserve everything I've got. I've served this country with my life!

KOLA: That's where you learned how to kill people. You thought we were easy meat? You thought wrong, Mr Bond. Every Englishman from Land's End to John o' Groats will curse your name when we take control. People will say, 'Oh that bastard Mike! May he and his family rot on a pile of BSE-infected cows for bringing hell to our green and pleasant land!' That is what they will say, and more.

MIKE: But I'm telling you I'm an employee just like you. I do what I'm told. It's the bosses of the agency. They're the ones you want. They're the fat cats making all the money off our backs.

OJO: Not only an assassin, a communist, too!

MAMA PAUL: You have been well-trained. Even I cannot keep up pretence this long. You are indeed a worthy opponent.

MIKE: Yemi, I can't believe you're part of this. You didn't say that when we were in the stock room and…

MAMA PAUL quickly slaps him.

Argh!

MAMA PAUL: When we what? Watch your mouth, oh! If I bring my gun down on your head the little brains that you have will spill on the floor. Bastard of dubious birth certificate.

OJO: Mama Paul, don't kill him yet. I've not finished questioning him. Mike. Mike! I want the names of all the operatives masquerading as supervisors in the agency. Your cohorts who do the dirty work.

MIKE realizes the ropes are loosened.

KOLA: No, it is we black people who do the dirty work.

MIKE: Yeah, right!

MAMA PAUL pulls his ear.

Yemi, what did you do that for?

MAMA PAUL: Your life is in our hands and you are laughing!

MIKE: I'm supporting what Kola said.

KOLA: Did I ask you for your support?

MIKE: I'm sorry. I don't want to die yet. Chelsea are playing tonight.

OJO: On Sky?

MIKE: Yeah.

KOLA: Who are they playing?

MIKE: Liverpool.

KOLA: Yeh! I have to be at my sister's house this evening.

OJO: There are more important matters at hand!

MAMA PAUL: Thank God, I thought you were going to fall for his strategy.

MIKE: It's true. Chelsea play Liverpool tonight and it's live on the telly. And if we don't get this mess cleaned up and go home, and do all things we need to do before evening, we're going to miss it. Ojo, you didn't clean the toilets. So the sooner we get cracking the better.

OJO: I don't know what trick you have up your sleeve but you are finished for still having the audacity to order me around.

MIKE: No, no!

MAMA PAUL: Mr Ojo, let me make him pay for his insult!

MIKE breaks free and lunges at OJO. MAMA PAUL and KOLA pile on top of him and proceed to pummel him.

OJO: He tried to kill me!

MIKE: Help! Somebody help me!

MAMA PAUL: You tried to kill our leader!

MIKE: Oh my God, somebody help me!

KOLA: We're in London, idiot! Nobody cares. Get him!

OJO: I have survived my first assassination attempt!

OJO stops KOLA and MAMA PAUL from beating up MIKE.

OJO: Enough. Enough! Let him live to see me triumph over him. You will clean this whole building from top to bottom. Give him a broom!

KOLA: *(Drags the battered MIKE up on to his feet.)* Are you deaf? Get the broom and sweep! Try anything 'gengentious'[5] again and I will shoot you! *(MIKE picks up the broom and starts sweeping.)* That's it. See what it feels like to be ordered around.

OJO: He knows what it's like, stupid. He is a government operative. *(Inspects where MIKE has swept.)* Good. I could not have cleaned it better myself. You see, I know how to supervise. But instead of acknowledging my talent, the agency sends an assassin to kill me. Their time will come. First, I must commemorate this seminal moment in my life.

MAMA PAUL: But I am yet to make my own speech.

KOLA: The time for making speeches has passed. Mike used a spy gadget to cut himself free. We must watch him carefully. We don't know what else he has on him.

MAMA PAUL: You did not secure Mike properly, Kola. That's how he…

---

5   Nonsense word for any act of daring.

KOLA: *(Hurriedly.)* Who says Mama Paul should not make her speech? *(To MIKE.)* You?

MIKE: No, no!

OJO: Kola, we will come back to that…

KOLA: Mama Paul, you are wasting precious time. Talk!

MAMA PAUL: In the name of Jesus, Alpha and Omega. All we niggers is gonna unite. We ain't gonna do no more shitty jobs. Hallelujah! We gonna get outta di ghetto an' live in da palace, Amen. We is gonna bring down Tony Blair and the Queen. Me is gonna replace dat broad an' become da new ho' on da block. Amen. Me is gonna fuck all di handsome niggers. Black woman's is gonna be free from baby fathers. All you runaway father's is gonna get hit. I say all you useless black men who leave the responsibility of your children to your women is gonna die! All you men who sit back at home in Nigeria waiting for wives slaving away in London and New York to send you money. You take the money to chase young girls around in our absence and leave our children to starve. We women is gonna…

OJO: Thank you, thank you, Mama Paul. God, where did you get this barbarian talk from?

MAMA PAUL: Don't you listen to the children on your estate?

OJO: Yes. They don't sound at all like that.

KOLA: As Minister for Education I will rid the streets of second-hand English. Education, education, education, that is the key to instituting Blackocracy. What would you do to Paul if you heard him talking like that?

MAMA PAUL: I would discipline them.

KOLA: Thank you. And I'm sure you did not understand half of what you just said.

MAMA PAUL: Now you want to insult me. I am older than your mother.

KOLA: What does 'ho'' mean?

MAMA PAUL: You say?

KOLA: You called yourself one. Tell us what it means.

MAMA PAUL: I did not. You are putting words into my mouth.

OJO: Mama Paul, you did.

MAMA PAUL: It means… It means…

KOLA: Yes…

MAMA PAUL: It means… It is short for Holy Virgin, Mother of God.

KOLA bursts into laughter.

MAMA PAUL: All right, Mr Voice of the Youths. Tell us what it means.

KOLA: You asked me to tell you, right?

OJO: Kola!

KOLA: So don't abuse my parents.

MAMA PAUL: How can I do that?

OJO: Kola!

KOLA: It is slang – for whore.

OJO: This boys is so stupid.

MAMA PAUL: *(Furious.)* Ehn! What did you call me just now? You are the son of a whore, do you hear me? All the females in your family are whores! Your father is a male whore! All the people in your village are whores! They will rape all the females in your family! Mr Ojo, hear how this boy used system to call me a whore.

KOLA: You see? You cannot abuse my family and my hometown and get away with it. No!

OJO: *(To MIKE who is inching nearer to the bag of guns.)* Hey! *(Grabs MIKE and ties him to the buffer.)* Stop your nonsense, both of you!

MAMA PAUL: Ehen, I abused your family, what do you want to do? I say I abused your hometown, what can a rat like you do about it?

KOLA: *(Puts down his gun and approaches MAMA PAUL menacingly.)* What do I think I can do? Did you not speak of rape just now?

MAMA PAUL: *(Puts down her own gun and approaches KOLA menacingly too. They meet in the centre.)* What do you want to do with that word? That word 'rape' in the mouth of a small boy like you. Can you mount your mother? *(Lands KOLA a vicious slap on the face.)*

KOLA: *(Is nearly knocked over by the slap.)* Yeh! You are finished! I will kill you with my bare hands!

Grabs MAMA PAUL by her neck. OJO looks on. There is a mischievous grin on his face. MAMA PAUL breaks free from KOLA's grasp, rolls him to the ground and holds him in a judo choke.

MAMA PAUL: Surrender.

KOLA: *(Gasping.)* Never!

MAMA PAUL: Surrender or else I choke you to death. *(Tightens her grip.)*

KOLA: *(Yells.)* Yah! Mr Ojo, help me. She is the one who abused my family, oh! Ah, I am going to die before my father.

OJO: Ah, well, you made the problem for yourself.

KOLA: *(Weakly.)* I am dead. You're right, Dad. I am a weakling. Goodbye. Mr Ojo, tell my father I went down fighting.

MAMA PAUL: You are not yet dead. Apologise while you are still in this world.

KOLA: S-s-sorry.

MAMA PAUL: I did not hear you.

KOLA: Mama Paul, I am sorry.

MAMA PAUL: Say that your mother and all the females in your family are whores.

KOLA: *(Pleading.)* Mr Ojo.

OJO: Mama Paul, it is enough. The boy has learned two lessons: one, too much knowledge is a dangerous thing and two: talk according to your muscle.

MAMA PAUL: *(Releases KOLA who runs to a corner sobbing and clutching his neck.)* God saved you. I would have snapped every bone in your miserable body before stamping on your head until your brains popped out.

OJO: No wonder you put down your gun. I was thinking that was a foolish thing for a person of your age to do even against a bone rattle like Kola.

MAMA PAUL: I stole a few judo lessons when the agency sent me to a sports centre. I told the coach I was a member of staff. If to say they left me there, I would have become a black belt.

OJO: You are my chief of security. Our youth are strong only when they are in front of Playstation. Kola, see how a woman your mother's age mishandled you. You're even crying! I wish your father could see you, threatening rape. Rape! Be honest. You were trying to get a cheap lay. And using your family honour as an excuse!

KOLA: I did not want to damage her because of her age. If not, I would have… *(MAMA PAUL approaches KOLA. KOLA jumps up and runs to hide behind OJO.)* Mr Ojo, save me!

OJO: Enough of this nonsense! Pick up your arms and settle down. *(MAMA PAUL picks up her gun. KOLA is preoccupied with his aching neck to pick up his own gun.) Oya*, come closer. The next phase is to…

KOLA: Yeow.

OJO: What is wrong with you now?

KOLA: My neck. It still hurts.

OJO: So?

KOLA: How am I going to contribute my quota if I am physically incapacitated?

OJO: Before you were shot by friendly fire, were you of any use? Stop whining before I set Mama Paul on you again.

MAMA PAUL: Let us leave that fool alone, President Ojo. Er, *(Nods in the direction of MIKE.)* what of *oyinbo*?[6]

OJO: *(To MIKE.)* So you enjoyed your ringside seat for the fight of the decade, *abi*? You have not seen anything yet. Mama Paul, Kola. Kola! Get up, you cry baby! *(They approach MIKE.)* Untie him. Hold him like a goat for slaughter. *(They hold him so that he is on his knees.)*

MIKE: Please, no, not again. I'll clean the whole building!

OJO: Oh but you will. *(Stands over MIKE.)*

MIKE: What are you doing? What are you doing?

OJO: Hold his mouth wide open.

6   the white man

MIKE: No, please no!

OJO: *(OJO urinates inside MIKE's mouth.)* Who's taking the piss now?

OJO zips up his trousers.

MIKE: *(Splutters.)* Oh God, Oh God, oh God.

OJO: You should be happy that I have blessed your mouth…

MAMA PAUL lands MIKE a vicious blow that renders him unconscious.

What is your problem, Mama Paul?

MAMA PAUL: Sorry Your Excellency, I got carried away.

OJO: No be only carried away. Leave him for now. For it shall be written in the chronicles of our Great Revolution that the enemy put up a brave fight. He showed the great bulldog spirit. But as always, it ended in heroic failure due to incompetence and tactical naïveté. Showing a lot of heart is not enough to win a war these days. Putting on too many strikers and leaving your defence exposed makes you vulnerable to counterattack. Possession is the key, especially when you are playing in the Champions League.

MAMA PAUL: What a strategiser! Mr Ojo the Field Marshal! We are going to conquer nations.

OJO: Na only nations?

MAMA PAUL: We are going to conquer planets.

OJO: Tell them, tell them!

MAMA PAUL: Mr Ojo is our salvation.

OJO: You didn't know that before?

MAMA PAUL: Mr Ojo is our heaven and earth.

OJO: Put am, put am!

MAMA PAUL: Mr Ojo is our god.

OJO: With a small 'g' – for the moment. And you, Mr Student, you have nothing to say? *(Picks up KOLA's gun.)* Did I not ask you to pick up your weapon? Your incompetence nearly allowed Mike to kill me the first time you want to give him another chance. Colluding with the enemy! For that I relegate you to caterer for the revolution, since you have sense for little else. Your position carries no gun. Go and get us tea. And don't take long! You cannot keep a god waiting, even one with a small 'g'.

KOLA exits.

MAMA PAUL: Idiot. The Other Way could have lost its way if Mike had picked up his gun.

OJO: Yes, yes. Our arms dealer cannot cope with our demand for weapons. I have a friend who cleans offices at the MoD. I will see if he can get us nuclear weapons.

MAMA PAUL: President Ojo, your friend will not have that kind of access, if that is what you are banking on.

OJO: He may know someone whose palm we can grease. If he can't help us we will have to go back to the underground network. My supplier might know some Russian ex-soldiers.

MAMA PAUL: I know some teenagers in my area. I will talk to them.

OJO: If only this country was like America. I would have bought rocket launchers and tanks from the high street. Then I would have taught my soldiers the Yeltsin manoeuvre.

MAMA PAUL: How to fall down drunk in public?

OJO: No. How to bomb parliament and remain a friend of the West.

MAMA PAUL: Mr Ojo, you know too much.

OJO: It is a problem. Time for tea break.

Enter KOLA with a tray of tea and coffee pots and mugs. He puts the tray in front of OJO. OJO looks over the tray.

What of biscuits?

KOLA: I didn't find any.

OJO: What? In the whole of that big staff room, you couldn't find any biscuits? Did you check the staff rooms on the other floors? How can we have a decent tea break without biscuits? I charge you with dereliction of duty. You call yourself Minister of Education, you cannot organise a proper tea break. So when students of the Revolution need a rest from their daily chores you will ask them to drink tea without biscuits? Is that not how the yeast of dissatisfaction rises into the bread of revolt? Even Thatcher did not dare try such a thing!

MAMA PAUL: Tell this idiot of rare distinction! Tell him!

OJO: Labour's greatest achievement was the tea break bill. The Tories lost the election over the abolition of tea break. Britain built its empire on tea – India for tea, the West Indies for sugar, Scotland for shortcake and China for china. And you can stand there offering us tea without biscuits. Abomination!

KOLA: Forgive me!

MAMA PAUL: Try him for treason! In the Great Book of the Revolution you are the fiery tea bag monster. There will be weeping and gnashing of teeth because the land has been cursed by a famine of custard creams! Oh, woe unto future generations, for our people have abandoned Canaan for Sheol!

OJO: Do you hear the prophecy of Mama Paul? Those who have ears let them hear!

KOLA: I am sorry! Please, forgive me!

OJO: You are forgiven – for now. One more mistake and you are finished. Go and look for the biscuits and make sure you find some this time.

KOLA: Yes sir, your Highness sir! I will lay down my life for this important mission.

MAMA PAUL: Be quick, before the tea goes cold.

Exit KOLA.

OJO: Stupid boy.

MAMA PAUL: Mr Ojo, are you sure he is up to the task of Minister for Education? I mean, if he cannot organise simple tea with biscuits how can he educate our youths? You know how our people love tea break, especially those lazy buggers on afternoon shift.

OJO: He nearly got me killed – twice! He is all we have for now, Mama. When others join our cause, we shall dispose of him quietly.

MAMA PAUL: I can use him as a training dummy. Never in his life will he call me a whore again.

OJO: You should be flattered that a young bobo[7] wants to wrestle with you. You should have given him a spin; he might be a stud.

MAMA PAUL: A man of your age!

OJO: Are we not adults? I am serious.

MAMA PAUL: You talk as if you don't know how lonely this London can get. *(Gets closer to OJO.)* I am on my own in another man's country working to support my children. The husband I left behind is a bastard. Where can a woman my age look to for comfort?

OJO: *(Edges away from her.)* Save your needs for when next you go home. A woman with pounds like you will find no problem in attracting young men. Or stick with your husband. I'm sure he stores enough firepower for you when you visit Ibadan.

MAMA PAUL: The husband who uses the money that I slave for to carry young girls around in my absence? The one who complains that I'm not sending enough for the family's upkeep? The last time I sent money was for repairs to the house. When I visited home what did I see? He had used the money to buy a new car and clothes to go around town acting the big man. My children were so poorly that I broke down in tears. I haven't slept with him for the past five years. But I still have my needs. If we fool around like you men you call us prostitutes. Or you don't know those girls you sleep with are also looking for comfort and not just money for one month travelcard?

OJO: Nonsense. They just need my penis inside them. When I open my trousers, they don't even care about my age. In fact, let us stop all this emotional talk – that is for white women. You are Mother Africa. You are strong and hardworking, and support your men and children under all circumstances. Who are you?

MAMA PAUL: I am Yemi.

OJO: Madam, you cannot first be breaking necks and the next minute be doing Indian film romance. The Revolution

---

7   young and hip man

does not need human beings. You have to be a god like me. There must be no weak link. Or else, goodbye!

KOLA enters unnoticed.

MAMA PAUL: Kola is our weakest link. Like all these book people, he dreams of a world where all fingers are equal. He's going to be a dissident anyway. Let's get rid of him here and now.

OJO: But who will be my Minister for Education?

MAMA PAUL: You will find better people to replace him when Blackocracy sweeps the nation.

OJO: *(Thinks.)* Fine! When Kola returns we finish him off. Where did he drop his gun?

KOLA tiptoes over and picks up his gun just as OJO finishes talking.

KOLA: Hands up! Too bad, you are too big to heed your own advice. You dropped your guns.

OJO: *(Startled.)* We were only joking, weren't we, Mama Paul?

MAMA PAUL: Yes, Mr Ojo. And wasn't it funny?

OJO and MAMA PAUL burst into uncontrollable fits of laughter. They edge towards their guns.

KOLA: Shut up! If you move one inch more, you will meet your ancestors. Stand against the wall. Come on!

OJO and MAMA PAUL move against the wall but do not put their hands up.

OJO: The most important thing is that you found the biscuits. Good job, I hereby appoint you Minister for Petroleum. That is in addition to your Education portfolio.

KOLA: Do you think I'm joking with you?

OJO: We don't know for sure but after tea break we will discuss it. Anybody want digestives?

OJO makes for the biscuits. KOLA cocks his gun. OJO stops.

Hey, as a true African it is disrespectful to tell us to raise our hands. What will you ask us to do next – close our eyes and raise up one leg?

Moves menacingly towards OJO and MAMA PAUL. They raise up their hands.

KOLA: This is not a matter of seniority. You were planning to kill me.

MAMA PAUL: Yeh, my arms. I have rheumatism in my shoulders.

KOLA: Oh, not in your bottom this time, Mrs Bruce Lee? Come forward. Keep your hands up! *(MAMA PAUL approaches.)* Yes, come slowly forward.

MAMA PAUL: Kolly-Bolly! My own firstborn! Kolly-Bolly for President! Kolly-Bolly for Prime Minister!

KOLA: Whose mother is a whore? Fat bottom! Whose mother is a whore?

MAMA PAUL: I don't associate with such people. As mother to son it's not good for you to go looking for prostitutes.

KOLA: Go back and stand against the wall. And keep your arms up! Mr Ojo, report for duty!

OJO: Yes sir! Honourable Minister for Education and Petroleum sir! Reporting for duty sir!

KOLA: That's right. Keep those sirs flowing like water. You'll need it.

OJO: Yes sir. In fact, we need to reheat the tea. Biscuit, sir?

KOLA raises his gun.

Don't shoot me sir!

KOLA: Me? Shoot a whole blackocratically elected President? Who born monkey? Just remove your shoes, please.

OJO: Remove my shoes sir?

KOLA: Yes, remove your shoes.

OJO: But I polished them this morning. You can see how they shine from where you're standing.

KOLA: True. But we've been working all morning. They must be dirty – especially the soles. If your soul is not clean, how can you lead a revolution? If your sole is not clean, how will it look to your genuflecting followers? They will become disaffected. Disaffection leads to counterrevolution. It's even worse if they cannot keep a cricket score.

OJO: That is why I use Odour Eaters in all my shoes. Not that my feet smell but you can't take chances in this cleaning job. That's how a leader should think. Don't take chances with yourself, only with others. *(Points to MAMA PAUL.)*

KOLA: *(Applauds.)* But of course. *(Slaps OJO, then lands gun on his head.)* This is a palace coup! Take off your shoes and lick the one with shit on it! Lick both the soles!

OJO: I am dead! My head is broken! Ah, Kola, please!

KOLA: 'I and the public know what all schoolchildren learn, those to whom evil is done do evil in return.'[8]

OJO: Please!

KOLA: Lick.

OJO licks the soles of his shoes.

Don't throw up.

OJO throws up.

You will swallow both my own and your own vomit today!

MAMA PAUL: What have we done to you, Kola? Have we not treated you like our own son?

KOLA: If that's how you treat your children I'm sorry for them.

MAMA PAUL: Are you saying that I, Mother Africa, am a bad mother?

KOLA: Who dash you 'Mother Africa'?

MAMA PAUL: So because you have a gun pointing at me I'm now a bad mother. All right, oh. There are some women, gun or no gun, if you call them a bad mother, they will rather die that accept such a slur.

KOLA: Are you one of those women?

MAMA PAUL: No.

KOLA: Then shut your bloody trap! *(Kicks OJO in the stomach.)*

OJO: Aargh!

KOLA: I am the Big Man now. I am the one people will line the streets for, the Blackocratic action hero gunning down my enemies single-handed. I am the hunter of white meat! I am no more the weakling. I was on your side, you treated

---

8   WH Auden, 'September 1, 1939'

me worse than Mike! Fucking hell, *you treated me worse than Mike!*

MAMA PAUL: But we held Mike down while he gargled on Mr Ojo's urine.

KOLA: Mama Paul, come here. It's your turn.

MAMA PAUL: But you've abused me already.

KOLA: I want to make amends by giving you another title.

MAMA PAUL: Oh thank you, my son! Thank you.

OJO: No, Mama Paul, you cannot desert me now.

MAMA PAUL: I saw you signalling to President Kola to kill me instead of you.

OJO: There was something in my eye! Mama Paul! Mama Paul, I love you!

KOLA points the gun at OJO. He holds his mouth with his fingers. OJO does likewise.

KOLA: That's right. I don't want to hear another peep from you. Now, Mama Paul. I just want you to do one tiny little thing for me.

MAMA PAUL: Ask and it shall be done.

KOLA: That is the spirit. Lie on the desk. *(Points to the one he polished.)*

MAMA PAUL: You want me to wipe it clean with my overalls? No problem. I can do it standing.

MAMA PAUL wipes the desk with her sleeve.

KOLA: One, two, three… *(MAMA PAUL lies on the table.)*

MAMA PAUL: Kola, please. You know your mother will not be too happy to see us in this position.

KOLA: She won't mind. She's a whore. *(Climbs onto the table and begins to unzip his trousers. He fumbles about.)*

MAMA PAUL makes to stand up. He pushes her down and continues fumbling about.

MAMA PAUL: *(Looks away, braces herself.)* Please, Kola, please I beg you.

He stops. He has ejaculated. He looks embarrassed, looking wildly at MAMA PAUL. Her face is still turned away from him. He looks at

OJO. OJO quickly looks away. Confused, he rips open MAMA PAUL's trousers and mounts her.

MAMA PAUL: God save me!

KOLA: *(Humps her viciously.)* Mother Africa! What does it feel like? Who's the whore now?

MAMA PAUL realizes KOLA has shot his load.

KOLA: Can you feel the power? *Can you feel the power?*

OJO watches the proceedings with disbelief.

MAMA PAUL: *(Unimpressed, jerkily.)* If you say so. Let me remove the keyboard underneath me.

KOLA: You feel the power now, don't you? You feel the power now, whore!

MAMA PAUL: *(In rhythm to KOLA's spasmodic movements.)* Kola, careful, now, I'm not a horse. Ah, my back! God! Oh! Ow!

KOLA: Hear her screaming with pain!

MAMA PAUL: Just one second, I'll get it out now! Yeow!

KOLA: *(Frenzied.)* She's feeling the power! She's feeling the power!

KOLA gets off MAMA PAUL. MAMA PAUL removes the keyboard from under her as she slides off the desk, her trousers covered in KOLA's semen.

KOLA: *(Gets off MAMA PAUL, his trousers soiled with his semen.)* Look how I gave it to Mama Africa. If only my father could see me now. Sending me here to study because he thought I was gay, saying that I was weak and would not be able to cope in Nigeria. But look at me now, father, look at me now!

OJO: Unbelievable. You're calling on your father to come and see you in action.

KOLA: I gave it to you, didn't I? Didn't I?

MAMA PAUL: *(Cleans the semen from off herself.)* Yes, yes. You really gave it to me good and proper. *(Looks at KOLA with pity.)*

KOLA: You hear that? You are jealous of me. So what if my father is a permanent secretary? Did he ask you not to go to university? My father is bigger than you, Little Man. I am bigger than you! I am too much for you. I am too much for any woman! I will be the father of generations.

OJO: What monster have I created?

MAMA PAUL: Kola.

KOLA: What?

MAMA PAUL: Your flies.

KOLA looks down to see his flies are undone. He has difficulty zipping them up using only one hand. The gun remains in the other hand, flailing about. OJO signals to MAMA PAUL. They move slyly towards the bag of guns

OJO: Look at you. How can you lead the revolution when you cannot even do up your trousers?

KOLA: *(Still struggling with his flies.)* Shut up! Nobody is leaving until I usher in the Other Way my way. *(Climbs onto the table.)* Now, I will bring to birth a true revolution.

OJO: How will it look in the Great Book of the Revolution, that you heralded the Other Way with your Brixton Market undies showing and your limp penis unable to make even a guest appearance through those soiled trousers?

KOLA: In your version, old fool. In my chronicles, you will be the impotent beast.

OJO: Next to the other great black men of history: Idi Amin, Bokassa, Sanni Abacha, you will look like a part-time pimp.

MAMA PAUL: You don't want your legacy soiled in this manner, do you? People will look upon you as the Anti-Christ. Please, for the sake of your adopted children.

KOLA: You sad, pitiful fools. Go for the bag. Go on. *(OJO and MAMA PAUL halt.)* No please, I beg you, take one more step so that I can end your miserable lives. This is the second time you're trying to kill me.

OJO: Ah, no, sir we were only trying…

KOLA: On your knees! Raise up your hands! *(OJO and MAMA PAUL fall on their knees and raise their hands.)* This is how blackocracy treats traitors, especially those from the wasted generation. The young shall inherit the Other Way. The Other Way is My Way.

OJO: OK, then. Do whatever you want with us. *(Stands up.)*

MAMA PAUL: Mr Ojo! This is no time for reverse psychology.

KOLA: Get back on your knees!

OJO: Dying in a failed revolution is a big thing, is it not? It is the sign of a Big Man. I will be remembered as one who fought to bring hope to our dirty, wasted lives. I could have stopped the flow of young black men and women paying their way here. Risking life and limb for second class lives, only to wonder in later years where their youth went.

MIKE stirs.

MAMA PAUL: Then let it be so. My children are now left to the wind. I only wanted to be a cash madam to give them a better life. Bye-bye, my children.

MIKE: What's happening? What's going on?

MAMA PAUL: What are you going to do with Mike?

KOLA: He'll die first and then you two.

MIKE: Kola, kill them but spare me! I've got my wife and kids to look after.

KOLA: Say your last prayers.

MIKE: Kola, you're not like Ojo and Yemi. You're different. You're better than them.

KOLA: You want to tell me how to be black, eh? Is that what they teach you at MI5?

MIKE: You're smart enough to see through Ojo's lies. I've never worked for MI5. Never!

KOLA: You people think you know all about me. You've never treated me with respect.

MIKE: *They* never treated you with respect! I've never done anything like what they did to you because *I* respect you. Because I know you're better than them. You've got your whole life ahead of you. You don't want to throw it all away on this foolish fantasy.

KOLA: Blackocracy is not a fantasy!

MIKE: OK, it's not a fantasy. It is not a fantasy.

KOLA: I am the king of blackocracy!

MIKE: That's right, you're the king. And soon you'll graduate and get a job in the city and be my boss.

KOLA: That's right.

MIKE: I started from scratch after I got discharged and look at me now, with no qualifications. Imagine what you can do with your degree!

KOLA: I will rebuild the Other Way from scratch.

MIKE: Exactly! Just like how I rebuilt my life. You won't believe this but eight years ago I was homeless. Never thought I'd be sleeping rough two years out of the army. But I pulled myself up, got a job as a cleaner and look at me now. I did it. You're going to do even better. But only if you stop this right here, right now.

KOLA: Cleaning supervisor, did you not say that people like me don't get plum jobs? Close your eyes.

MIKE: *(Pleading.)* Don't do this, Kola!

KOLA: Goodbye Mr Bond.

KOLA squeezes the trigger. It does not fire. As he fiddles with the safety catch OJO and MAMA PAUL grab their guns just as KOLA turns round to face them. Stalemate.

OJO: So we have come to a deadlock. Extra-time. Golden goal. First to shoot.

MAMA PAUL: Still the idiot. You forgot to unlock the safety catch. Your counter-coup is over!

OJO: Kola, if I shoot you your father will be relieved. Drop your gun and surrender. I might consider extenuating circumstances.

KOLA: I know the quality of your mercy. I don't trust you two. Not after what you did to me.

OJO: When you held the reins of power, did you not do worse?

MAMA PAUL: Don't mind him, Mr Ojo. He is as stupid as ever. Surrender and stop wasting our time.

KOLA: You keep calling me all these names but you are the ones who are stupid. Stupid and weak-minded. You

couldn't keep your eyes on the ball and get the job done.
Now look at where we are. The revolution is botched.

MAMA PAUL: Show this traitor no mercy, Mr Ojo. James Bond
must always have a partner. This time it's the turn of the
gay black man.

KOLA: Whatever.

MIKE: Kola's not my accomplice. Look, I'll give you my
tickets to the match.

OJO: What match?

MIKE: Chelsea-Liverpool. They're in my case in the Executive
Suite.

OJO: Oh yes, the match. The tickets, are they for the director's
box?

MIKE: No, but my mate's a steward at Stamford Bridge. He
can get them upgraded. We can go together.

KOLA: You said you could not afford to watch football.

MAMA PAUL: Another trap!

OJO: The tickets might be in an exploding briefcase. Still
trying to kill us, eh?

MIKE: I'll open the case for you!

KOLA: Sorry, but I don't trust anybody in this room.

MIKE: I'll help. I can be Mama Paul's assistant in military
strategies. I can…

OJO: Shhh! Footsteps.

MAMA PAUL: The workers. It's time for work. What do we do
now?

OJO: The enemy's reinforcements have arrived. *(He points his
gun down.)* Are you with me, Mama Paul?

MAMA PAUL: I am right beside you. *(She points her gun away
from KOLA.)*

OJO: Kola, we must patch our differences or else the battle is
lost before we've fired a bullet.

KOLA: *(His gun swings between OJO and MAMA PAUL.)* I'd rather
die!

OJO: We will all die one day. But not in this way, or what am I saying, Mama Paul? All right, maybe we were a bit strict with you.

KOLA: You made me lick your shoes! You wanted to kill me!

MAMA PAUL: Why did you bring tea without biscuits?

OJO: Kola, look, now is our opportunity to correct our mistakes. You will inherit the revolution if we do it right. Come on, we cannot proceed without you.

MIKE: Don't do it Kola! You've come this far! Don't do it!

KOLA: *(Wavering.)* I say I'd rather die!

MAMA PAUL: *(Approaches KOLA and envelopes him in a hug.)* My own Kolly-Bolly! A-Kolly-Bolly-baby. Who is a whore?

KOLA: Mr Ojo!

MAMA PAUL: I'm joking! We must restart the revolution. We can get the job done. All of us, together.

OJO: In the process, Kola, you might even make your father proud.

KOLA: I do it for myself, with my zip undone.

OJO: *(Laughs.)* Yes, my son, anyhow you want it. This is your moment. Mr Mike, your fifteen minutes of fame just keeps getting longer.

MIKE: Are you going to let me go?

OJO: In a manner of speaking. You'll be our military strategy: our Son of Star Wars.

They tie MIKE to a chair.

MIKE: No, please don't. Please!

KOLA: We can still redeem the blackocracy. We can still bring change to our people.

MAMA PAUL: Now is the time for action.

OJO: Order within the ranks! *(MAMA PAUL and KOLA stand to attention.)* Today marks another dawn in our glorious revolution. The blackocracy was threatened by the germ warfare of distrust and the atomic bomb of disunity. But we have proved that we are greater than that. We have proved that we are not gods. Our job now is to take the fight to the

77

enemy, to bring down the forces of imperialism and global capitalism. Right now the enemy is making his approach and we must counter him with the power of the Other Way, for the Other Way is the only way. There is no going back, there is only going black.

MAMA PAUL/KOLA: There is no going back, there is only going black!

OJO: Attention! *(MAMA PAUL and KOLA stand to attention.)* Assume attack position! Human shield in place!

They wheel a pleading MIKE in front of them.

Charge!

They charge.

The End.

THE ESTATE

The Estate was commissioned and produced by Tiata Fahodzi. The first production was at The New Wolsey Theatre, Ipswich on 11 May 2006, with the following cast:

EKONG	Wale Ojo
ABASINA	Ayo-Dele Ajana
AFOLABI	Nick Oshikanlu
PAKIMI	Femi Elufowoju Jr
HELEN	Ellen Thomas
SOJI	Kwaku Ankomah
SOLA	Yvonne Dodoo
SAMSON	Wale Ojo
YINKA	Richard Pepple

Director, Femi Elufowoju Jr
Designer, ULTZ
Costumes Consultant / Builder, Moji Bamtefa
Lighting Designer, Trevor Wallace
Composer, Akintayo Akinbode
Sound Designer, Simon Deacon
Casting, Nadine Hoare
Dramaturg, Neil Grutchfield
Assistant Director, Vernon Douglas
Assistant Director, Rachel Briscoe

The London run was at Soho Theatre in June 2006.

Characters

HELEN ADEYEMI
Late Chief Adeyemi's second wife, Mother of Sola

YINKA ADEYEMI
Eldest son of Chief Adeyemi and his first wife, Toyin

SOJI ADEYEMI
Yinka's brother

SOLA ADEYEMI
Helen's daughter, half-sister of Yinka and Soji

PASTOR LOMI PAKIMI
former driver to the Adeyemi family

ABASINA
House-girl

SAMSON
Abasina's elder brother

EKONG
The Adeyemis' driver

AFOLABI
The Adeyemis' caretaker

All the action takes place in the living room of the
Adeyemi Mansion.

Note
A / indicates an interruption.

THE WAKE

Early morning. The sitting room of the Adeyemi mansion. It is in a state of upheaval. Offstage right is the front door. The kitchen door is behind the sitting-room. Stage left, a small flight of stairs leads up to the landing which leads to the bedrooms. Faded 1980s ostentation drips from everywhere – except for the chandelier, which is missing a few bulbs. There is a crude vase on the cabinet, which is incongruous with the opulent surroundings. Chief Adeyemi's portrait hangs on the wall. He wears a full Yoruba outfit. Two smaller portraits hang on either side. One is of Chief Adeyemi with his first wife and their two sons, Yinka and Soji. The other is of Chief Adeyemi with his second wife Helen and their daughter, Sola.

AFOLABI and EKONG rush in and out of the kitchen with crates of drinks. ABASINA drags along a heavy bag of rice.

HELEN is on the phone.

HELEN: If you're double-booked, nko? That is my problem? Look! The food arrives on time or no payment! *(Slams down the receiver.)* Idiot. *(Clocks ABASINA dragging the bag.)* Look at this lowlife. Because I allowed you to pass through the sitting-room, that is why you want to spoil my carpet?

ABASINA lifts the bag. AFOLABI enters from kitchen. He goes to help ABASINA.

Mr Afolabi. You've finished off-loading the drinks?

AFOLABI leaves ABASINA to carry the bag on her own and exits through front door. ABASINA exits into the kitchen with the rice.

HELEN removes a pair of scissors from off the sofa and puts it on the centre-table before she sits on the sofa. Beside her, her head-tie and handbag. Samples of fabric litter the sofa, centre-table and floor. Copies of 'Ovation' lie on the centre-table. HELEN flicks through each magazine, checking that none of the fabrics worn in the photos match the samples.

ABASINA enters from front door with a crate of drinks. HELEN snaps her fingers. ABASINA puts down the crate and stands attentively beside HELEN.

HELEN: *(Points to a sample next to ABASINA.)* Let me see that one.

ABASINA picks the wrong sample.

That one! Abasina, you are blind?

ABASINA: *(Picks up correct the sample.)* Sorry ma. *(Treads on a sample on the floor.)*

HELEN: Get your charcoal feet off my material!

ABASINA: Sorry ma. *(Curtseys as she hands the sample to HELEN.)*

HELEN: You are a good for nothing. If not that Papa pitied your cursed family, I should have flung you back into the bush. Animal. *(Snatches the sample from her, flings another sample at her.)* Tell the designer: this one is for the wake. *(Gives ABASINA another sample.)* For the funeral. *(Another sample.)* For the first half of the party. *(Another sample.)* For the second half of the party. *(Another sample.)* For the Thanksgiving. I want them ready by this evening.

ABASINA waits. EKONG passes into kitchen with drinks. AFOLABI exits through front door.

Ehen?

ABASINA: Mr Ekong never finish.

HELEN: What is your business with Ekong? *(Claps her hand in disgust.)* Can your father afford a driver? Mind yourself. *Mind yourself!* Get out!

ABASINA curtseys and exits through kitchen.

Let me find a speck of dust on them, you will see.

HELEN heads for the stairs.

EKONG enters from kitchen.

EKONG: Eh, madam, Alhaji say 'no money, no diesel'.

HELEN: And it is just now you're telling me?

EKONG: Madam, you say I should bring the drinks inside.

HELEN: You told Alhaji that *I* say I will pay him later?

EKONG: I tell am, madam. He say you never pay am for the last diesel.

HELEN: *(Puts on her head-tie, grabs her handbag.)* I have to do everything myself. *(Her mobile phone rings.)* Sola. What are you still doing on campus? … No, no! Start coming now… Ekong is busy… Charter taxi! Hold on. *(Snaps her fingers at EKONG.)* Get the car ready. *(As EKONG exits.)* Fool.

AFOLABI enters with a suitcase and a travel bag. SOJI follows behind him sweating profusely. He is dressed in a short-sleeved shirt, jeans trousers and sandals. SOJI makes to say hello to HELEN. HELEN waves to him but does not stop. She exits through front door, continuing her conversation with SOLA.

Is that not Wale's voice I'm hearing? Ask him to bring you home now…

SOJI, miffed, looks at AFOLABI.

AFOLABI: Brother Soji, everything is rush-rush. *(Puts down the bags.)*

SOJI: That shouldn't stop her from saying hello properly.

AFOLABI: She go to buy diesel for the generator. You know Power Holdings is always withholding power. They change their name from NEPA[1], still is the same no light.

SOJI: *(Looks around.)* Bloody…! Nothing is ready.

AFOLABI: Is the labour strike causing all sorts of delay. And fear did not allow us to go out on weekend. See soldier and police shooting each other.

SOJI: You're serious?

AFOLABI: They want to collect bribe from the same person. Twenty civilian die from stray bullet. Ehn, person leave his house to follow his own business…

SOJI: Yes, yes, yes…

AFOLABI: A-ha. Is only yesterday we buy the cow. Caterer has not deliver the *mede-mede*[2]. And no fuel. Ekong queue for three days at petrol station.

SOJI: So? She couldn't send Sule or Edward to the airport to pick me up?

AFOLABI: You don't know? They sack them.

SOJI: At a time like this?

AFOLABI: Is Pastor tell Madam to sack them. But I am happy to see your face. You don't even ask of me on your last visit. Is Papa not tell you I am in the hospital?

SOJI: It was a flying visit.

---

1   National Electric Power Authority
2   Slang for foreign food.

AFOLABI: Is OK. As you are big professor, Nigeria's problem is on your mind. You remember when you are student you are saying you will help us poor people. The English that Wole Soyinka cannot talk, you will talk it and save our country. I suppose to retire since but I have to support my children when there is no work for them. Nigeria is too tough even more than before.

SOJI: It's tough for all of us…

AFOLABI: A-ha. You remember when you are small child. I drive you in wheel-barrow. I carry you on my back. You are laughing, calling my name: 'Afolabi, do it again! Afolabi, carry me again!' Of all Papa children, you are the one who treat me well. Just like Papa. That's why nobody else in my life I work for. As Papa do me, I know you will do me well, too.

SOJI puts his hand in his pocket. AFOLABI waits expectantly. SOJI brings out a handkerchief and wipes his face. AFOLABI is disappointed.

SOJI: Oh. I don't have naira on me.

AFOLABI: Even poor man like me, I know how to spend pounds.

Enter SOLA from front door. AFOLABI runs to collect her bag from her.

Little sister, welcome!

SOLA: Thank you, Baba. *(Gives him money.)*

AFOLABI: Allah will replenish your pocket! *(Looks through the door.)* Ah, is that not Uncle Wale?

SOLA: The canopy is here.

AFOLABI: A-ha! Please help me tell Pastor the canopy have arrive. *(Bows as he exits.)*

SOLA: Hi.

SOJI: Hi. How are you?

SOLA: Fine.

SOJI: And your studies?

SOLA: Fine. So. You got your full-time appointment.

SOJI: Uh-huh. You. You look good.

SOLA: London is doing you favours.

SOJI: When it wants to.

SOLA: When did you land?

SOJI: A few minutes ago. And you? Of course, of course, just now. Um, yeah, um, good to see you.

SOLA: You didn't keep in touch.

SOJI: *You* never kept in touch.

SOLA: You were supposed to send me your new email address.

SOJI: You have my number. You could have called.

SOLA: *You* should have called. Then I remembered; it's Soji. If I don't call, you won't call. So…

Awkward pause as SOLA waits for SOJI to respond. Realizing he's not going to say anything she picks up her bag and heads for the stairs.

SOJI: Sola.

SOLA turns around to face him.

I'm working on it.

Enter PASTOR LOMI PAKIMI from upstairs, on his mobile phone. He comes to a halt on the landing.

PAKIMI: What inflation? Am I the Minister of Finance? You deliver the chickens at our agreed price or I go elsewhere!… Better. No African time! *(Hangs up.)* What a delight! *(Comes down the landing.)* Brother and sister together! Dr. Adeyemi, welcome. The Lord answers our prayer for your safe arrival. *(They shake hands.)*

SOJI: Yinka isn't here yet.

PAKIMI: Living amongst unbelievers makes our brother cynical. Brother Yinka will arrive safe and sound, in Jesus' name.

No response from SOJI or SOLA.

In Jesus' name.

SOLA: Amen.

PAKIMI: You are fine, Sola?

SOLA: Yes, Pastor Pakimi, thank you.

PAKIMI: Architect to be! That will be in addition to another coveted title. If you know how many of our young church men wish to confer on you the honourable title of Mrs, your head will swell like overripe paw-paw. I can picture it: the society event of the century. It will be just like the Royal Wedding.

SOJI: And we all know how that ended.

PAKIMI: Brother Soji, don't wish ill for your sister.

SOLA: I've still got my final year to go.

PAKIMI: Of course but you must meet a suitable partner now.

SOLA: I'd like to stand on my feet first. I don't want to rely on any man.

PAKIMI: But you need your other half to complete you. More so for you, Brother Soji. I keep saying it. My London branch overflows with good Christian girls. When was the last time you went there to fellowship?

SOJI: I attended the singles programme, the one where Pastor Michael joked that he could smell the oestrogen.

PAKIMI: In time our heavenly Father will cleanse Pastor Michael of his vulgarity.

SOJI: I'd better pop back into his service before the Lord washes out his mouth.

PAKIMI: You will come out of God's house with something greater.

SOJI: Fela will be playing on my iPod.

PAKIMI: The choir will drown out that idol worshipper's pagan music.

SOJI: It doesn't bother you, referring to our traditional beliefs as pagan?

PAKIMI: Some things are beyond human understanding.

SOJI: Such as why we denigrate our own beliefs…

PAKIMI: The caterer must have arrived by now.

SOLA: Mother has a list of things for me to do. Pastor. *(Exits upstairs.)*

PAKIMI: My sister. Brother Soji, I've not even proffered my condolences. Your father was a rarity: an honest businessman. Like Abraham Papa was obedient to God's every wish. And like Abraham God blessed him with abundance and with you wonderful children. You will say you don't believe in prayers. But we pray for you constantly that your academic career blossoms. That you remain a worthy son of Papa.

SOJI: Um, thank you.

PAKIMI: And so a fitting, trouble-free send-off is the only compensation we mortals can honour Papa with. My ultra-modern Church is fully prepared. I hope every other arrangement is to your satisfaction.

SOJI: *(Looks around at the mess.)* Um, ye-ah.

PAKIMI: Papa was my Godsend. Who could have imagined me becoming the leader of Nigeria's biggest Church? If Sule had not taken ill I would not have driven Papa to his business lunch with the Lord's anointed, Reverend Billy Robertson. I will always be part of this house. So please let us make things go smoothly.

HELEN by the front door, yelling at someone offstage.

ABASINA enters through kitchen and waits to be noticed.

HELEN: When you put the canopy on the driveway how will our guests enter? Or what kind of idiots are you? Pastor, I asked you to supervise these people now.

PAKIMI: *(Testily.)* I told Afolabi to tell me when the canopy arrives. *(Exits.)*

SOJI: Oh, yeah. He told Sola to…

HELEN: Brother Soji, welcome. Sorry I couldn't stop before. Those lazy unionists, they are causing us all kinds of problem.

SOJI: I thought we were getting a marquee. Papa would have wanted a marquee.

HELEN: We were late in hiring it. The Odibos and the Jimohs, they too are having parties today. The canopies are made in London. They are to Papa's taste.

SOJI: Where is Ekong?

HELEN: He's been busy all day. Sola is here?

SOJI: Upstairs. Will Ekong be too busy to pick Yinka from the airport?

HELEN: If there is work to do.

SOJI: Oh, OK. I'll be here to see that.

HELEN: But you can see for yourself… *(Notices ABASINA. Harshly.)* What is it?

ABASINA: The designer say the cloth go ready by this afternoon. Welcome sah/

HELEN: Take Brother's bags upstairs then join the aunties in the backyard to prepare the rice.

ABASINA curtseys and exits upstairs with SOJI's bags.

SOJI: I thought we'd already sorted out the clothes.

HELEN: The material we decided on; the Oloidi's wore one for their son's birthday. The Inyangs wore another for their child-naming.

SOJI: You've gone for a whole new batch?

HELEN: We cannot wear cast-offs for your father's funeral. When people see our photographs in 'Ovation', you want them to mock us? People must know that we remain a family to reckon with.

SOJI: Tell me at least Yinka knows.

HELEN: Not yet.

SOJI: You know he was furious with you having the service at Pakimi's church.

HELEN: That is where Papa fellowshipped until he left us now, *abí*? *(Hopefully.)* You will talk to him for us.

SOLA enters from upstairs.

(To SOLA.) Mama Buky says the pastries are ready.

SOLA: Good morning, mother.

HELEN: Ekong!

SOLA: I said good morning.

HELEN: Morning, morning! *Oya*, there's no time to waste.

ABASINA enters from upstairs. Exits through kitchen as EKONG enters from kitchen.

SOLA: *(To EKONG.)* I will drop by my friend's…

HELEN: *(To EKONG.)* Join Afolabi and cut the grass behind the shed.

EKONG hands over the keys to SOLA. He lingers, trying not to show his annoyance.

What?

EKONG: Madam I never chop breakfast.

HELEN glares at EKONG. EKONG withers under her glare and exits.

HELEN: *(To SOLA.)* Ekong is busy. Drive yourself.

SOJI: I'll drive you there.

HELEN: And don't stop at any friend's house! The wake…

SOJI looks at HELEN.

It's Sola I'm talking to.

SOLA exits. SOJI follows.

Brother Soji!

SOJI stops.

It will help if you support me. Papa wanted all of us to be one. I shouldn't have to remind you of that.

SOJI: Right. You can start by telling Yinka about the cloth yourself.

HELEN: Yes. When he arrives. Look, sorry about Ekong. Honest drivers, you can't find them. Leave anything in the car they will steal it. That's why we sacked the other drivers. Ekong too is a first-class criminal. We are just managing him. I should have come to pick you myself. Sorry my brother. My big brother.

SOJI: Yeah, yeah… Your moneychanger is near Mama Buky's?

HELEN: *(Searches her bag. Hands SOJI a business card.)* You are learning. Dashing your money to the banks when the black market offers a better rate.

SOJI: I was helping Nigeria.

HELEN: Helping Nigeria? *(Laughs uncontrollably.)* Dr. Adeyemi!

SOLA: *(Off. Angrily.)* Are you coming?

PAKIMI enters from front door.

SOJI: Pastor Pakimi. *(Exits.)*

PAKIMI: I see we are in good humour. Do we have time for your morning prayers?

HELEN: There is always time for God in this house. *(They exit upstairs.)*

ABASINA enters from kitchen. She looks at Chief Adeyemi's portrait and sighs as she pats her stomach. A noise from the kitchen. ABASINA tidies up the sitting room. EKONG enters wearily from the kitchen with a container of food. He holds it up as he makes a sign of appreciation to ABASINA. He collapses onto the sofa.

ABASINA: Mr Ekong, no let madam see you for sitting-room.

EKONG: Na only shout she go shout. Because Papa die, make we follow am to him grave? *(Opens the container.)*

ABASINA: No be only for you, oh. Mr Afolabi's food dey inside.

EKONG: Where you go before?

ABASINA: I dey for backyard. See the time. When you go go collect Uncle Yinka?

EKONG: *(Closes the container.)* Work no dey finish for this house.

ABASINA: Is work we are here to work.

EKONG: I am driver, not gardener. You never hear of division of labour? We suppose to join the union to strike.

ABASINA: Mr Ekong, no start that one again.

EKONG: I beg, no talk like Afolabi. Upon all his loyalty what is his reward? Abasina, I always tell you: you have no future with these people. Nothing you can get from them.

ABASINA: Make I follow you return to village? That one is not my future.

EKONG: Why not? We will support ourselves instead of doing slave to rich people.

ABASINA: Everyday you dey talk this kind talk. But everyday you return to work.

EKONG: Soon.

ABASINA: 'Soon'. Since how long you dey sing your revolution song? Mr Ekong, this life is matter of money. And na here money dey.

EKONG: And where the money come from? Oil pipeline dey run through my backyard for village. But our people, na so-so housemaid and driver we dey do for Lagos. When is people like your brother Samson dey carry you and your people come do slave for here.

ABASINA: He dey help us. Nothing dey for village.

EKONG: So, is not you I hear abusing Samson last time he come collect your salary from Madam? No be you tell am say you no come Lagos to do house-girl?

ABASINA: Mr Ekong, that is between me and my brother. Opportunity is here. When the chance come I will take it. That is how Nigeria is. That is how we have to live.

EKONG: How things go better when poor person like you dey talk this kind talk?

ABASINA: So what are we poor people suppose to do? Make we secede from Nigeria?

EKONG: Why not? Hausa man have secede already.

ABASINA: *Mr Ekong*! Where you hear dat one?

EKONG: Hausa man do Sharia law for their state, which is unconstitutional. Dat one no be secede? The thing wey dem no let Igbo man do. Fela talk am. Our people, we fear too much. Even when we have to look after ourself.

ABASINA: I fit look after myself. I know wetin I dey do.

EKONG: I know say, one day-one day, things go change for this country. When that time come, hey, I will line up Madam, all the rich people, politicians, army generals *(Makes a firing squad gesture.)* …

The front door opens. EKONG snatches the container and dashes into kitchen. ABASINA cleans hurriedly. AFOLABI enters and stands by the entrance.

ABASINA: *(Laughs, stops cleaning.)* Baba, na you…

AFOLABI: Where is Ekong?

ABASINA: He don carry the food go meet you for backyard.

AFOLABI: He don't know that hunger is killing person? Madam will soon come down now, ah! *(Heads back through front door.)*

ABASINA: Baba, Madam dey upstairs. You fit pass through the sitting room.

AFOLABI: Is all right, my daughter.

ABASINA: By the time you reach backyard, Ekong go don finish the food.

AFOLABI hesitates. His hunger gets the better of him. He walks through the sitting room. He is halfway across when HELEN and PAKIMI enter from upstairs. AFOLABI tries to run.

HELEN: Papa never wasted money on homemade, so check those napkins well.

PAKIMI: This dealer is my church member. All his stock is imported… Ah, Afolabi, any problem?

AFOLABI: No sah.

PAKIMI: No? How long have you been working here? It is now you decide to set a bad example to the other staff. Because Papa is no longer with us, *abi*?

AFOLABI: Sorry sah. *(Walks back across the sitting room to exit through front door.)*

PAKIMI: *(Thinking AFOLABI has come in through the kitchen.)* Afolabi! *(Points to the kitchen door.)*

AFOLABI bows apologetically and exits through kitchen.

HELEN: *(To ABASINA.)* The clothes are ready.

ABASINA: Yes, ma.

PAKIMI: The designer is on my way. I'll drop you there. (*Exits through front door.*)

ABASINA follows PAKIMI. HELEN eyes her. She exits through kitchen. HELEN looks sadly at Chief Adeyemi's portrait. A knock at the door.

HELEN composes herself.

HELEN: Yes, who is it?

SAMSON, ABASINA's elder brother, enters, carrying a box of balloons. He wears fake designer sunglasses.

(Unenthusiastic.) Oh. Samson.

SAMSON: Good morning, Madam. Sorry I couldn't come sooner. About Papa…

HELEN: It's all right. Thank you.

SAMSON: I brought balloons for decorating the canopies. International quality.

HELEN: I will open Sola's room. Blow them up in there. *Oya,* there's no time.

SAMSON: *(Not expecting to be told to work.)* Er, yes, Madam.

They exit upstairs. AFOLABI enters with suitcases. YINKA enters. He is dressed in a suit.

YINKA surveys the sitting-room with disgust. HELEN enters from upstairs, mobile phone in hand.

HELEN: What is the time that it's now you're just coming… Oh, sorry, I thought it was the hairdresser. Welcome, Brother Yinka.

YINKA: Morning.

HELEN: *(To AFOLABI.)* Tell Ekong to go and collect the hairdresser. I will inform her he's on his way.

AFOLABI exits.

HELEN: How is your computer business? Papa was so proud when you opened a new branch.

YINKA: Fine.

HELEN: Yes, em, I wanted to tell you but there was no time. I had to get new material for the family uniforms.

YINKA: What of Soji?

HELEN: Brother Soji loves it. He says I have done Papa proud.

YINKA: Where is he?

HELEN: Oh. He and Sola, they went out. They should be back soon.

The front door opens. SOJI enters.

(Relieved.) A-ha.

SOJI: Hey! The Black Republican has landed!

They hug.

YINKA: I want to talk to you – in private.

HELEN: *(Makes to leave reluctantly.)* What of Sola?

SOJI: She branched at her friend's. Wale…?

HELEN: *(As she exits upstairs.)* But I told her! What is wrong with this child? *(Phones.)*

YINKA checks to see that HELEN has gone upstairs.

SOJI: So Joyce couldn't make it after all.

YINKA: I know you can leave your sick mother to travel halfway round the world.

SOJI: You could have let the twins come.

YINKA: They're prepping for their exams. America doesn't reward failure.

SOJI: Living the dream, eh? Just like their father.

YINKA: *(Faces Chief Adeyemi's portrait.)* And like their grandfather. Soon the Adeyemi name will be as American as apple pie. So. The material.

SOJI: Yeah, um, it should be all right. Knowing Helen's taste in clothes.

YINKA: It's not the material we agreed on.

SOJI: She says they've all been worn before.

YINKA: She discussed it with you?

SOJI: Time was against her. She had to make a decision.

YINKA: That's why you should get married. You control the house. What other decisions has she made behind my back?

HELEN enters from upstairs.

HELEN: Brother Yinka. You didn't give me chance to explain about the material.

YINKA: There's no point now.

HELEN: There is, oh. I can never go behind your back. No one can replace you as Papa's eldest son. *(Goes on her knees.)* Please, forgive me.

SOLA and PAKIMI enter through front door. SOLA looks at HELEN with disgust.

ABASINA enters through the kitchen with the clothes.

PAKIMI: Brother Yinka, your stepmother accords you the respect your position deserves. Whatever she might have done, forgiveness is your only option.

YINKA: *(Stiffly.)* OK.

HELEN stands up.

PAKIMI: God is in this house! Abasina bring the… Abasina!
(Sees ABASINA. Beckons to her.)

ABASINA approaches. PAKIMI takes one of the clothes, a buba[3], from her. ABASINA puts the rest of the clothes on the sofa.

HELEN: Don't crease them, bush girl.

PAKIMI: You see how lovely they are? Fit for a king. *(Hands the buba to YINKA. YINKA turns his face. SOJI takes it from PAKIMI.)*

SOJI: Not bad.

YINKA glares at SOJI. SOJI hands the outfit to HELEN. HELEN smiles proudly as she unfolds the buba.

YINKA heads for upstairs.

PAKIMI: Brother Yinka…

YINKA: I need to take a shower. *(Exits upstairs.)*

ABASINA takes YINKA's bags upstairs.

PAKIMI: Well! I'd better keep an eye on the arrangements outside.

HELEN: Thank you, Pastor. *(Looks after YINKA.)*

PAKIMI exits.

SOLA: Back to being the housemaid, eh?

HELEN: Choose your words carefully my dear.

SOJI: She's got Yinka on board.

SOLA: I am talking to my mother.

HELEN: Don't be rude to your elder brother! You are naïve. You cannot understand.

SOLA storms upstairs. SAMSON passes SOLA by on the landing.

SAMSON: Good morning, Sister Sola.

SOLA ignores him. She exits.

SOJI: Excuse me. *(Goes after SOLA.)*

HELEN watches SOJI with suspicion.

SAMSON: Good morning, sir.

SOJI: Samson. *(Exits.)*

SAMSON waits, expectantly.

HELEN: Oh. *(Gives SAMSON a wad of notes from her handbag.)*

---

3   traditional jumper

SAMSON: Thank you, ma. I should be going. *(Heads for the door.)*

HELEN: Ehen. Abasina!

ABASINA enters from kitchen. SAMSON is irritated.

HELEN: I'm checking on the aunties. When the hairdresser arrives… *(Exits through kitchen.)*

ABASINA curtseys.

SAMSON pockets the money. He brings out two mobile phones. He checks them for messages.

ABASINA: Brother Samson. You dey avoid me?

SAMSON: I have a business appointment. I cannot stay to chat.

ABASINA: When you go give Mama her allowance?

SAMSON: Soon.

ABASINA: Which one be soon? Which money Mama dey take maintain herself?

SAMSON: *(Testily.)* I said soon! What is it? Ah! Because you live in big house you've become big madam?

ABASINA: So when I dey leave this big house?

SAMSON: You can't leave. The funeral.

ABASINA eyes him defiantly.

SAMSON: OK if not for the Adeyemis, what of we your family? The bakery is not yet finished.

ABASINA: That one is for you and your family.

SAMSON: So your nephews are not your family any more? The boys should not go to school because you are too lazy to work?

ABASINA: Papa pay your school fees/

SAMSON: Don't tell me how to look after my children! If you don't want to contribute your share tell me.

ABASINA: I need money.

SAMSON: What for?

ABASINA: Na me work for my money.

SAMSON: You cannot spoil my progress because you want to wear new dress…

ABASINA: …I talk say I wan' buy dress?

SAMSON: …What of the new dress I gave you last month?

ABASINA: That rag wey your wife throw'ay?

SAMSON: My wife's name is Anna. You can patch it up.

ABASINA: Why Sister Anna no patch am for me?

SAMSON: My wife is not your tailor.

ABASINA: Last year you say Madam will allow me to learn trade. Patience next door don learn tailoring. She don get shop. Next month she go marry.

SAMSON: This your salary, I'm saving it for you.

ABASINA: When value of naira dey fall every day?

SAMSON: Once I start my export business we will be cashing pounds and dollars.

ABASINA: Why you no do that business first?

SAMSON: You ask too many questions that don't concern you.

ABASINA: E concern me. Even if naira na one thousand to one pound, inflation go useless di money. Na because everything too cost dat's why di workers dey strike. No save my money for me again. Tell Madam to pay me direct.

SAMSON: How can she pay you direct? I am the one who brought you here.

ABASINA: Na me dey work! Na my money.

SAMSON: It's because you are around these book people. You don't understand what they are saying. Your wings are getting too big. So I your elder brother, I cannot control you? That is very bad, Abasina. That is very bad. Small. After the funeral I will find you another house. If you go now Madam will not patronise me again. You don't know how lucky you are. I'm coming from Ikoyi. Patrick rumpled Chief's *aso oke*.[4] Chief scraped his head with a broken bottle. *(Smirks.)* His head is like the map of Nigeria.

ABASINA: *(Glares at him in response to his lack of sympathy.)* Tell Mama to send medicine for Patrick.

---

4   expensive woven cloth

SAMSON: This is the best time to be around. People will spray money. *(Phones.)*

ABASINA: Who go spray house-girl?

SAMSON: You have eyes. Shake your bottom at the right man. If you were as smart as your Madam you could have become the next Mrs Adeyemi… *(On the phone.)* *Omo*-boy! Which one, now? Di consignment, e don land?

SAMSON exits through kitchen. ABASINA looks after him in disgust. She looks at Chief Adeyemi's photograph. SOJI and SOLA enter from upstairs. ABASINA exits to kitchen.

SOLA: I should have stayed away.

SOJI: Just because of a few balloons?

SOLA: See how they messed up my room.

SOJI: What's really bugging you? … Talk to me.

SOLA: You know why I liked your mother?

SOJI: You didn't know her.

SOLA: She had self-discipline. You couldn't mess with her. That's what everyone says about her.

SOJI: She was a hard woman, all right.

SOLA: Hard. Not harsh. Papa was harsh.

SOJI: Helen's easy-going. I'd have thought any child would love that in a parent.

SOLA: Isn't that why Papa replaced your mother with mine?

SOJI: You don't know what you're talking about.

SOLA: Oh yeah. I'm naïve.

SOJI: That's not what I meant.

SOLA: I've never felt I belonged. Papa, he just… It's like I was something that happened by accident.

SOJI: Papa treated us all like that. Where do you think Yinka gets his attitude from? The funeral's getting to you. Come here. *(Drags her into his arms. Gives her a comforting hug.)* London's not as easy as people think.

SOLA: It's easier than Nigeria. I can be myself.

SOJI: Being yourself is even harder.

SOLA: Write me the letter of invitation now.

SOJI: I told you, after the funeral. OK?

SOLA: Promise.

SOJI: I promise.

SOLA squeezes SOJI excitedly.

SOJI: Ah! You do know it's our Father we're burying.

SOLA: You're the only one who makes me feel I belong. You're my one source of light. Erratic like NEPA…

SOJI: Oh, thanks.

SOLA: You may be nonchalant most times but you step up when it really matters.

SOJI: Will this Wale guy be coming with you to London?

SOLA relaxes her hold.

YINKA enters. SOJI and SOLA let go of each other.

SOJI: Hey, bro'.

SOLA: *(Stiffly.)* Welcome Brother Yinka.

YINKA: It's now you decide to greet me?

SOLA: *(As she heads for kitchen. To SOJI.)* I'm getting a drink. Do you want one?

YINKA: *(Enraged at the slight.)* Ehn? *(Chases after her.)*

SOLA runs round the sofa. SOJI restrains YINKA.

SOJI: Yinka! Yinka!

YINKA: What an insult!

SOJI: Come on, man!

YINKA: I will show you your place! You and your mother!

SOJI can barely restrain YINKA.

SOLA: *(Runs to centre-table, grabs the scissors.)* I am not like my mother.

YINKA: Oh, you think you're strong, eh?

SOJI: Yinka!

YINKA: I swear on my father's corpse, after the funeral you will not spend one more night in this house! *(To SOJI.)* And what the hell are you doing with this interloper?

SOLA: You are a bastard.

YINKA lunges at SOLA. SOJI barely restrains him. PAKIMI enters. YINKA calms down.

PAKIMI: Is everything all right?

SOJI: Everything is fine.

PAKIMI: I heard a commotion.

SOJI: How are the preparations going?

PAKIMI: We are almost done. The caterer has arrived, thank God. Sola, can I talk to you for one minute?

PAKIMI leads SOLA into the kitchen. SOLA drops the scissors on the table.

YINKA pushes SOJI.

SOJI: Hey!

YINKA: Your mother's usurper swans around like she owns the place and you're playing big brother to her bastard.

SOJI: Sola is our half-sister.

YINKA: You know how these things go when you're dealing with these parasites.

SOJI: This isn't the time.

YINKA: When will it be the time? When they steal everything Mother worked for?

SOJI: Helen can't go against Dad's will. What are you afraid of?

YINKA: She stole Dad from Mother. This time, no way! This is a fight to the death.

SOJI: We don't even know what's in the will.

YINKA: One kobo is too much for her. *We* are the true Adeyemis. Remember that.

SOJI: Living in New York's turned you into a drama queen.

YINKA: You want history to repeat itself? You'll see when that usurper and her…

HELEN enters from front door.

HELEN: My big brothers, you are here… Abasina!

ABASINA: *(As she enters from kitchen.)* Ma!

HELEN: Is this how to clean up?

ABASINA tidies up around them. She is in discomfort.

Brother Yinka, I was going to ask. How is Joyce's mother?

YINKA ignores HELEN. PAKIMI and SOLA enter from kitchen. SOLA goes straight upstairs. SOJI gazes after her.

SOJI: … Erm, where's Ekong?

HELEN: I sent him to the hairdresser. They have both disappeared… Abasina. *(Points to the clothes.)*

ABASINA takes HELEN's outfit and follows HELEN upstairs. SOJI and YINKA make to leave.

PAKIMI: Just a few words. Please. *(Beckons to them to sit down.)*

SOJI: I don't know what Sola told you but…

PAKIMI: This is another matter.

SOJI: Oh.

PAKIMI: I don't want to poke my nose in your family's affairs but I like to think I'm very close to you.

YINKA: You're our former driver.

PAKIMI: *Papa's* former driver.

YINKA: Same thing.

PAKIMI: *(Composes himself.)* In your absence the sands of time have not reduced the pressures of running the estate. There are those who are not satisfied with their God-given lot. Afolabi wants an astronomical rise in his salary.

SOJI: Afolabi was here before you. He knows this place inside out.

PAKIMI: Which is why we cannot afford for him to organise thieves to ransack the estate.

SOJI: Afolabi is not that kind of person.

PAKIMI: And King David did not plan for[5] Uriah. I know how dear he is to you but the estate needs young blood to maintain it effectively.

YINKA: You invited us to discuss Afolabi?

PAKIMI: As perceptive as ever. Just like your father… Er, you know how messy sharing property can get. I would like to help make a smooth transition.

---

5   scheme against

SOJI: The days of miracles are long gone.

PAKIMI: I…my church, would like to buy land of the estate. Just enough to build a new church. I'll pay the going rate.

YINKA: But you only just moved into a new building last year.

PAKIMI: My congregation has grown exponentially. We live in dire times. People need direction. They recognise me as God's true voice.

SOJI: This has nothing to do with the New Evangelicals? They've just bought the Owoloju's estate down the road.

PAKIMI: Visibility in a prime location such as this will accelerate my God-appointed mission. Selling some land will make you liquid. Money can be shared much more easily than property.

YINKA: This family has money. The land is not for sale.

SOJI: We've enough land to make the Duke of Westminster look like a sharecropper. It's an offer to consider.

PAKIMI nods vigorously. YINKA eyes SOJI.

YINKA: *(Stands up.)* There is nothing to consider. God has blessed you. You have risen above your station, fair enough. But trying to get your hands on our father's land? You're stretching too far.

PAKIMI: I'm just saying that with you and Helen…

YINKA: Tell Helen my mother built this estate. She will not carve it up. *(Heads upstairs.)* Soji.

PAKIMI: It has nothing to do with Helen, Brother Yinka.

SOJI: Afolabi made the garden. He bought this vase as a gift to Papa when I was born. Dad hated it but he kept it here as a sign of respect for the old man…

AFOLABI enters, stands by front door.

AFOLABI: E' Pastor, the canopy is making jigi-jigi.

PAKIMI: *(Testily.)* There was nothing wrong with it before. *Oya.*

They exit through front door. ABASINA enters from upstairs.

YINKA: *(From upstairs.)* Soji!

SOJI: Bring our uniforms up to my room. *(Goes upstairs.)*

HELEN and SOLA enter from downstairs. HELEN is half-dressed.

ABASINA: Yes sah. *(Takes the clothes.)*

SOLA and SOJI smile at each other. SOJI exits to upstairs. HELEN clocks them. She gestures to ABASINA, to ask if the clothes are for SOJI and YINKA. ABASINA nods. HELEN signals to ABASINA to go upstairs quickly.

ABASINA exits upstairs.

HELEN: *(Dances as she sings.)* 'They took them, they took them,' *(Notices that SOLA is looking upstairs.)* Hey, I don't like the closeness between you and your brother.

SOLA: You say you want us to be a family.

HELEN: I also say you should be wary of them. He will try and tear us apart.

SOLA: Mama.

HELEN: Yes now. They are the true sons of their mother.

SOLA: The true sons of their father.

HELEN: You too you are the true child of your father, even more than them… *Oya, oya,* change. You cannot be late for your father's wake. *(Finishes dressing up.)*

SOLA: You turned my room into a store.

ABASINA, tired, enters from upstairs.

HELEN: You didn't see my own room? It's a small sacrifice to make for your father. Hurry up!

SOLA: Abasina. *(Exits upstairs.)*

HELEN: Suit yourself.

ABASINA stumbles as she takes SOLA's clothes.

(To ABASINA.) What is wrong with you? *Abi,* those garage boys have been putting their penises inside you that you cannot walk properly again? Prostitute. Let me see pregnancy on you, you will be out on the street where you belong. Get out!

ABASINA exits.

HELEN puts on make-up.

PAKIMI enters. HELEN gestures to him that SOJI's and YINKA's clothes are gone.

PAKIMI: They took them? Hallelujah! The Lord has ordained it that today shall go without problem.

HELEN: Amen!

PAKIMI: *(Looks at HELEN appreciatively.)* The trouble with beauty is that it is beautiful.

HELEN: When last did I hear that?

PAKIMI: Papa said it enough times. How he kept so honest… I'm sorry. I didn't mean it that way.

HELEN: Lomi, we are not children. They put kola[6] in my mouth, I should not chew? Those boys cannot understand. Their father came to me.

PAKIMI: Every child thinks their mother is Virgin Mary.

HELEN: Mama Yinka[7] was no Virgin Mary. Not to us.

PAKIMI: She was not an easy woman.

HELEN: You've not forgotten.

PAKIMI: Still, we are examples that anybody can rise above their station, no matter what any man thinks.

HELEN: You mean no matter what Yinka thinks. I washed the wet dreams from his pants. And he wants me to continue worshipping him like that house-girl of before.

PAKIMI: *(Looks up warily to the stairs.)* Before you came in I was talking with him.

HELEN: I am ready for them. My daughter will claim her rights to the estate.

PAKIMI: The idea is not to divide the estate like gamblers casting lots.

HELEN: My husband will not leave me empty-handed.

PAKIMI: We do not know what Papa left for you. We need to be sure you are catered for in any eventuality.

HELEN: I am not like Mama Yinka. I'm not a prim sexless killjoy. She turned the whole house to monastery. You saw how much Papa and I enjoyed life together. It was then that people knew how rich he was. I set him free.

PAKIMI: Still, his mind was on other things. He told me…

6   kola nut
7   Yinka's mother

HELEN: Lomi, I will bury my husband like a king. That is how he lived. They will read the will. I will claim my share. His sons have no choice…

PAKIMI: Listen to me, for once! God! See now, you've made me take the Lord's name in vain.

SOLA and ABASINA enter from upstairs. SOLA is dressed in her aso ebi.

Ah, my daughter. Any man who sees you will proclaim he has seen an angel.

HELEN: Pastor is complimenting you. You can at least smile.

The sound of the funeral trumpet. Singing. YINKA and SOJI, on the landing. They are wearing identical attires, made from the old material. HELEN and PAKIMI look at them in alarm.

HELEN: Brother Yinka, I thought we had resolved the matter.

PAKIMI: Brother Yinka. This is your Father's funeral. It is not right for the family to wear different uniforms. People will pick up the wrong signal.

HELEN: Brother Soji. Help us to beg Brother Yinka. Not today. Your father will not look kindly on us…

YINKA takes Chief Adeyemi's portrait. Nods to SOJI to take their portrait with Toyin.

HELEN: I begged you on my knees…

YINKA and SOJI exit through front door. SOLA lets out a cynical laugh and exits after them.

PAKIMI: Don't worry. We will sort this out. *(Sings, gestures to HELEN join in.)*

HELEN goes up the landing and takes her family portrait off the wall.

PAKIMI and HELEN exit through front door.

The music fades.

THE FUNERAL

The following day, afternoon. ABASINA and AFOLABI enter from kitchen with party utensils. They adorn the walls with balloons. ABASINA puts up on the wall a funeral poster of Chief Adeyemi. She is still feeling queasy.

AFOLABI: Don't worry. When the party start and the big men spray you with money, your stomach will settle.

ABASINA: Baba!

AFOLABI: Big man doesn't care if you are from village or you are groundnut seller. If he like your face…

ABASINA: Baba! Heyi-ay!

AFOLABI: Abasina. You are good girl but don't pretend that you are little child. As Madam was house-girl yesterday, see her today. Fine girl like you, you just have to know the right man. Have patience.

ABASINA lingers, looking at Chief Adeyemi's poster.

EKONG enters.

EKONG: Your own kind of patience, even Job did not have.

ABASINA: Mr Ekong! Dem don finish for church?

EKONG: Madam say make I help you. She go phone when service end. *(Puts on music.)* Party don start! *(Dances. Takes a bottle of beer. Raises a toast to Chief Adeyemi's poster.)* To the Big Man! Abasina, dance with me.

AFOLABI: What is wrong with this man?

ABASINA: Mr Ekong!

EKONG: *(Swirls ABASINA around.)* For now, we are the owners of Adeyemi Estate. Afolabi, boogie down. *Ariya!*

AFOLABI: I know my place.

EKONG: Stay there, then. *(Continues dancing with ABASINA.)*

ABASINA: Oh! Mr Ekong, I no well.

EKONG: Your illness is too much work. Enjoyment is the cure. *(Releases her. Dances on his own.)*

AFOLABI: Some people don't know their place.

EKONG: What-ti! You that you know your place, what is your gain?

AFOLABI: Wait and see.

EKONG: *(Laughs in derision.)* See this old man. You think say Papa put you for him will?

AFOLABI: You can laugh. But you will see who will laugh longest.

EKONG: A fool at forty is a fool…

ABASINA: Mr Ekong!

AFOLABI: Your father is a fool!

EKONG: Yes! *My* father is a fool! He was doing 'yes sah, no ma,' all his life, just like you!

AFOLABI: I pity your father for having you as a son.

EKONG: Your own children will pity you! You no dey shame? House-boy at age of seventy! Abasina, don't listen to this Yoruba man. Na so dem dey do for their country.

AFOLABI: And your father who is doing 'yes sah, no ma', he is Yoruba?

EKONG: Shut up!

ABASINA: *(Turns off the music. Firmly.)* Stop this nonsense! Mr Ekong, we don finish for here. Make you return to church.

EKONG: *(Mock salute.)* Yes 'Madam'. *(Exits with the beer.)*

AFOLABI: You young people. You don't listen to your elders. Have patience or all your hard work, another person will reap your reward.

ABASINA: Baba. I've heard you. I am not a small girl.

AFOLABI: You are siding with your countryman. Is OK. *(In anger exits through front door.)*

ABASINA: Baba…

Funeral trumpet. AFOLABI runs back in and exits through kitchen.

The noise of people outside partying. Enter HELEN, SOLA, YINKA, SOJI and PAKIMI. ABASINA takes the portraits and hangs them back on the wall.

HELEN: Thank God. Power Holdings has not taken the light.

PAKIMI: They know what day today is.

HELEN: I've just buried my husband.

YINKA glares at HELEN. EKONG enters.

EKONG: E sa, Lawyer Anike have arrive.

YINKA: Er, all right. *(As he passes EKONG, hisses.)* Broadcast it to the whole world!

EKONG scratches his head apologetically. YINKA and EKONG exit. HELEN looks at PAKIMI. She is agitated.

PAKIMI: He can't do anything about the will. Come on. Papa is looking down upon us from Heaven. He will not like this nonsense… Okay, I'll keep an eye on him.

AFOLABI peers through the front door.

Yes?

AFOLABI: Retired General Olowolonjaiye, sah.

PAKIMI: Ah! *(Exits through front door. Off.)* My General! Welcome. Helen!

HELEN eyes SOJI, eyes beseeching. SOJI looks at her blankly. HELEN exits through front door.

SOLA flops onto the sofa.

SOJI: We'd better join them outside.

SOLA: When I come to London the first place I want to see is your office. Then I want to ride on the Millennium Wheel.

SOJI: It might be a good idea to finish your studies. There's no point running away to start all over again.

SOLA: That's not what we agreed on.

SOJI: Yeah but one more semester won't kill you.

SOLA: You know what. I don't want to wait until after the Thanksgiving. Let's go up to your room. You can write me the letter of invitation now.

HELEN enters.

HELEN: People are asking of you. Sola, Wale is here.

SOLA gets up.

(Jokingly.) I don't want grandchildren yet, oh!

SOLA ignores her and exits.

HELEN: Brother Soji. Brother Yinka is paying too much attention to the lawyer. He should show respect for your father. The will we can sort out after the party. People are talking.

SOJI: Not even Yinka can get Lawyer Anike to change the will. Don't worry.

ABASINA enters from kitchen.

HELEN: All our guests have been served?

ABASINA: Yes, ma. E' sa, your uncles want to see you.

HELEN: *(Prepares to leave.)* Ah, I've not seen them since the funeral.

ABASINA: Es' ma. Is only Brother Soji and Brother Yinka they ask for.

HELEN, slighted, waves ABASINA away.

ABASINA exits through kitchen.

SOJI: *(Stands up.)* He's like a soldier. Papa always joked that Yinka should have been named Soji.

HELEN: But he is going beyond a joke. People will say Papa has died, the family is falling apart.

SOJI: That's their problem. *(Heads for front door.)*

HELEN: Remember: Sola is also your flesh and blood.

SOJI pauses briefly. PAKIMI enters. They greet each other. PAKIMI waits for SOJI to leave. SOJI exits.

PAKIMI: He's still with Lawyer Anike.

EKONG enters through kitchen with a tray. He takes some drinks and exits.

From outside a song singing praise to the late Chief Adeyemi and his wife HELEN ADEYEMI. HELEN looks at PAKIMI. Her confidence grows.

HELEN: You hear that? They are singing my name, not Toyin's.

PAKIMI nods.

Yinka can scheme all he wants. Chief Adeyemi will do me right. We have prayed over it.

PAKIMI: It is in times of uncertainty that our faith is tested. I too believe that Papa will treat you fairly. But what fair means to Papa we don't know.

HELEN: Now you are making me worried again.

PAKIMI: You know better than any one how volatile Papa could be.

HELEN: I know he would not make his wife a laughing stock.

PAKIMI: That is our prayer… I have a proposal. Something that will secure your future and Sola's in the event of the unexpected.

HELEN: Yes? *Oya*, Pastor, I have to see to my guests…

PAKIMI: Marry me.

HELEN: *(Cannot believe her ears.)* Sorry?

PAKIMI: It makes sense.

HELEN: Lomi! I've just buried my husband!

PAKIMI: Stop playing games! This is what we've always wanted.

HELEN: *(Points outside.)* And you've forgotten about Mrs Pakimi, and your children.

PAKIMI: They will understand.

HELEN: What about your church?

PAKIMI: I am the church, the church is me. My members will kick a fuss but dust settles.

HELEN: You see me fighting one battle you want me to fight another?

ABASINA enters. Takes one of the coolers and exits.

(Defiant.) Yinka is not the only person who can talk to the lawyer! *(Exits.)*

PAKIMI: Helen! Helen!

PAKIMI exits.

YINKA enters from kitchen, with a whisky bottle. He makes sure no one is around. He exits upstairs, taking a swig along the way. Enter ABASINA, with a tray. She puts drinks on it and waits to see if anyone is coming in. She tidies herself as she exits upstairs.

HELEN and PAKIMI enter, followed by EKONG.

HELEN: You are sure Brother Yinka came in here?

EKONG: Yes madam. Maybe he is upstairs.

HELEN: Who asked you? *(Clocks the tray.)* Why did you leave the tray there?

EKONG: Not me madam…

HELEN: Take it out, idiot!

EKONG takes the tray and exits. HELEN marches upstairs.

PAKIMI: Mama Sola…

The lights go out. A cry of 'NEPA!' fills the air. A generator roars into life. The lights come back on. The lights flicker violently and go out. An explosion.

Commotion.

HELEN: Jesus! What was that?

EKONG enters from kitchen with a torch, candles, lanterns and matches.

EKONG: E' sa, the generator has blow!

PAKIMI: *(Takes the torch from EKONG.)* Stay here.

HELEN and PAKIMI exit.

EKONG makes sure they are gone and stuffs salad from a tray into his mouth. He spits it back into the tray. He grabs a candle. ABASINA creeps downstairs, smoothing her clothes. He lights it just as ABASINA collides into him.

EKONG: Yah! Abasina! You want to kill me?

ABASINA: Sorry, Mr Ekong.

EKONG: Ah-ah. Where you hide yourself?

ABASINA: Sister Sola send me errand.

EKONG: Is not the drinks she ask you to collect? Abasina, answer me.

YINKA enters from upstairs. He smoothes his clothes.

YINKA: What was that?

EKONG: The generator, sah.

YINKA: For goodness sake. *(Exits.)*

ABASINA makes to leave.

EKONG: Abasina. *Abasina. Chei*! No say I no tell you. The game you dey play with these people, ehn? Okay-oh. When the grass fight the elephant suffers, *abi* how dem dey talk am?

ABASINA exits.

Sound of the family seeing off guests by the front door. EKONG quickly wipes his mouth. HELEN, SOJI, SOLA, PAKIMI enter with AFOLABI, who is smiling. HELEN leads AFOLABI to sit on the sofa.

HELEN: *(Forlornly.)* They're all going to the other parties now.

AFOLABI: *(Makes himself comfortable.)* Thank you, madam.

HELEN: Abasina! Ekong, call Abasina.

EKONG: Yes, madam. *(Exits through kitchen.)*

EKONG eyes AFOLABI with envy. AFOLABI returns a jeering look to him.

SOJI: *(To AFOLABI.)* If you hadn't ripped out the plug…

HELEN: Don't blame me! Alhaji has never sold adulterated diesel. Everybody knows that.

SOJI: And I suppose this is a new kind of diesel?

HELEN: You, big Professor, ask your useless president why there is petrol shortage. I only wanted to give your father a proper burial.

SOJI: He really went out with a bang!

SOLA: Who are you to talk? You didn't do a thing to organize the funeral.

ABASINA and EKONG enter.

PAKIMI: If we can just calm down…

HELEN: *(To ABASINA.)* Where did you go? I will deal with you later. Serve Mr Afolabi food.

ABASINA gets food from the cooler.

(To EKONG.) Ehen? You didn't see what happened? Go and help!

EKONG exits. AFOLABI smirks.

PAKIMI: Afolabi. Join him.

SOJI: Let the old man eat now.

PAKIMI: He should be helping Ekong to clear up. *(Claps his hands at AFOLABI.)*

AFOLABI exits through kitchen.

HELEN: Pastor…

PAKIMI: A befitting ending to his triumphant entry.

SOLA takes the food from ABASINA and exits through kitchen.

SOJI: You didn't need to do that. He saved us.

PAKIMI: *God* saved us.

SOJI: What is it with you and Afolabi…

PAKIMI: We should exert our energies more productively other than talking about the help.

HELEN: Thank God nobody is injured. What a day.

SOJI heads for the front door.

Brother Soji…

SOJI: I'm going to see off my uncles. *(Exits.)*

HELEN: People will say look at the send-off I gave to Papa.

PAKIMI: Those same people who said Papa lowered his standards when he married you? Forget them, my dear.

HELEN: This way I could have showed them who I am. I would have showed them that Papa made the right choice.

PAKIMI: You cannot change people's minds. Better to look to the future, Helen. *(Reaches out to hold her hand.)* I meant what I said…

HELEN: *(Jumps up.)* Hepa! They are with the lawyer. *(Makes to storm out.)*

YINKA and SOJI enter.

Why don't you stop playing games? We are all adults.

YINKA: If saying goodbye to our uncles is a game to you…

HELEN: I am not a fool. Let us call Lawyer Anike and the accountant. We will settle everything tomorrow.

YINKA: Why wait? They are still here. Soji, go and get them.

SOJI reluctantly exits back out.

There is blood and there is blood. Tonight we will find out which is which.

Music.

Later that night. All the family except for YINKA. The atmosphere is glum. Some lanterns and candles provide light. Suddenly the lights come back on. A cheer of 'NEPA!' in the distance. Documents dangle from HELEN's limp hand. ABASINA takes out the lanterns and returns to clean up. AFOLABI takes some coolers and exits through kitchen.

HELEN: Today should have ended in darkness. It would have been appropriate.

SOJI: Don't let Rafiu hear you say that. Ekong is not wise, oh. You don't tell a hungry man who's just loaded his plate, '*oya,* start going home'. Especially when his teeth are as sharp as Rafiu's.

HELEN: This is not the time for jokes.

SOJI: But you're all smiling now. See, see, see…

They burst out laughing. YINKA walks in, torch in one hand, a whisky bottle in the other. He is drunk. ABASINA takes the torch from him. She puts it in the kitchen and returns to clean.

YINKA: You've done your job. You can now laugh over my parents' graves.

HELEN: Me? What have I done?

YINKA: Looter!

SOLA: Don't insult my mother!

YINKA: Shut your mouth!

SOJI: Yinka calm down.

YINKA: You heard the accountant! She bankrupted Papa.

HELEN: I didn't have access to his accounts. I asked for money, he gave me.

YINKA: You asked for everything! My dear, all the gold in Ghana cannot cover up your background.

HELEN: Your jealousy has turned your head.

YINKA: *(Approaches.)* Who are you calling mad?

HELEN: *(Stands up. Ties her headgear round her waist.)* Who is a looter?

SOJI: *(Restrains YINKA.)* For God's sake, both of you! Sola take your mother upstairs. Go on!

HELEN: I'm not leaving this room for anybody! This is my house!

YINKA: This is my father's house.

SOLA leads her mother upstairs.

HELEN: This is my house! Nobody can take it from me!

SOJI: *(To ABASINA, who continues cleaning.)* Madam, you want your own invite?

ABASINA exits.

Man what's your problem?

YINKA: I told you this would happen.

SOJI: It's not as bad as it looks.

YINKA: Were you deaf? Didn't you hear the accountant?

SOJI: After Thanksgiving we'll talk to him. There has to be something left. He was drunk.

YINKA: If you had to inform your biggest client that they are now paupers, would you do it sober? We are not selling the estate. No way.

SOJI: He was only suggesting it. We could sell the office blocks off to those South African investors.

YINKA: I thought dealing with Afrikaners was anathema to you.

SOJI: We're all Africans now. Or those Chinese businessmen. The factories are just what they're looking for.

YINKA: The factories are shells. They've been dormant for the past five years.

SOJI: You're joking!

YINKA: You never concerned yourself.

SOJI: Every time I asked Dad how is business, he'd say things were looking up.

YINKA: Trust you to take his word for it. So long as nothing bothered your life you couldn't care less.

SOJI: But he was spending money like he owned the Mint.

YINKA: Bank loans.

SOJI: But if he wasn't creditworthy how was he…

YINKA: For goodness' sake, Soji!

SOJI: … We still have the mansion in London. With property prices what they are we'll clear some of the debts.

HELEN: *(Off.)* I say I don't need to lie down!

YINKA: I can't be dealing with this woman now. *(Exits front door.)*

HELEN and SOLA come down the stairs.

HELEN: After all I've done for you boys. Treated you like my own brothers. Abasina!

ABASINA: *(From the kitchen.)* Ma! *(Enters.)* Ma?

HELEN: Is this how to clean up?

ABASINA resumes cleaning. A loud crash comes from the front yard. Yeh! What is that again?

HELEN and ABASINA exit through front door. SOLA heads for the front door. SOJI grabs her arm.

SOJI: You all right?

SOLA: Yes.

SOJI: How will you cope?

SOLA: *(Squeezes his hand.)* I'll stay a bit longer, to look after Mum…

HELEN and PAKIMI enter holding YINKA who clutches his head. ABASINA gets a first aid box. HELEN tends to YINKA.

HELEN: Why didn't you come out? *(To HELEN.)* Tell Ekong to get the car ready.

ABASINA exits.

YINKA: *(Stiffly.)* I said I'm fine.

SOJI: What happened?

PAKIMI: The work of your friend Afolabi. Brother Yinka leaned against the canopy.

SOLA smirks.

HELEN: If you're sure.

SOLA: *(Angrily.)* He says he's fine! *(Exits upstairs.)*

HELEN: I'm only asking. If you need me. *(Exits upstairs.)*

SOJI: Thanks, Mama Sola.

PAKIMI: Mama Sola was only looking after you, as she has done in the past… Perhaps I too can play a similar role in a more perilous situation.

SOJI: How did you…

YINKA: Don't be dim. Helen has gone blabbering to him. *(To PAKIMI.)* Forget it.

PAKIMI: Once the banks turn on you, you will find them hard bargainers.

YINKA: The banks can't touch this property.

PAKIMI: This estate is the jewel in the crown. The debts are in the family name. You are liable.

YINKA: We will pay what we owe the banks once we sell Papa's London mansion.

PAKIMI: Papa already sold it to service his foreign debts.

YINKA looks at SOJI.

SOJI: The estate agent was in charge of it.

YINKA: And you never thought to check on the place?

PAKIMI: My offer still stands. I need only a few plots.

SOJI: Thanks but we are still considering other options.

YINKA: … Let's say I agree to sell the estate?

PAKIMI: For the amount of land I need at today's evaluation…

YINKA: I meant all of it.

SOJI: Woh, woh, woh! All of it?

PAKIMI: *(Eyes light up in surprise.)* I would table a suitable offer… There will be lots of paperwork.

YINKA: I'm not in a hurry to return to New York.

PAKIMI: What about Helen?

YINKA: I'm head of this family.

Pause. They shake hands.

PAKIMI: I will have a word with her, if you don't mind.

YINKA shrugs, starts drinking whisky.

Brother Soji. *(Exits upstairs.)*

SOJI looks accusingly at YINKA.

YINKA: With all our debts, the estate is a burden. Not another kobo is going on maintaining her. She has stolen enough already. We pay her off, she finds her way.

SOJI: What about not breaking up the estate that our mother built?

YINKA: I'm doing this for Mother. Helen does not get to win.

SOJI: And Joyce and the boys? Who's looking after your business in New York?

YINKA: That's my problem. It's time I had a branch in Nigeria, anyway.

SOJI: What about me?

YINKA: When I built my house, what were you doing? Too busy playing *Baba* London.

SOJI: And now that we have to sell Dad's other properties do I build my house in the sky?

YINKA: You can stay in my guest-house when you visit.

SOJI: I was hoping... You know that government programme? The one that brings home professionals from abroad?

YINKA: You applied for it?

SOJI nods.

Your reason being?

SOJI: I just want to come home.

YINKA: It's a good gig. You get paid in dollars, right? I thought you were happy in London with your new job.

SOJI: Yeah, well. Don't tell anyone yet. I've not finalised things.

YINKA: Anyway, you'll help me sort out this mess. One thing is certain: you won't be living here. *(Looks at his watch.)* The boys are expecting me to call.

Exits upstairs with the whisky. He passes PAKIMI and HELEN on the landing.

PAKIMI: Brother Soji, I hope all is well.

SOJI: I'm fine. The air conditioning needs fixing.

HELEN: We're giving it a rest. What with the light coming and going.

SOJI: It's as if mother's back in charge.

PAKIMI: Times have changed.

SOJI: The driver is in the driving seat. *(Exits through front door.)*

HELEN looks at PAKIMI questioningly.

PAKIMI: *(Dismissive.)* He's talking Professor talk. I didn't want Sola to hear us, that's why I wanted us to come downstairs.

HELEN: I still don't feel comfortable about letting Afolabi go.

PAKIMI: He has served his time.

HELEN: I have a father. How is he going to feed?

PAKIMI: He has children. Let them perform their God-given duty and take care of him.

HELEN: The country is tough. Children are kicking their mothers out of their fathers' houses.

PAKIMI: And that is your number one problem?

HELEN: Honestly I didn't know about Papa's finances. He never breathed a word to me. Where did it all go? Honest money should be solid as a rock.

PAKIMI: Papa was a businessman.

HELEN: Are you saying he was not honest? His body is not yet cold you dare speak ill of him! You a pastor. Were you not the one who drove him to his business meetings with foreign businessmen?

PAKIMI: So? Oh, because they are white they are honest?

HELEN: *(Heads for the stairs.)* If this is the nonsense you brought me down to hear…

PAKIMI: Yinka is selling the estate.

HELEN: *(Stops and turns round.)* Now you are trying to be funny.

PAKIMI: I will help you negotiate a decent pay-off.

HELEN: I am not a harlot that you can pay off! I am Chief Olanrewaju Adeyemi's lawfully wedded wife!

YINKA appears on the landing.

YINKA: Stop shouting in my father's house.

HELEN: You cannot make me homeless, you hear?

YINKA: I am the man of this house.

HELEN: Man? Who made you into a man?

YINKA: Spread your poisonous lies.

HELEN takes off her wrapper.

PAKIMI: Helen! *(Holds her arm.)*

HELEN: *(Breaks free. Shouts.)* Everybody come and see the woman who made Yinka Adeyemi into a man! *(Removes her buba.)*

PAKIMI locks the front door. EKONG puts his head through the kitchen door. PAKIMI waves EKONG back into the kitchen. SOLA appears on the landing. YINKA trembles.

Adeyinka Adeyemi, come down and see! *(Removes her petticoat. She is down to her underwear.)* Small boy!

YINKA: Bitch.

HELEN: Your mother is a bitch!

PAKIMI: Helen it is enough!

YINKA descends the stairs. PAKIMI comes between them. HELEN pushes PAKIMI aside. She stands face to face with YINKA.

HELEN: What? What do you want to do? Everything my father this, my father that! My father my father my father! Go back to Yankee, small boy! You should have seen him on our first night, *(Points at his penis.)* 'Where do I put it?' Me and you. God punish you…

YINKA: You are leaving this house today.

YINKA marches back upstairs. SOLA smirks at him. YINKA glares at her as he walks past. SOLA descends. She kisses her mother and exits. HELEN puts her clothes back on.

PAKIMI: You and him?

HELEN: Don't pretend you don't know.

PAKIMI: Was that before or after you cheated on me with Chief?

HELEN: Does it matter? It is in the past.

PAKIMI still finds it hard to take in.

Lomi, help me find out who they sold the estate to. Maybe I can do a deal with them.

PAKIMI: I think that offer has expired.

HELEN: Just help me find out.

PAKIMI: I have to prepare for the Thanksgiving.

PAKIMI heads for front door.

HELEN: You were going to tell me something.

PAKIMI: It will keep.

HELEN: What of our prayers?

PAKIMI: Tomorrow, tomorrow. *(Exits.)*

An hour later.

ABASINA and AFOLABI enter from kitchen with coolers and other items from the party. She makes sure no one is around, puts rice in a container and gives it to AFOLABI.

AFOLABI: …Doing as if he is the owner of the estate. And I am the one who save them, oh. I risk my life.

ABASINA: God will reward you, Baba.

AFOLABI: Is not Allah reward I'm looking for now.

ABASINA: Why Pastor no like you?

AFOLABI: I don't know what I did for him.

ABASINA: Maybe you know his secret when he is doing driver for Chief.

AFOLABI: I am not gossip like woman. *(Eats.)*

ABASINA: OK, gossip like man. He dey tief?

AFOLABI shakes his head.

ABASINA: He dey tell lie?

AFOLABI shakes his head.

ABASINA: He sleep with Mama Yinka?

AFOLABI glares at her.

ABASINA: So wetin he do now! … Eh, Baba, you sure say you wan' chop for this house again?

AFOLABI: *(Smiles.)* He and Mama Sola…

ABASINA: That one na history now. I even believe say dem dey bang each other before Papa die.

AFOLABI: Abasina!

ABASINA: How many special prayer does person need?

AFOLABI: When you are talking nonsense talk why madam will not treat you bad?

ABASINA: You, *nko*? You talk nonsense talk about Pastor?

AFOLABI: That is different. Now that Papa's sons are here, Pastor have no role in this house again. That's why I don't say anything to him. My time has come.

ABASINA: Ah, Baba, you never hear about the will…

EKONG enters. His hand is bandaged.

EKONG: The triumphant entry! That is your nickname from now forever.

AFOLABI: That is your grandfather's nickname!

ABASINA: Wetin! *(Points to upstairs.) Oya,* everybody outside.

EKONG: *(Serves himself rice in a container.)* Any news?

ABASINA: About what?

EKONG: The will now. Is it not the reason why Madam and Brother dey fight?

AFOLABI: Fight? When?

ABASINA: Dem dey sell the estate to Pastor.

EKONG: Talk true!

AFOLABI: That is lie.

ABASINA: I hear Pastor and Brother Yinka as dem make agreement.

AFOLABI: I say that is lie!

YINKA: *(On the landing.)* Who is there?

ABASINA and EKONG scramble into the kitchen. YINKA with the whisky bottle descends. He is drunk. The truth dawns on AFOLABI.

AFOLABI: Is me sir. I'm looking for Brother Soji.

YINKA: You see him here?

SOJI enters.

Ah, Afolabi. You are a conjurer. *(Prostrates to AFOLABI.)* All hail, Afolabi, the Professor Peller[8] of Adeyemi Estate!

SOJI: Come back later.

AFOLABI exits. SOJI pulls YINKA up onto the sofa.

YINKA: Yo! What's up, man?

SOJI: Pull yourself together.

---

8   Famous Nigerian magician.

YINKA: *(Laughs.)* Hey, look at that. Soji is being responsible for someone other than himself. The world has truly turned upside down.

SOJI: You need to sober up.

YINKA: You are right not to marry! Women, they are a curse. They will poison you. When they do this *(Waves his finger and rolls his head.)* run! Run!

SOJI: *(Tries to take him upstairs.)* Come on.

YINKA: *(Pushes SOJI away.)* I must warn all men. Run, guys or they will kill you! *(Collapses into the sofa.)*

SOJI: Get a grip!

YINKA: There I am building a wing of the Adeyemi dynasty in God's Own Country. In God's Own Goddamn Country.

SOJI tries to pull up YINKA. YINKA at first goes with SOJI, then wrests himself away from SOJI.

YINKA: My friend! I love my boys. But they pledge allegiance to the Stars and Stripes. And their women, ho, ho! You think marrying an African American is the same as marrying an African? You are wrong! Don't believe them when they tell you we're all from the source. They are American, end of story. It's amazing. So, because a man has a ring on his finger he cannot look at another woman, eh?

SOJI: Yinka, you're not making sense.

YINKA: …A man cannot have a meaningless fling, just to keep his manhood ticking? Except that his own wife must pull him down.

SOJI: *(Shakes YINKA.)* Yinka. Yinka! What's going on with you and Joyce?

YINKA: Who? Oh, *Joyce*! She's filed for divorce. She is taking everything. The house, the kids, the business. She meant nothing to me I pleaded with this woman. It was a harmless fling. Sixteen years of marriage, burst like a bubble. Papa warned me: don't get involved with foreigners. They don't understand our ways. Papa. Papa, Papa, Papa…

SOJI: Get up.

YINKA: I'm OK here.

SOJI: The others will see you.

YINKA: Let them. They've stripped me naked already.

SOJI: Come on…

YINKA shoves SOJI away. YINKA puts his head in his hands and sobs. ABASINA enters from kitchen.

ABASINA: Is not good for people to see you like this, sah. *(She holds out her hand.)*

YINKA takes her hand. SOLA enters through front door. ABASINA leads YINKA upstairs.

YINKA: I've told you. When we're alone don't call me sir.

ABASINA and YINKA exit.

SOLA smirks.

SOJI: Not a word.

SOLA: Did I say anything?

SOJI looks at her. SOLA bursts out laughing.

SOLA: Good for Joyce!

SOJI: You think it's funny?

SOLA: You should have been here a few minutes ago. Your brother wants his women subservient. Just like Papa.

SOJI: Give it a rest, Sola.

SOLA: No man will hurt me the way Papa hurt me and Mother. I won't let any man take from me and not give me even the bare minimum of respect.

SOJI: Oh you're a feminist now.

SOLA: I thought you were enlightened. But I forget your head is buried in your books so how would you know about real life? You're not married. Do you even have a girlfriend? So how would you know how to listen to a woman, let alone know what she needs? How would you know how to respect a woman?

SOJI: Does your man Wale know about your plans for London?

AFOLABI enters.

AFOLABI: I will come back, sah.

SOJI: No, no, it's all right. How can I help you?

SOLA goes upstairs.

AFOLABI: I hope I'm not disturbing you.

SOJI: No, no. Please sit down.

AFOLABI: I don't want to dirty the chair.

SOJI: Something to drink?

AFOLABI: Thank you, sah. I can take stout back to boys quarters. Big stout.

SOJI: What can I do for you?

AFOLABI: Pastor want to sack me.

SOJI: He's not sacking you. He's laying you off.

AFOLABI: What is the difference? I am the one who make the garden and the lawn. The tree that you and Brother Yinka are using to make swing. I am the one who plant it.

SOJI: I know.

AFOLABI: *(Picks up the vase.)* And this vase! I am the one who buy it for Papa the day you are born.

SOJI: Yes, yes.

AFOLABI: I don't know what I did for Pastor. Person who work suppose to reap his reward. I work very hard for your father. Of all his children you are the one I am close to. That's why I come to you, nobody else.

SOJI: I know, Mr Afolabi.

AFOLABI: You remember you say you are going to save the whole Nigeria? You remember? I am not even asking for that one. Just help me talk to Pastor. Is only this work that is keeping me alive.

SOJI: I'm sorry, Afolabi, I can't help you.

AFOLABI: Please now! *(Weeps. prostrates at SOJI's feet, grabbing onto SOJI's leg in desperation.)*

SOJI: Mr Afolabi!

AFOLABI: Please, I take Allah beg you!

SOJI: Mr Afolabi, please stand up. Please.

AFOLABI: Where can I go after this? Where can I go?

SOJI: *(Pulls him up.)* I'll talk to Pastor. Just get up. Afolabi! Get up.

AFOLABI: (*Stands up. Still weeping.*) Thank you, sah. As you have spoken, Allah has already reward your good heart.

SOJI: Uh-huh, uh-huh.

AFOLABI: Thank you, Brother Soji.

AFOLABI exits through kitchen.

SOJI sees that AFOLABI has left the stout behind. He picks it up.

SOJI: Mr Afolabi!

AFOLABI is gone. SOJI puts down the stout and goes upstairs.

ABASINA comes down. SOJI looks at her. ABASINA averts her gaze.

SOJI: Make sure you turn off all the lights.

ABASINA curtseys. SOJI goes upstairs, turns round and looks at ABASINA. ABASINA turns off the lights, leaving SOJI in darkness.

THANKSGIVING

The next morning. ABASINA is tidying up. Enter HELEN. She is dressed to go out.

HELEN: You are sure Pastor has not called this morning?

ABASINA: Yes madam.

HELEN takes the car keys. ABASINA heads for kitchen.

HELEN: Where are you going?

ABASINA: To call Ekong, madam.

HELEN: *(Gives ABASINA a dirty look.)* Did I ask you to call him? *(Exits.)*

ABASINA continues cleaning. EKONG rushes in, chewing-stick in mouth.

ABASINA: She no ask for you!

EKONG returns, looks at his bandaged hand.

EKONG: Dat Rafiu na animal. If you see am yesterday. He nearly chop my hand comot.

ABASINA: You no say hungry man, na angry man.

EKONG: Madam must have big problem to leave so early when we have Thanksgiving. Maybe is to look for where she and Sola go live.

ABASINA: I beg. Me too I get my own problem.

EKONG searches the table. He pockets an ash tray.

Mr Ekong, you keep something there?

EKONG: Abasina, you have sorted yourself.

EKONG goes over to the cabinet to continue his search. He pockets the TV remote control.

ABASINA: Mr Ekong, wetin you mean?

AFOLABI enters.

AFOLABI: Has Brother Soji come down?

ABASINA: Not yet. Sorry Baba…

EKONG picks up the vase.

Mr Ekong!

EKONG: This na my compensation. Afolabi, you no go take something for yourself?

AFOLABI: *(Blocks EKONG's path.)* Put it back.

EKONG: Brother Soji cannot help you, my friend.

AFOLABI: Put it back!

EKONG: Old man, you want to fight me?

AFOLABI: I'm telling you now!

EKONG: *(Puts back the vase.)* Is not me that will kill you. Is your blindness that will kill you. *(Exits.)*

SOJI and SOLA on the landing. SOJI sees AFOLABI and retreats, pulling SOLA back.

AFOLABI: I will come back later. *(Exits.)*

SOLA and SOJI come downstairs.

ABASINA: Good morning sah, good morning sista.

SOLA: Morning. Get our food.

ABASINA enters kitchen.

(Looks about the house.) This could be our last breakfast together in this house.

SOJI ponders. There is something on his chest he needs to get off.

SOJI: London's not all rosy. My life's not going the way I thought it would.

SOLA: Look at how messed up this country is. Everybody wants to check out. Didn't your friends tell you?

SOJI: Home is home isn't it? For better for worse.

SOLA: Nothing can be worse than not knowing where your next meal is coming from.

SOJI: I don't think our situation is that bad.

ABASINA enters with the breakfast. She avoids SOJI's gaze. She exits to kitchen.

SOLA: I hope she hasn't puked in it.

SOJI looks quizzically at SOLA.

You wouldn't know morning sickness if it dropped on you. Too bad she can't pass it off as your brother's. Not that I'd wish any woman on him.

SOJI: Yeah, well, um, I was saying we should start thinking, um, thinking of what kind of country we want…

SOLA: You're no longer a student union leader. The soldiers are back in their barracks. Job done.

YINKA enters from upstairs and exits to kitchen. He has a hangover. SOLA smiles as she bows her head. YINKA enters with a cup of coffee and goes upstairs.

My father, my father, my father…

YINKA: *(Stop. To SOJI.)* You see how this thing shows me no respect?

SOLA: You want me to fear you. Who does that remind me of? Oh yeah, my father, my father, my father. 'Sola has no respect, Sola has no discipline. I caned her, she didn't cry. She has no remorse. I will beat you until you bleed.' You want to see the scars?

YINKA: Oh great. Another strip-show.

SOLA: You'd love that. It would remind you of what you couldn't keep. Dear Daddy must have the beautiful house-girl for himself. Junior should go find himself another plaything.

YINKA: Dad did me a favour. I'd hate to have had you for a daughter.

SOLA: It's your sons I'm sorry for.

YINKA: You'll never be a true Adeyemi.

SOLA: Like I care?

YINKA: You're a pig in a house of diamonds. No name, no future.

SOLA: Brother Soji is taking me to London. I'll get away from this godforsaken family for good.

YINKA: Which London? *(To SOJI.)* Please let me tell her. Please.

SOLA: You hate seeing me happy. You just have to try and…

SOJI: The university is reviewing my position. Funding has been cut. My department did poorly in the research assessment. I was one of those whose research work was deemed inadequate.

SOLA: So what? Return to your former college.

SOJI: Never. People were being promoted over me.

SOLA: No problem. Find another job…

YINKA: He's not going back. He's got a job here.

SOLA: Rubbish. Lies.

YINKA: Soji.

SOJI: I'm sorry, Sola.

SOLA: You led me on!

SOJI: I didn't know how to tell you.

SOLA: I made plans!

SOJI: You can always go by yourself.

SOLA storms upstairs.

YINKA: What's this rubbish about taking her to London?

SOJI, not in the mood, heads for front door.

YINKA: Come here! I said come here!

SOJI stops. YINKA goes to him and hugs him.

YINKA: Why didn't you tell me about your work problems?
Ah, it doesn't matter. This other job is a sure banker.
Return to London and pack your things. We'll be together
again. Enim's sister was sizing you up at the funeral.
Abasina!

ABASINA: *(Enters from kitchen.)* Sah!

YINKA: My breakfast.

ABASINA curtseys and enters kitchen.

SOJI: For how long have you been sleeping with Abasina?

YINKA: None of your business.

SOJI: Do you know that she's…

AFOLABI enters from kitchen.

AFOLABI: Sah, I am wait for you this morning.

HELEN and PAKIMI enter. AFOLABI exits quickly.

HELEN: Morning, oh. Up so early?

*YINKA scowls at HELEN. He takes his breakfast and exits upstairs.
HELEN shakes her head.*

SOJI: Morning. You're out and about early.

HELEN: You won't believe it. I went to the church not knowing Pastor was here already.

SOJI: Surveying your property, I see.

HELEN: Oh, you've agreed to sell Pastor some of the land. That's very kind of you. At least part of the estate will remain a part of us. Even better, it will be used to God's greater glory.

SOJI: You haven't told her? *(Laughs, makes a bow and exits upstairs.)*

HELEN looks quizzically at PAKIMI.

PAKIMI: I wanted to tell you.

HELEN: They've told you the person they're selling the rest of the estate to?

PAKIMI: It's me, Helen.

HELEN: Be serious… I don't believe it!

PAKIMI: What can I say?

HELEN: You should have told me!

PAKIMI: I tried but do you ever listen when you get agitated?

HELEN: When?

PAKIMI: We're sorting out the paperwork this evening.

HELEN: The driver is in the driving seat. *(Heads for upstairs.)*

PAKIMI: *(Holds her.)* Stay as long as you like. You know that I would never throw you out.

HELEN: They've won. They've used you to make me the harlot.

PAKIMI: Nobody's won. You'll get the settlement you deserve, I'll make sure. You are Chief Mrs Helen Adeyemi. No one can take that away from you… It's funny. We both used to dream: what would it be like to be Chief and Chief Mrs of the estate. I never thought we'd have to take it in turns. *(Looks up at the chandelier.)*

HELEN: About your offer…

PAKIMI: …Mrs Pakimi will want to redecorate.

HELEN: Oh, of course.

PAKIMI: You said?

HELEN: The car was making a funny noise this morning… *(Heads to kitchen.)*

PAKIMI: Let Ekong to see to it.

HELEN: I have to explain to him. *(Exits.)*

SOLA enters from upstairs with her bags.

PAKIMI: You're leaving us? The Thanksgiving…

SOLA: I'm behind in my course work.

PAKIMI: OK, erm. We haven't had the chance to talk. How are you?

SOLA: I'm fine.

PAKIMI: You can't be fine if you're not attending your own father's Thanksgiving.

SOLA: I really don't have the time to talk.

PAKIMI: There's something wrong with the car. Let me drop you off.

SOLA: I'll charter a taxi.

PAKIMI: It's no problem. I need to talk to you. I don't want this issue to spoil our relationship. Whatever happens I guarantee you will not suffer.

SOLA: I'm sorry, Pastor. I don't know what you're talking about.

PAKIMI: Ah. I'll tell you on the way.

AFOLABI enters from kitchen. He sees PAKIMI and makes to retreat. PAKIMI sees him.

PAKIMI: Afolabi!

AFOLABI: Sah.

PAKIMI: *(To SOLA.)* I'll meet you in the car. *(Ushers AFOLABI into kitchen.)*

SOLA looks around the house briefly then heads for the front door. SOJI enters from upstairs.

SOJI: What are you going to do now?

SOLA: What does it matter to you?

SOJI: When I return to London I'll get my lawyer friend to write you the letter of invitation.

SOLA: Why didn't you think of that before?

SOJI fumbles around for an explanation.

SOLA: My mother was right. You're all the same.

SOJI: That's not true, Sola.

SOLA: What happened to you? I thought you'd be the next Fela, standing up for what is right. You can't be honest with me. You can't be honest with yourself. Please, everybody should just stay on their mother's side.

PAKIMI enters.

PAKIMI: Sorry for keeping you. Brother Soji… *(Exits through front door.)*

SOJI is downcast. EKONG enters through kitchen.

EKONG: Sorry sah. I'm looking for Abasina.

SOJI: I don't know where she is.

ABASINA enters from kitchen with washing.

Oh, there you go.

ABASINA: You dey find me, sah?

SOJI: No, no. *(Exits through front door.)*

EKONG: How the fallen are mighty, I mean, how the mighty are fallen.

ABASINA: Dem still dey inside house, oh.

EKONG: Pastor don serve Afolabi notice. Come see as e dey cry for backyard. I no tell am? All his years wasted. To help the rich get richer. But Abasina, money dey for this church business, oh. I know how to pray for people. *Oya,* kneel down.

ABASINA: Mr Ekong. Everything to you is joke.

EKONG: What can I do? Pastor dey find me too. How your stomach? No more morning sickness?

ABASINA: I no get morning sickness.

EKONG: My wife have born me three children, including the one who resemble my next door neighbour. So. You play the game. You win. As one Adeyemi door close, another one open.

ABASINA: As you talk am, we have to look after ourself… So you know about me and Papa?

EKONG: *(Nods.)* You lucky say Brother Yinka resemble Papa. If the baby no resemble dem, make you take am go do plastic surgery. If you get driver and house help, no treat dem like dirty, oh.

They hug.

Abasina! You no be small girl, oh.

ABASINA: Mr Ekong. What of you?

EKONG: Madam say make I carry the car go mechanic… *(He winks mischievously and throws the car keys up in the air. He exits through the front door like a king. Sings.)* 'Revolution is coming, one day-one-day…'

ABASINA: *(Looks after him.)* Mr Ekong… *(She looks at Chief Adeyemi's portrait and touches it. She pats her stomach.)*

HELEN enters.

HELEN: Ah-ah. How long does it take you to put the washing away? Ehn? God knows you will soon be out of a job, then you will see. Bastard.

ABASINA quickly exits upstairs.

PAKIMI and SOLA enter.

PAKIMI: That is wrong. That is totally wrong.

HELEN: What is it?

PAKIMI: Sola has something very important to say to you.

HELEN: *(Sits down.)* What is it?

PAKIMI: I didn't realise she hadn't said goodbye to you. I brought her straight back.

HELEN: Sola, is this true? You see our situation yet throughout you've behaved so badly. I'm disappointed in you. I'm only trying to give you a better life. Is that my crime that you are punishing me for?

SOLA: I didn't ask you to do anything for me.

PAKIMI: Sola! Apologise to your mother.

HELEN: That is how she talks to me. Because I did not go to university, you are too smart to take correction from me.

Because my friends are not the children of lawyers and doctors.

PAKIMI: Sola apologise.

SOLA: You wanted me to have a heart to heart with my mother. If you don't like it, too bad.

PAKIMI: What has come over you?

HELEN: It is only now that you are noticing this her behaviour? I did not want you to end up a house-girl like me, this is the thanks I get.

SOLA: Whatever.

PAKIMI: You are starting to sound like Soji.

HELEN: Abi, oh. It is too late for him to be playing big brother to you. *(To PAKIMI.)* Remember Papa's 70th. He didn't even recognise her. The fool was toasting her.

SOLA: *(Testily.)* Why do you keep bringing that up?

HELEN: Because his dirty ideas are infecting you. You know *oyinbo* people. We see them on Jerry Springer. That you are brother and sister he would say after all you are not of the same mother.

SOLA: *(Cannot believe her ears.)* You think me and Soji… Wow. OK. Can I go now?

HELEN: I don't blame you. You've never known suffering. I've been looking after you too much.

SOLA: When did you look after me? Was it when you dumped me in boarding school? Oh we must keep the house-girl's child out of sight so you could play Chief Mrs Adeyemi.

HELEN: You are a child. That's why you keep looking at the past in that manner.

SOLA: Oh and you don't?

HELEN: I did what I thought was right.

SOLA: Because now Papa is dead and the estate is gone the society invites will dry up.

HELEN: I was protecting you.

SOLA: You were protecting your lifestyle. You left me behind! All because of him! *(Points at Chief Adeyemi's portrait.)*

PAKIMI: Sola!

SOLA: I will never be like you. I don't need any man to make me somebody. Imagine, getting pregnant to steal him from his wife…

HELEN grabs her shoe. She grabs SOLA by the neck and beats her with it.

PAKIMI: Helen!

PAKIMI intervenes. He cannot get HELEN's hand off SOLA's neck.

HELEN: How dare you! If I had not pushed Chief into marrying me you'd be a house-girl! I suffered the slights of your father's family and friends! I took his beatings without fighting back, wondering if this was the time he would send me packing! All for you. All for you!

PAKIMI: Helen! *(Finally wrestles HELEN off SOLA.)*

HELEN: I will kill you and I will kill myself! You ungrateful child. If you want to go, go! Get out! Don't come back here if you know what is good for you! *(Storms back upstairs, tears streaming down her face.)*

PAKIMI: Of course she doesn't mean that, Sola.

SOLA calmly takes her bag and exits through front door.

PAKIMI: Sola!

Evening.

YINKA and PAKIMI are sitting on the sofa, passing documents between them. SOJI and HELEN sit watching the proceedings. Enter ABASINA with a tray of drinks, which she serves to everyone.

HELEN: You're sure Ekong did not tell you where he went?

ABASINA: I no see am since the time he go mechanic, ma.

PAKIMI: The Lord's work is done.

YINKA: *(Reads the document.)* The Lord is generous. *(Passes it to HELEN.)*

PAKIMI: *(Looks around, as if he is seeing the place for the first time.)* Indeed.

HELEN: *(Reads the document and signs.)* I will phone the mechanic.

HELEN passes the document to YINKA, who puts it in his briefcase and stands up.

SOJI: You can phone later. One last drink.

YINKA: What for?

SOJI: Sit.

YINKA: *(Sits.)* One drink.

HELEN: The future brings the unknown but our Saviour guides us. To the Lord.

They knock glasses and drink. ABASINA enters kitchen.

SOJI: To the unknown… Sola?

HELEN: I apologized to her. She refused to come back.

YINKA: *(Drinks up. Stands.)* Afolabi is coming with me. Soji…

SOJI: I'm spending a few days with Enim. I'll phone you when I'm ready to come over.

YINKA: Suit yourself.

HELEN: So when are we seeing Joyce and the boys?

PAKIMI: Oh yes. I learn that you want to return home permanently. That is wonderful news.

YINKA: Once I've sorted out the house and the business. I need Abasina to clean my house.

HELEN: She can't stay too long. I need her to help me pack.

YINKA exits to kitchen.

YINKA enters from kitchen. Takes the portrait of Chief Adeyemi. HELEN wants to protest. PAKIMI gestures to her not to.

SOJI: So, Pastor. What are you going to do with the house? Tear it down?

YINKA: *(To SOJI.)* Bring the other one when you're coming. *(Exits through front door.)*

PAKIMI: Tear down? God forbid. I will use it for the Pastor's quarters. Once the surveyor does his job, I'll know where to build the church.

SOJI: So the mansion has become quarters. Wow.

PAKIMI: Of course I did not mean to belittle the mansion. Preserving it will be in remembrance of Papa. You are always welcome to visit.

HELEN: When is your friend coming to pick you?

SOJI: Soon. So…

HELEN: Abasina!

ABASINA: *(Runs out.)* Ma!

HELEN: Get Brother Soji's bags from the bedroom.

ABASINA exits upstairs. She returns with the suitcases and exits through kitchen.

SOJI: So, you're now the proud owner of my father's house.

PAKIMI: The way of the world.

SOJI: Take care of the place.

PAKIMI: First thing to do is to renovate the interior. With your permission, of course.

SOJI: You'll make a great diplomat, Pastor.

The sound of a car driving up the driveway. A horn honks.

That'll be Enim.

SOJI and PAKIMI shake hands.

PAKIMI: The Lord is patient. He waits for you with open arms.

SOJI: Better than Ogun waiting for me with an axe, eh? Say bye-bye to Sola for me. Tell her… Never mind. The Adeyemis have left the building! *(Exits.)*

HELEN: Well.

PAKIMI: Well.

HELEN: Look after this house.

PAKIMI: Will you be all right?

HELEN: You know me.

PAKIMI: If you and Sola ever need anything. Anything…

HELEN: I will need a stick to break Ekong's head when he returns.

PAKIMI: But seriously.

HELEN: Eh, I'm fine. Papa was careless with his chequebook. A sensible second wife always saves for a rainy day.

PAKIMI: Nigerians, Nigerians.

HELEN: What? You took my house. Did I complain?

SOLA enters. There is a plaster on her face.

PAKIMI: The prodigal returns!

HELEN: Did you think they'd be waiting for you?

SOLA: Soji's gone?

PAKIMI: To his friend's.

A car horn.

HELEN: Tell Wale to come in.

SOLA: We have to get back to campus. Where are you staying?

HELEN: I'll phone you when I've decided.

SOLA exits.

PAKIMI: That your daughter is just like you.

HELEN: You're telling me? I need prayers on some matters.
(Goes up the stairs.)

PAKIMI hesitates. HELEN turns round at the middle of the landing. She holds out her arms.

PAKIMI smiles. They hold each other as they exit upstairs.

The End.

THE CHRIST OF COLDHARBOUR LANE

The Christ of Coldharbour Lane opened on 31 May 2007 and was produced by Soho Theatre, with the following cast:

OMOTUNDE (OMO)	Jimmy Akingbola
SARAH GREEN	Kay Bridgeman
MARIA MAUDLIN	Dona Croll
DONA	Nadine Marshall
ROBBIE WEDDERBURN	Mark Monero
GREG / KINGSTON / JASON	Javone Prince

All other characters played by members of the cast

Director, Paulette Randall
Designer, Libby Watson
Lighting Designer, John Bishop
Sound Designer, Dan Steele
Costume Designer, Susannah Henry
Choreographer, David Leighton
Fight Director, Terry King
Casting, Nadine Hoare
Assistant Director, Antoinette Lester

Characters

OMOTUNDE
Black-British, late-twenties

DONA
Black-British, late twenties

SARAH GREEN
Black-British, late-twenties

MARIA MAUDLIN
Black-British, early forties

GREG
Black-British, mid-thirties.

KINGSTON
Jamaican, early sixties

JASON
Black-British, mid-thirties

ROBBIE WEDDERBURN
Black-British, late-twenties

CITIZENS OF BRIXTON
BOHEMIAN, DRUNK, WOMAN,
BAG LADY, PUNTERS, ETC.

UNDERGROUND PASSENGERS

Note
A / indicates an interruption.

Autumn, bordering on winter.

Soundscape: Street noises, loud music from passing vehicles, police sirens.

OMO, DONA and KINGSTON, outside Brixton Prison. OMO is dressed casually in jeans, and a white shirt. At his feet lies a box with his possessions. DONA wears a sweater with the words 'The Mission' on it. She holds a bag containing DVDs, Christian tracts, books. OMO surveys his surroundings as if he is experiencing the world for the first time. KINGSTON, the prison warden, drinks from a bottle of water. He glares at OMO. His glare dissolves into a smile when he faces DONA. He wipes his eyes intermittently.

OMO: Thank you Sister Dona.

DONA: Dr. Gupta wasn't happy with us settling you back in Coldharbour Lane. He felt you needed a complete break from the past to help your recovery. Blah. He's a man of science. Anyway Brixton's gone all toney since you've been away. It's all the new money moving in. *(Rummages through her bag.)* The high street's like any other high street now. Except for that buzz. That's one thing you'll never bleach out of Brixton. Doesn't matter how many wine bars and patisseries they put up, you know you're in Brixton. I didn't give you my folder, did I?

OMO: No, Sister Dona.

DONA: I must have left it at the front desk. One minute. *(Exits.)*

OMO touches the ground with his hands.

KINGSTON: I warn that girl 'bout you and still she is helping you.

OMO: *(Still looking at his palms.)* Sorry?

KINGSTON: In her presence you is pretending that she have convert you. Behind her back you preach heresy.

OMO: You call it heresy to justify locking up a political prisoner.

KINGSTON: You were locked up for impersonating the Prime Minister. You is Rory Bremner? You so stupid you didn't even chalk up your face. Is no wonder Dr Gupta say you is mad.

OMO: They do not understand that I work for the Father.

KINGSTON: Pah!

OMO: I came first on The Mission's 'Born Anew' programme.

KINGSTON: Exam standards aren't what dey used to be.

OMO: I have honour in my home town. I will return to my people. They will acknowledge me.

KINGSTON: Is obeah or is juju you use on Dona, is why she believe you is from Brixton?

OMO: You treat your opinion as fact, Kingston.

KINGSTON: Your home is a mud hut Bob Geldof can't find time feh visit. Is just dat I'm feeling lucky. I woulda bet my pools coupon you is an illegal immigrant. Dey should ship you straight to Heat'row.

OMO: The world is my Father's temple. Coldharbour Lane is its foundation.

KINGSTON: Me can't believe it! From Prime Minister you graduate to Christ! Chris Rock say dere is black man and dere is nigger. Nigger is the filthiest word to come from a black man mouth. Is you he was talking 'bout. I don't know why the police didn't kill you in custody.

OMO: Are you the one crying in the wilderness?

KINGSTON: You is an offence to humanity to ask me that question. Move from here! *(Shoves OMO.)*

OMO: *(Catches KINGSTON's hands.)* The thought that a black man could be your saviour repulses you. Deny your self-hatred. *(Tries to lay a hand on KINGSTON's head.)*

KINGSTON: *(Breaks free of OMO's grasp.)* Lay that hand on me and you will see black on black violence! Go preach your lunacy to your African brethren. Is dem believe in voodoo. Why you nah say you is a reincarnation of Shango? Why is the white man's ting you always have feh mash up?

OMO: Your eyes are blinded and your heart is hardened by the establishment.

KINGSTON: Who gave birth to you, you foundling?

OMO: *(Losing his cool.)* You are the king of your own ignorance.

KINGSTON: You blank page. I peeped inside your file! Place of birth unknown!

OMO: *(Raises his hand skyward.)* Father…!

The town hall bell rings.

Alfred! His is the voice crying in the wilderness.

KINGSTON: Town crier Alfie Howard? Alfie dead. Is the town hall clock. Your ears are deaf to reality, and you expect people to believe your falsehood.

OMO: What can I do to make you believe?

KINGSTON: Me is a focus group? Wait! OK. *(Holds up the bottle of water.)* Turn this water into rum. Appleton, not Malibu.

OMO: You seek a sign?

KINGSTON: *(Tastes the water.)* Me thought as much.

OMO: My people will acknowledge me, those who have been left behind. They have no need for a sign. For too long they have been waiting for me to fulfil my manifest destiny.

KINGSTON: Your manifest destiny is to roast in hell. Me willing to send you dere! *(Approaches OMO to assault him.)*

DONA enters, waving her file. KINGSTON retreats and smiles at her.

DONA: Found it! Let's go, Omo. See you tomorrow Kingston. God bless. *(Exits.)*

KINGSTON: God bless, Dona. See you tomorrow. Omo!

OMO stops.

KINGSTON: For whom the bells toll, they toll for thee.

OMO exits.

That should put the fear of God into that Walter Mitty fantasist. It's his Robert Powell eyes. Stare at them too long he'll mek you believe anyting. Him say him cured and everyone believe him. Dey've let a mad communist loose.

Changes his clothes to GREG's.

…If there's one thing people of the book agree on is that communists are heretics. Dey want to turn the world upside down so that dey can become boss. Is my duty as a Christian and a patriot ah dis country to report him to the authorities. I'll call Greg. He knows people in high places and he wants to join dem up dere. Ever since him graduate from Oxford him have dis overbearing sense of entitlement. Learn from the Prince of Wales, I tell him. If he was like Greg he woulda poison his mother by now. Me nephew refuse to do a feature on Brixton.

KINGSTON morphs into GREG.

GREG: That's because it's typical they'd give their one black reporter the job. How should I know what it's like living in an inner city? I live in Muswell Hill for God's sake. The South Bank's as far as I go south of the river. I went to school with guys who're moving up in high places, guys who can get me scoops. *(Sighs with resignation.)* I might as well take Uncle Kingston's advice. Start from the bottom and work my way up. I bet the Duke of Westminster never had that problem. Luck of the draw.

The scene morphs into Brixton High Street.

A roadside preacher enters, spreading her message. GREG approaches her.

GREG: Excuse me! Are you…

Another roadside preacher enters followed by another, spreading their messages.

I'm wasting my time chasing up on Uncle Kingston's anarcho-messiah. I mean, take your pick. I need another story fast so I can get the hell out of here. *(Sees a patisserie.)* Is this a patisserie I see before me? *(Goes to it, excited.)*

GREG exits.

Soundscape: Noises of the street. Coldharbour Lane, Brixton.

OMO and DONA are engulfed by the roadside preachers who set up OMO's bedsit: a single bed, a table, a TV and a DVD player. SARAH, in a wheelchair, wheels by. GREG, a camcorder, in one hand and a cappuccino in the other wanders around looking for something interesting to shoot. The street noises subside as everyone exits leaving DONA and OMO in the bed-sit.

DONA: What do you think?

OMO: *(Approvingly.)* Nice.

DONA: *(Unpacks her bag.)* Ready meals in the fridge. And I got you some more copies of Prayer Request Live. *(Hands him the DVDs.)*

OMO: You are to the collar born.

DONA: With The Mission gender's no barrier to becoming a minister. Did I tell you? I've made the shortlist for the next promotions.

OMO: This is the third time you've made the shortlist.

DONA: The church elders think my Prisoners Reform Programme is my best idea yet. Imagine you, my *protégé*, rising through the ranks as my right hand man.

OMO: If I can convert my fellow inmates inside prison, I can convert people anywhere.

DONA: Exactly what I told the elders. Your talent for reaching people's souls makes up for your inexperience. It's those eyes of yours. No one can resist them.

OMO: Once I open the eyes of the people the choice is made.

DONA: The outside world has many distractions. You'll need to move the earth to get peoples' attention, never mind convert them. Our survey shows that Brixtonians are preached to on average twelve times a day. They learn of a new religion twice a month. They hear preaching from six denominations every day. And that's just between Coldharbour Lane and Electric Avenue.

OMO: What's with the statistics?

DONA: It's good to know the people you're competing with. You've seen the high street. It's like the floor of the stock market.

OMO: The word spreads.

DONA: That's my point. Everyone's getting in on the act. Forget Jerusalem and Mecca. Brixton is the most religious place on earth. The people are getting jaded. If Christ landed in Tate Gardens today, Brixtonians would be like, 'Join the queue'.

OMO: I can convince them. They will recognise the Lord in their midst.

DONA: Too right. People need reminding this is a Christian country.

OMO: Everyone knows that.

DONA: Christianity is the whipping boy of the chattering classes. You'd be amazed at how many times The Mission has been slated by the liberal press. I'd like to see them attack Islam the same way.

OMO: Your father is a big influence on you.

DONA: So you keep reminding me. Yes. I'm Daddy's little girl, the lastborn in my family so I had it easy with the old dragon. My Mum says I'm just like him. I hope not. He's solid C of E. He hates The Mission. 'Your preaching is junk food for the soul.' Something profound happens to you, it should transform you, right? You accepted the Lord. Don't you feel like a new person?

OMO: In many ways, yes.

DONA: And what about worshipping the Lord with all your heart and mind and soul? You can't do that sitting in some cold church listening to a man in robes droning on. Reverend Williams has done great work in bringing the Lord's riches to us. Hello! We're in the twenty-first century. No one wants to live in penury. Dad doesn't get it. I'm sorry. You know how I go on when I get started.

OMO: Please. I love hearing you go on. I empathize with your relationship.

DONA: I was insensitive.

OMO: So long as the Father loves me I am not an orphan.

DONA: That's the spirit, Brother Omo. *(Looks about.)* Oh, did I get you the Good News handbook?

OMO holds up the handbook.

Great, you can brush up on your skills. Get ready to convert Brixton.

OMO: I am ready for Brixton. Is Brixton ready for me?

DONA: Sorry?

OMO: Just gearing myself up for the work ahead, Sister Dona.

DONA: Oh. Right, I'm off. *(Hugs him. Pulls away and brings out the chain around OMO's neck. The pendant is a piece of rock.)* I thought you'd done away with all this.

OMO: I have. I'm keeping it as a memento.

DONA: Where's the rest?

OMO goes to his box and brings out a cowries-studded ankle bracelet, two white handkerchiefs and a white caftan.

DONA: *(Reaches for them.)* I'd better take these.

OMO: No! I'll dispose of them. I am a new person. *I am.*

DONA: Brother Omo, you are not a spirit child.

OMO: I know.

DONA: When you are born again, that is it. You are not trapped in some silly life and death cycle.

OMO: That was another life, another me, Sister Dona. My search for myself is over.

DONA: What about your crucifix?

OMO produces a crucifix from his pocket.

Brother Omo!

OMO: *(Puts it around his neck.)* The rock is around my neck but the Lord is always on my mind.

DONA: Uh-huh.

OMO: Revelations 21:19 to 20. The stones that are the bedrock of Jerusalem. We are the foundation of the New Jerusalem here in Brixton. First Brixton, then the world.

DONA: You've an answer for everything. OK, see you tomorrow.

OMO: Tomorrow, Sister Dona.

DON: *(Points to the handkerchief, caftan and bracelet.)* And you will…?

OMO: *(Removes his rock pendant. Puts it with the handkerchief, caftan and bracelet and gathers them up.)* Certainly.

DONA exits. OMO leaves the handkerchief, caftan and bracelet. He takes off the crucifix and puts it in his pocket. He puts the rock pendant around his neck. He flicks through the handbook. He puts it on the table. He puts the Prayer Request Live DVD on. OMO changes his top. On his chest we see a tattoo of a crucifix. The DVD comes on – the Texan drawl of Reverend Williams, preaching:

DVD: Ask the Lord, He will answer your prayers. He will transform your lives. Touch the screen. Touch the screen. Bob in Utah needs a new car. God is answering your prayer right now. Mrs Baker in Houston, God is curing your son of his homosexuality as we speak.

OMO goes down on his knees. He mimics Rev. Williams:

Touch the screen. Touch the screen. Jose in New York is asking for the return of prayers in school. Eugene in Ohio, a million dollars is coming your way today in Jesus' name. Amen and amen. That's all on Prayer Request Live, folks. Remember: we are all God's children. Ask our Father whatever you want. Belief is the key that unlocks the door to heavenly and earthly riches. We will create a new world in the image God wants us to, a new world of prosperity for all his children. Until next time, this is Reverend Williams saying, stay blessed and stay with The Mission. *(Music.)*

OMO sways violently as if he is being pulled between two forces. He reaches for the bracelet of cowries and puts it around his ankle. The sound of a baby crying is punctuated by singing in Yoruba of the Celestial Church, followed by frantic praying. OMO calms down, as if he has won the tug of war between two worlds, plumping for the middle ground. His demeanour is of sober realisation. He takes the handbook and throws it in the bin, along with the DVDs. The music and praying stop. All we hear is the music from the Prayer Request Live DVD.

The CITIZENS OF BRIXTON change the set. The music from the DVD fades into the noises of Brixton High Street.

The following day, outside Brixton Station. People going to work. DONA and OMO preaching. DONA hands out tracts. CITIZENS pass by, ignoring them.

DONA: *(Preaching.)* Brother, do you want everlasting happiness? All you have to do is accept Christ as your Lord and saviour…

OMO: You must wipe your soul of sin before you can enter the kingdom.

DONA: *(Looks at OMO.)* All else shall be added on to you. Accept Christ and the riches of the earth shall follow.

OMO: Transform yourselves, cast off your earthly possessions.

DONA: *(To a CITIZEN.)* Brother. Brother! One second. Don't be shy. *(CITIZEN approaches cautiously. DONA presses a leaflet into his hand.)* I'm with The Mission, the true gateway to Heaven. We've over one thousand members in London alone, saved for Heaven and prospering on earth.

OMO: Prepare to enter the New Jerusalem. Leave your earthly desires at the gates.

CITIZEN leaves, dropping the leaflet.

DONA: Brother, wait! Brother Omo, let's catch a break.

OMO: It is easier for a camel to pass through the eye of the needle…

DONA: Brother Omo.

OMO: … than for a rich man to enter my Father's home!

DONA: Brother Omo! Break. Now.

OMO: *(Looks at his watch.)* Um, OK.

DONA: What happened to our Good News Approach?

OMO: I don't think we are preparing the people properly.

DONA: We haven't signed up anyone to prepare.

OMO: We should be letting people know that the road ahead is hard. The material things of this world will weigh them down.

DONA: We must tread lightly. Remember how people perceive us.

OMO: We are here for the Lord.

DONA: With The Mission as his true church.

OMO: We must spread His true message. The people must make the effort to come to Him.

DONA: You're starting to sound like my Dad. God's love is unconditional otherwise we'd all be on a budget flight to hell because we've all fallen short. Christ died for us because we cannot help but sin. You can try to be like Christ but you can never be Christ.

OMO: We must try.

DONA: You can't turn yourself inside out. You still have to live in the world and give unto the Treasury what is the Treasury's. Remember we're lambs in the midst of wolves.

OMO: Transforming ourselves completely, that is our only way to break the cycle, to change the world. These lost souls, they will follow the true leader once they hear his voice.

DONA: You're not going to impersonate Reverend Williams, are you? Sorry! Not funny. I must admit though, on my own I'd have signed up a fair few converts by now.

OMO: By appealing to their material needs.

DONA: I was like you when I first found Christ. I wanted to convert the whole world by appealing to spiritual needs. I had to learn that you must appeal to the soul through the body. You'll learn the process when you train to become a minister.

OMO: This process feels too corporate.

DONA: It isn't corporate. The Good News Approach is psychology-based. You responded to it.

A homeless woman sits on the ground, puts her hat down and starts begging.

OMO: Not for material gain. My Father called me and I heeded his voice.

DONA: You're saying that now.

OMO: I have always said it. God considered me according to my need. The call was for me, no one else.

DONA: When I was young my family lived outside of London. The old parish priest was retiring and so they brought in this new priest. Was I happy? For the first time I met a black man in a position of authority. The parishioners wrote to the Archbishop. They weren't comfortable with him leading the service.

A smartly dressed man passes by. DONA waves to catch his attention. He ignores her and exits.

The next week he was gone. I hear you. We're all special in God's eyes. What you like those parishioners forget is that He also made us the human race. Extend your idea of uniqueness all you're doing is shredding the world into a billion pieces, each and everyone with their petty wants that you decry. In the spirit we are one. You of all people should be happy that we believe in one family.

OMO: Sister Dona!

DONA: I know! That was below the belt. But I need you to understand what we're doing…

SARAH GREEN passes by.

Sister Sarah! Hold up.

SARAH: *(Not eager to stop and chat.)* Dona.

DONA: You've not been coming to Church. What happened?

SARAH: Nothing. That's why I stopped going.

DONA: You must keep believing, Sister Sarah. If the Lord wants you to walk again you will walk. But it can't be to your schedule.

SARAH: *(Shrugs.)* Well then.

DONA: Don't be like that. When the time comes, you will be lifted even higher.

SARAH: Time is essential in my line of work.

DONA: Which is why you must never give up hope. Or maybe God has another plan in store for you. Come back to service. We shall work out another prayer plan for your miracle healing.

SARAH: Been there, done that.

DONA: Give yourself another chance with God.

SARAH: You mean give God another chance.

DONA: Sister Sarah! God loves you anyway. The door is always open.

SARAH: I think I'll pass on that.

OMO: Believe.

SARAH: And you are?

DONA: This is my colleague, Omo.

SARAH: That's an African name, isn't it?

OMO: Yoruba. It's short for Omotunde. It means the child returns.

SARAH: Ah. Welcome back.

DONA: Brother Omo is Brixton born and raised. He's never been to Nigeria. He's The Mission's latest success.

SARAH: *(To DONA.)* You might want to tell your ministers to sort out disabled access.

OMO: First believe, Sarah. First believe.

SARAH looks curiously at OMO. She shakes her head as she exits.

DONA: Well said, Brother Omo. 'Give God a chance.' You get what I'm saying about your 'I'm unique' idea? You end up like her, rejecting the Lord, bitter and lonely. I bet when she won her gold medal she thought she was invincible. She's a lesson to be learned from. (*Spots the homeless woman, in a manner of her being the only one left. Approaches her.*) Sister! For how long will you stay in the cold when the Lord offers you shelter?

WOMAN: I haven't eaten for a week.

DONA: The Lord will not let his chosen go hungry. *(Opens her purse. Brings out some money.)* How does a nice beef pattie sound?

WOMAN: It don't sound like KFC to me.

DONA: *(Reluctantly digs into her purse for more money.)* The Lord answers your prayer even before you ask.

WOMAN: The Jews, they have English blood. Is why Jesus feed the five thousand fish an' chips. But Jesus know if he land in Brixton, is a Family Bucket he hav' feh conjure.

DONA: Have you heard about The Mission?

WOMAN: Is only now you telling me. Who you wan' me feh kill? The mayor?

DONA: What? No!

WOMAN: When me nose block me kian buy Vicks because me kian afford di congestion charge. I kill him for you for free.

DONA: I'm talking about *The Mission*. The Lord's one true church.

WOMAN: Ah, is like Tom Cruise. He hav' feh join Scientology before him get him license to kill in *Mission Impossible*…

DONA: Sister! I'm not asking you to kill anyone…

DONA and WOMAN exit.

OMO remains where he is.

The following day.

Rush hour. People going to work, rushing past OMO. He looks around in wonder. Left with OMO are the CITIZENS OF BRIXTON, those left behind: the homeless, the unemployed, the drug dealers, the single mothers pushing their prams. MARIA MAUDLIN, on her way to work. SARAH wheels after MARIA. They freeze. OMO bends down and wipes his hands on the ground.

OMO: The touch of home, my home, Brixistane, where streetlights first lit up the London night, the rock upon which New Jerusalem will be built. Brixton, a spill over of excessive dreams. Anonymous masses, dancers of the dying beat. I come with the strong arm to ignite the rhythm, to drive again your passion for life!

The passers-by and loiterers remain frozen.

(Sighs.) You will claim your birthright as I have done. I will fulfil the task the Father has sent me to do and He will be pleased with me. *(Looks around at those left behind.)* I will find my apostles and they will follow me. Then I will take my message to Brixton and to the world.

The town hall bell rings. The CITIZENS as one look to the town hall clock. They go about their business as normal.

MARIA exits. SARAH tries unsuccessfully to catch her attention. She exits angrily in the opposite direction.

OMO: The voice of the one crying in the wilderness! Alfie!

CITIZEN: Where you been, man? Alfie's dead. *(Exits.)*

OMO: *(Breaks out of his reverie.)* Ah, Tate Gardens. Here's where I should be, with my people who need me.

CITIZENS set up Tate Gardens with a bench as OMO walks into the scene. OMO turns round to look at the CITIZENS chilling, drinking, doing drugs. He spots BOHEMIAN, dressed in scruff-bag chic, sitting on a bench. OMO nods at him.

BOHEMIAN smiles, beckoning OMO to join him. OMO sits beside him.

BOHEMIAN: Welcome to the One Seat Theatre. Admission is free. To justify my non-funding I need your participation.

OMO: I am not an actor.

BOHEMIAN: Obviously. I'm Paul.

OMO: Hello Paul. I'm Omo.

BOHEMIAN: For this performance you shall be Peter. Search inside my coat pocket and bring out whatever you find. Go on.

OMO brings out a five pound note.

Now say the line.

OMO: What?

BOHEMIAN: 'I've robbed you, Paul, to pay me, Peter!'

OMO doesn't get it.

(Sighs. Takes back the note.) An artist is not recognised on his own street. Fame will come. One day.

OMO: You seek fame?

BOHEMIAN: Money, really. I tell you, this starving artist lark is so *Fin de siècle.* God knows why I feel guilty about wanting a life. Brixton itself has had such a facelift my mates are buying houses here. I've held out against the tide but now I'm holding up my hands. Fame's the easiest way out of poverty. Slap your face on TV for the viewing pleasure of folks and you're off to a decent pension.

OMO: And if you run out of money?

BOHEMIAN: Turn the other cheek.

OMO: Why would you do that?

BOHEMIAN: Don't know about you but I find it galling whenever I see chancers race up the celebrity ladder to fortune. I've tried to stay true to the profession. The philistines have scaled the wall. I have no choice but to surrender to the big pay day.

OMO: You would dehumanise yourself to line your pocket?

BOHEMIAN: I'm human: anything I do can't be dehumanising. I'll play the game like everyone else.

OMO: But what if you could make your own game, play by your own rules?

BOHEMIAN: You pan through the same dirt to get to the gold.

OMO: It's not worth losing your dignity over.

BOHEMIAN: Dignity went out with the socialists. Who were never in, by the way.

OMO: Think about securing a foothold in our new world.

BOHEMIAN: I'm still trying to sort out my life in this world, my dear idealist. Anyway I dirty my body but I keep my soul clean.

OMO: But if I told you that body and soul are inseparable, that one is the other.

BOHEMIAN: I'd say there is one and there's the other. I'd say one thing at a time.

OMO: A man can be many things at once.

BOHEMIAN: I suppose so. I'm not only an actor. I write as well.

OMO: You place faith in uncertainties when I offer you a new life set upon the bedrock. Follow me and as I change the world so shall your desires change. You will become a new person. *(Holds BOHEMIAN.)*

BOHEMIAN: Steady!

ROBBIE WEDDERBURN enters with briefcase and mobile phone. He looks around furtively.

ROBBIE: *(Approaches.)* Hey! Jude Law! You got a pound?

OMO lets go of BOHEMIAN. BOHEMIAN seizes his chance to escape from OMO.

BOHEMIAN: Yes! Here you go. *(Gives ROBBIE a coin and dashes off.)*

ROBBIE: Oi! This is a penny, you stingy arse ham! *(Eyes OMO.)* You got a pound?

OMO: I don't have any money.

ROBBIE: Of course you don't, black man. How long you going to rely on Live Aid? All I'm asking for is a lousy pound.

OMO: I wish I could help. Sorry.

ROBBIE: Stuff your sorry, yeah? I need to top up my mobile. I got to spread the word. Something big is going down.

OMO draws nearer. ROBBIE shows him the briefcase.

Copped this off an MI5 agent while she was downing chicken wings in Nando's.

OMO: You sure she's an agent?

ROBBIE: She's the harbinger. I've found out the biggest secret. *(Beckons OMO to come closer. Conspiratorially.)*

This government, yeah, are you listening! Jeez… This government is plotting to sterilize the Melanites.

OMO: The who?

ROBBIE: The thirteenth tribe of Judah. You. Me. Black people!

OMO: Oh, sorry. Is that true?

ROBBIE: Baby fathers are gonna make like 1066. We're gonna be history.

A cheer from all the nearby females.

(Yells.) You'd like that wouldn't you? Bitches.

WOMAN: Fuck you!

OMO: You should take your information to the police.

ROBBIE: Are you stupid?

OMO: Go to the media, then.

ROBBIE: They're all involved! Didn't you see *Notting Hill*? That's the vision of a future Britain, man. It's all in here, in black and white. Long time man's been telling brothers about The Project for the New Anglo-Saxon Century.

OMO: What happens next?

ROBBIE: You really are stupid. Just like the rest of these sleepwalkers. *(Points around. Yells.)* They're coming for all of you. Yeah! You too white trash! Don't think you're safe. The Berkeley Plan is going to take care of you.

OMO: The Berkeley Plan?

ROBBIE: Who's going to clean the streets when we're gone? Bridewell Corp.'s signed the contract. Says so right here, man. *(Taps the briefcase.)* Should have happened years ago but the Prime Minister set back the timetable when he said we're all middle-class.

OMO: He's called a halt to this project.

ROBBIE: For fuck's sake. *For fuck's sake.* He was off message. Things are back on track now. It's only a matter of time.

OMO: So how do we fight this plan?

ROBBIE: You got a bomb?

OMO: After the suffering, through peaceful means. If we rally the people…

ROBBIE: You shit: you're the establishment's foundation. Peace is built into the system to keep us down. Be grateful for your lot when they feed you scraps. Be the bigger man when they shit on you. Show dignity when the foot is on your neck. And we buy into it wilfully. Peace my arse.

OMO: The wilful peace…

ROBBIE: Trickle down economy? More like tinkle down economy. We're getting pissed on.

OMO: The wilful peace…

ROBBIE: Call it what you like. The house always wins yet we keep playing their game.

OMO: The wilful peace…

ROBBIE: Yeah and you're part of it. I'm having none of that. I'm opting out of society.

OMO: But you want to tell the people.

ROBBIE: Just my mates and then I go offline.

OMO: Who will tell the rest?

ROBBIE: Look around you! You think this lot want to wake up to face reality? Nah man, they can dream in their sleep. You open their eyes to see they've got fuck-all that's too much information. Because then they have to do something about it. They can't pretend ignorance no more. They can't hide behind the god of that's your lot.

OMO: But what if I told you that I can help destroy the wilful peace?

ROBBIE: You ain't got a bomb!

OMO: I do not need one, brother. I will gather the meek of Brixton in a union of souls. Everybody, black, white, Asian, male, female, the young, the old, the gay, the straight, the sick, the disabled, the healthy. We shall all speak with one voice as citizens, not subjects.

ROBBIE: You still riding that peace and love mule? Why not perform a miracle while you're at it.

OMO: A miracle is a sign, nothing else.

ROBBIE: Oh yeah? I'd like to see you convince this lot how you're going to topple the ogre without waving your magic wand. Believe me, I've tried.

OMO: Belief is the key, and action soon follows. Believe.

ROBBIE: I believe in opting out. Steer clear of the establishment. That's action, man. That's me saying and doing. If you can't blow this place to kingdom come, yeah, keep your mouth shut. There's already too many talkers. You sure you haven't got a pound on you?

A BAG LADY enters.

BAG LADY: Robbie Wedderburn! You still here? Giro office shuts in ten minutes.

ROBBIE: Shit! *(Jumps up.)* You don't have a pound on you, do you?

BAG LADY: *(For the umpteenth time.)* No, Robbie. I don't have a pound.

ROBBIE dashes off. He leaves behind the briefcase.

OMO: *(Picks up the briefcase.)* Robbie!

BAG LADY: He's read too many books. They ought to shut down the library. It's a mental health hazard.

OMO: He forgot his briefcase. He said there's secret information inside it.

BAG LADY: Robbie's the tallest tall tale teller.

OMO: He sounded like he was telling the truth.

BAG LADY: Sonny, never trust a man who's on pay as you go.

OMO: He had such conviction. A man like that can move mountains.

BAG LADY: You can make bread from clouds if you believe. But can you eat it?

OMO: Would you like to learn the truth?

BAG LADY: *(Contemplates.)* Nah. I don't want to end up like Robbie. *(Exits.)*

OMO makes to open the briefcase. A DRUNK passes by.

DRUNK: All right?

OMO: (*Shuts the briefcase.*) I'm fine. And you?

DRUNK: Nothing like a can of Special Brew to make you feel special. *(Drinks.)* That's my working day over. Unless I can cadge a fag off you.

OMO: I don't smoke.

DRUNK: I don't smoke either but if you pushed me to the wall, dunked my head in water, put a gun to my head, I'll inhale.

OMO: A question. What if I said I could help you overthrow the wilful peace that is holding you down?

DRUNK protects his beer, turns round and starts swinging his fist at the imaginary figure holding him down. OMO holds him.

OMO: What if I said I would no longer wait for the one crying in the wilderness, would you drop your can and follow me? Would you change your life and follow me if, if I showed you proof?

DRUNK: *(Points to the briefcase.)* Ah! You got your fags in there. *(Tries to take the briefcase off OMO.)*

CITIZENS run excitedly across the stage chanting:

CITIZENS: Maria's on, Maria's on.

DRUNK: *(Lets go of the briefcase.)* Maria's on!

OMO: Maria?

DRUNK: Everybody knows Maria Maudlin, the Union Jack. *(Exits.)*

OMO: Maria Maudlin. Is she the one crying in the wilderness? *(Exits.)*

A woman in a trench coat and wearing sunglasses, with a half-eaten chicken wing enters, frantic. Attached to her collar is a Nando's napkin. She sees the briefcase and grabs it. She checks the contents, sighs with relief and exits with it.

CITIZENS: *(As they set up the gentleman's club.)* Maria's on, Maria's on.

The gentleman's club.

Music. A crucifix descends. MARIA MAUDLIN, in a Union Jack bikini, wrapped in the Union Jack, dances around a pole. PUNTERS – male, female, hermaphrodites, gay, straight, transvestites – sway and groan to the music as they ogle her, their hands down their trousers' fronts. OMO looks around at the different people gathered. He stares at MARIA.

MARIA: I hate the day shift. Too many prying eyes with empty wallets. My boss thought he'd hit the mother lode. Catch the giro junkies just after they cash their cheques. Too bad, Brixtonians aren't that desperate to hand over their money. Another of my boss's bright ideas was to convert this old church into a gentleman's club. Gentrification will bring in new money. Someone should have told him the rich have their clubs where they worship their lucre. The poor just keep on coming. I hate this place. But I can't stop dancing.

PUNTER 2: It's my first time here. Why is she called Union Jack?

PUNTER 3: She makes us ejaculate in unison.

The PUNTERS ejaculate in unison.

PUNTERS: Ah. *(They hum 'God Save the Queen'.)*

OMO: Maria Maudlin. Maria Maudlin!

MARIA: My g-string's empty. Fill it up or shut up.

OMO: Maria Maudlin. I have come.

MARIA: Glad to help, cheapskate.

OMO: Kiss my feet.

MARIA: Is that street for give us a blow-job?

OMO: Kiss my feet.

MARIA: Kiss my arse.

OMO: Kiss my feet.

MARIA: Fuck yourself.

OMO: Kiss my feet.

MARIA: Go to hell.

OMO: Maria Maudlin, know yourself. You are not a cunt.

MARIA MAUDLIN eyes him, furious.

I will return.

MARIA: The bouncers will be waiting. Fuckwit.

The PUNTERS ejaculate.

PUNTERS: *(Sigh.)* Ah…

MARIA: I'm on form.

OMO, by the Underground.

OMO: Maria Maudlin is the one. But she does not believe.

He watches people exiting and entering the station.

I see it now. A prophet must make good abroad before his people recognise him. I will gather my apostles from among the Gentiles. I will return to claim Maria and then Brixton.

Soundscape: The music from the gentleman's club morphs into the sound of the Underground. All that remains from the previous scene is the pole.

OMO in the tube. Rush hour clogged. PASSENGERS jammed up around the pole, some with their heads stuck in newspapers, magazines, novels, under another passenger's armpit. They avoid making eye contact with each other.

PASSENGERS: *(To the sound of the train.)* 'Grin and bear it. Grin and bear it. Moan and Groan. Grin and bear it. Grin and bear it…'

The train grinds to a halt.

DRIVER: *(Over the PA.)* This is your driver speaking. There is a signal failure at Victoria Station. We're being held here until further notice.

PASSENGERS groan collectively. They shake their newspapers and continue reading. They avoid making eye contact with each other.

OMO: So many people yet such loneliness. Today begins the union of souls. *(To a PASSENGER.)* Acknowledge me.

PASSENGERS move one step round the pole to avoid OMO.

OMO: *(To the next PASSENGER.)* Acknowledge me.

PASSENGERS move one step round the pole.

OMO: *(To the next PASSENGER.)* Acknowledge me.

PASSENGER: *(Scottish.)* And you are?

OMO: I am the one.

PASSENGER: Nice to meet you, the 'one'.

OMO: You are a Gentile?

PASSENGER: Glasgow.

OMO: You don't live in Brixton?

PASSENGER: I used to. I've just moved to Kilburn.

OMO: Nice area?

PASSENGER: It's all right. It's got enough Celts to make devolution feel like a good idea.

OMO: There is strength in the union.

The train moves.

PASSENGER: You're not a *Sassenach*. Why do you care about the Union?

OMO: Return with me to Brixton. Be part of the new foundation that is being laid.

PASSENGER: If you're talking about buying property I missed the boat. I cannae afford to live in Brixton.

OMO: Ask.

PASSENGER: Sorry?

OMO: Ask.

PASSENGER: I'm not religious.

OMO spreads out his arms.

Oh ask you.

OMO: Shrug off your unbelief and follow me.

The train moves.

PASSENGER: I beg your pardon?

OMO: *(Holds PASSENGER's face.)* Don't beg: take. Know yourself. Acknowledge me as your redeemer…

PASSENGER: *(Pushes OMO's hand off.)* Could you step away from me, please?

PASSENGER 2: That's the problem with jocks. They talk to anybody.

OMO: *(Advances, arms outstretched. In the voice of Rev. Williams.)* Touch the screen! Touch the screen and your wish will come true! Together we shall destroy the wilful peace and you shall toil uselessly no more…

PASSENGER presses the emergency alarm. The train shudders to a halt.

PASSENGERS: For fuck's sake!

Soundscape: The sound of the underground morphs into the sound of Brixton High Street.

A STATION ASSISTANT escorts OMO from Brixton station.

ASSISTANT: You understand what I told you? You're banned from the underground.

OMO: The concerns of the flesh prevail in the hearts of the fallen everywhere. *(Looks heavenwards.)* I was wrong. The work must start with the truth here in Brixton.

MARIA MAUDLIN passes by with shopping bags.

OMO: Maria Maudlin!

MARIA: Oh. It's you. Are you stalking me?

OMO: Maria Maudlin, there is work to be done.

MARIA: This lady's doing just fine as she is. Stop following me.

OMO: I cannot break the cycle without you, Mother of the End Times.

MARIA: Too bad I'm not the mother type.

OMO: Look into my eyes.

MARIA: They're beautiful, I know.

OMO: I see into your soul. It is full of beauty and light.

MARIA: I don't know who you think you are but…

OMO: You know who I am.

MARIA: Honestly I don't, OK? Now I'd love to stay and chat but I've got work to do.

OMO: The real work will begin. Soon we shall cross the river hand in hand and we shall shake off the wilful peace. Become, Maria. Become!

MARIA: You look like a nice guy. My advice, get a job and settle down. That's all there is to a happy life. No one's buying the new world you're peddling. *(Brings out a few coins.)* Here, buy yourself a meal. And don't come looking for me any more.

The town hall bell rings.

OMO: You *are* the Mother! Thank you, Alfie!

MARIA: Alfie the town crier? Alfie's dead. *(Exits.)*

Soundscape: Market noises.

DONA and OMO in Brixton Market.

DONA is talking to CITIZEN. OMO looks on but he is not paying attention. He holds a file and pen.

DONA: …That's where you're wrong. God doesn't want us to live in dignified penury. He wants us to have the best things in life.

CITIZEN: So there's no catch? No charges, like inheritance tax?

DONA: *(Laughs.)* The Father's gifts are unconditional. He does not give with one hand and take with the other.

CITIZEN: So what do I have to do to buy into this scheme?

DONA: You don't have to buy into any scheme. All you have to do is give your life to the Lord.

CITIZEN: Yeah but I still don't see how I'm going to pay off my mortgage. And with the Olympics coming/

DONA: All these worries mean nothing when you put your faith in the right place.

CITIZEN: *(Pauses, trying to make up his mind.)* You're from The Mission, right? You were in the news. You're a cult.

DONA: The media are the world's biggest junk mailers. Don't believe what you read in the press. Believe this: seventy per cent of our members are homeowners. Sixty per cent of us have our children in private schools. Forty percent of us are debt-free.

CITIZEN: Hm, sounds phenomenal.

DONA: Phenomenal it is, Brother. If I can just take your name… Brother Omo. *Brother Omo.*

OMO wakes up from his reverie. He hands DONA the file and pen.

DONA: *(Hands CITIZEN the file.)* Here you go.

CITIZEN writes down his name. Hands DONA back the file.

See you in church on Sunday.

CITIZEN exits.

DONA: Brother Omo. You're making me regret that I chose you to partner me.

OMO: Sorry, Sister Dona. I was remembering my time in the Prisoners for Christ Programme.

DONA: Yes. And?

OMO: Thinking about it has made me understand the Good News approach.

DONA: So what's the problem?

OMO: First you were luring the vulnerable.

DONA: Excuse me. I was not luring the vulnerable. They're the ones who need to hear the good news the most. You said you understood…

OMO: Now you're attracting the new money, those who are gentrifying Brixton.

DONA: Brother Omo.

OMO: You offer them a conscience-free life.

DONA: How do you think we raise money for the prisoners programme? If not for our high income members giving generously we would not have met and you would not have been saved.

OMO: Our Father willed that I should be saved through you.

DONA: Exactly. But we live in the world. Our Father knows that and he rewards us in the world. If you calculate Abraham's net worth in today's terms, Bill Gates couldn't touch him.

OMO: The rewards that the Father gives us are different.

DONA: To those who have even more shall be added.

OMO: Meaning the rich can make money guilt-free while the poor get poorer and must beg charity from the rich.

Enter two CITIZENS OF BRIXTON, those left behind, arguing over a parcel.

DONA: The poor will always be here with us. This is the only way we can help them.

OMO: By making gods of the rich.

DONA: He's not rich…!

The CITIZENS glare at them. DONA leads OMO to a corner.

Brother Omo, I know all the troubles you've been through. You're trying to find order in your life and that's fine. The Mission provides that for us. It's pointless you questioning everyone and everything. You'll only get confused. You must submit yourself to us to direct you. Jesus said we must be like children.

OMO: Children always ask questions.

DONA: And you know how annoying that is. (*Pause.*) You cannot drink from the pond if you muddy the water, Brother Omo. Life is simple. Don't overload it with unnecessary complications. You want to change the world? That's not our job.

OMO: Whose job is it?

DONA: God's. And until He creates a new kind of human being that change you're hankering after is a pipe dream. *(Pause.)* Go home, have a lie down. I'll come by later and we'll pray together, all right? *(Squeezes his arm.)* Go. *(Sees GREG, walking by with camcorder.)* Brother, have you heard the good news?

GREG ignores her and passes by. She goes after him but backtracks when he stands by the CITIZENS. He focuses his camera on them. He gets too close to the CITIZENS and gets entangled with them. He shields his camera from damage. He gets shoved to one side as the CITIZENS become more aggressive with each other.

The homeless woman enters. She sees DONA and backtracks. DONA sees her.

DONA: Sister! Sister! You promised me you'd come to service… *(Exits after WOMAN.)*

OMO: *(Restless.)* Change. Transform the world. Unfold the folded lie. Surely the time has come. *(Looks heavenwards.)* Show me the sign. *(He exits.)*

GREG re-focuses his camera as the CITIZENS OF BRIXTON fight over the parcel.

The parcel comes apart, releasing white powder into the air. The CITIZENS inhale deeply. They dance with each other, singing 'Make love, not War'.

Police siren. A gunshot. GREG dives to the ground. Everyone else freezes.

GREG: I've called it the Brixton Challenge. How to inscribe Brixton without the usual signposts of drugs, violence and the shining white knight called gentrification. It is hard work trying to see the world except through the grand narrative bestowed on us, them, from on high. The longest way up the mountain is by taking the route less travelled. And from where I'm standing, my friends in high places seem even further away. *(Stands up.)* Fuck it. I'm calibrating my lens to normal focus. Let some other mug search for the 'real' Brixton. What would I gain from humanising these beasts of England? They're wild life, primetime fodder. And I shall serve them to you in a tale of the expected. It's what you want, isn't it? *(GREG films the CITIZENS.)* Come on you animals, fight! *(Disappointed, he puts down his camera.)*

Police siren starts again.

The CITIZENS OF BRIXTON unfreeze. Quickly, they set up the gentleman's club and become the PUNTERS. They jerk off to MARIA dancing around the pole.

PUNTERS: *(Sing.)* 'Maria Maudlin, Maria Maudlin, Maria Maudlin…'

GREG: 'Maria Maudlin'. Is that your real name?

MARIA: Who wants to know?

GREG: My name's Greg. I'm doing a feature on Brixton. I'll make you the centrepiece. What do you say? Have Middle Englanders wet themselves over you.

MARIA: Thanks but no thanks.

GREG: I can make you the angel of Brixton.

MARIA: You missed me by a lifetime. This angel's face is way too dirty now.

GREG: Get a face wipe and join the queue. How did you become a pole dancer?

MARIA: Don't ask me stupid questions.

GREG: Stupid questions get the truth.

MARIA: The truth or the answers you want.

GREG: Same thing.

MARIA: In your book. The way you look at me through that camera. The contempt sandblasted onto your face. Is that your SW4 sneer?

GREG: I look this way all the time.

MARIA: You're a shit stirrer. You're a voyeur.

GREG: One or the other. A little of both. Hey, I'm a journalist. I like you, Maria Maudlin. You make good copy.

MARIA: That's made my day. Now take your box of tricks and go play in someone else's garden.

GREG: You're turning down an opportunity to change your life.

MARIA ignores him. GREG focuses his camcorder on MARIA. The PUNTERS stand up.

GREG: *(Films them.)* Scowl for the camera, boys. Show me that urban grittiness.

PUNTERS adopt gangsta poses.

That's it. You. Move one step to the left. You're blocking Maria.

The PUNTERS smear GREG and his camera lens with their used tissues.

GREG: Ah!

PUNTERS laugh and return to their seats.

You fucking wankers! *(Brings out a hankerchief. Cleans himself and the camera.)*

GREG cursing retreats, bumping into OMO.

Don't touch me!

GREG exits.

MARIA: *(Sees OMO.)* Oh for God's sake!

OMO: Maria Maudlin I have come.

MARIA: Haven't you got your work to do? Shake off the wilful willy.

OMO: Maria Maudlin did you attend Oxford?

MARIA: Is today Stupid Questions Day? I'm a pole-dancing prostitute. What do you think?

OMO: You are the foundation of the wilful peace.

PUNTERS: Matriculate, graduate, ejaculate. Ah!

OMO: *(Points to PUNTERS.)* You lock them in the cycle. You prevent them from unfolding the folded lie.

MARIA: And how do my origami skills stop you from getting a job?

OMO: The scales will fall from your eyes. You will be the angel. And then the work begins.

MARIA: That's twice in one day I've been called an angel. Hate to spoil your fantasy but you were wrong. This angel is a cunt.

OMO: Every harlot was a virgin once.

MARIA: No one can live with their fantasy. Reality gets in the way.

OMO: *(Joins her. Looks her straight in the eye.)* Maria Maudlin, you are my reality.

MARIA: I can't stop dancing.

OMO: Then I shall dance with you.

They dance together. OMO traps MARIA with his eyes. They slide to the floor, wrapped in the Union Jack. The PUNTERS whoop and catcall.

Windrush Square, in front of Brixton Library. CITIZEN 2 enters, singing.

CITIZEN 2: I'm gonna get paid

I'm gonna get paid

I'm gonna get paid

And after get laid

CITIZEN 1 enters. He wears African beads around his neck. CITIZEN 2 looks at him with disbelief.

CITIZEN 1: How you doing, my man?

CITIZEN 2: See why I don't believe in God? You've joined another cult, haven't you?

CITIZEN 1: Light the incense, bro'. Afrocentrism's the true path.

CITIZEN 2: For how long this time?

CITIZEN 1: This is it. My search is over.

CITIZEN 2: So what, you gonna call yourself some name I can't pronounce?

CITIZEN 1: You'd better start learning, African. From now on I'm Oladipupo Olugbolahan Titilola Olatunde.

CITIZEN 2: What's wrong with Cuthbert?

CITIZEN 1: That was my slave name, a noncey one too.

CITIZEN 2: You been listening to 'acknowledge me' guy again. Why is he different from all the other nutters who've conned you?

CITIZEN 1: He's from Bahia. They mix Christianity with Orisha.

CITIZEN 2: He ain't from Bahia, blood, trust me.

CITIZEN 1: But what if, just for the sake of argument that Omo's the real deal. If he could grant you one wish, what would you ask for?

CITIZEN 2: You know I don't believe in that shit.

CITIZEN 1: Humour me.

CITIZEN 2: Let's see – one wish… I'd wish for world peace.

CITIZEN 1: What are you, Miss World?

CITIZEN 2: OK, I'd wish for land reform. No one can own land, not even forty acres. You can be the Ponce of Poncebury or the Bum of Bumsville.

CITIZEN 1: Hell will freeze over. England don't belong to the peasants.

CITIZEN 2: What would you wish for?

CITIZEN 1: I'd wish to be white.

CITIZEN 2: For real?

CITIZEN 1: Yup.

CITIZEN 2: You serious?

CITIZEN 1: With the bluest eyes.

CITIZEN 2: Man, you shook off your Afrocentrism quick time.

CITIZEN 1: Black people ain't even kings in Africa. All those queens got their head-wraps on too tight, they are gonna be in for a shock when they get to the pearly gates.

CITIZEN 2: *(Eggs CITIZEN 1.)* You saying God's racist?

CITIZEN 1: None of the disciples was called Amantutanerfertiti.

CITIZEN 2: Oh come on!

CITIZEN 1: Don't matter how many times you attend service, we're pre-fabbed to keep hellfire burning.

CITIZEN 2 laughs.

CITIZEN 1: Coal fire for hell, bruv. By the oven there's this giant shovelling us in. That's all we're good for in the white man's faith. We can't even get into hell. You can sing so you might have a chance.

CITIZEN 2: I'm telling the guys you want to be white.

CITIZEN 1: I knew you'd fall for it!

CITIZEN 2: Yes 'cos you're not joking.

CITIZEN 1: I was winding you up, brethren. I'm black and I'm proud.

CITIZEN 2: You'd better be.

CITIZEN 1: For real. But seriously. Equal opportunities hasn't reached the church and I ain't sure it's reached the Great Upstairs. On earth as it is in heaven. There ain't no black messiah in my bible. Better we go with the black man's god. Edumare ain't gonna use me for coal.

They continue talking.

SARAH enters with shopping. Her shopping bag falls from her lap. She struggles to pick up the fallen items. OMO enters. He helps her.

SARAH: Thanks. Dona let you off her leash for today?

OMO: I am not a prisoner, Sarah Green.

SARAH: You could be doing something more useful than standing on Coldharbour Lane getting on everyone's nerves.

OMO: Do you know that you are good for so much more, Sarah Green?

SARAH: Oh I've been good all right. Good for lots more than you could ever imagine. Don't you know who I am?

OMO: Do you know who I am?

SARAH: What are you doing with Dona and her people?

OMO: What were you looking for with them?

SARAH: You really must have Nigerian roots. You answer a question with a question. *(Goes off.)* I've got to see my therapist.

OMO: If you only believe.

SARAH: *(Stops.)* I was chockablock with belief. Look at me now.

OMO: You have tried and you have failed on your own.

SARAH: Me, a failure? You really don't remember me. The 'English Rose'? You watched me on TV running the hundred metres for Great Britain, winning Olympic gold, draped in the Union Jack. You called me 'Our Sarah'. *Our Sarah*. I thought: this is only the beginning. I'm going onto glory representing my country. I put Brixton on the map. I am the English Rose, I can never wilt. Then I woke up one morning and my legs were gone. And I cried. I cried so hard my pupils turned red. I asked every god known to man, why me? The driver said he didn't see me. Yet he testified that I didn't look before I stepped onto the road…

OMO: You can be the flag bearer of this nation again. You can help raise the people so that their day of glory will not pass them.

SARAH: Tell Dona I'm never coming back. I'm a person. I'm not a marketing tool for your church.

OMO: I am not talking on Dona's behalf.

SARAH: First that prostitute uses my image to entertain those dogs, then you lot. This is how you treat a sister when she's down? *(Goes off.)*

OMO: Sarah! *(Goes after her.)*

CITIZEN 1: Brother Omo! Say the word.

OMO: *(Stops.)* You would like to hear the word?

CITIZEN 2: We ain't going nowhere.

OMO: Acknowledge me.

CITIZEN 2: Sure, we acknowledge you.

CITIZEN 1: Yep, you're you.

OMO: The stone of Brihtsige… Brixton to you… Anonymous masses, incredible mavericks, indistinguishable, yet each one of you unique. Every step draws us closer to the crossing of the river to overthrow the wilful peace. I am the one you prayed would come and revoke your life sentence of second-class citizenship, the one who will smash the cycle of pain. You must transform yourselves, now when it is time for the meek to inherit the nation. Come out of your Otherness. Like a butterfly breaking out of its chrysalis, reveal your true selves. Revel in your reflection. The middle passage, the criss-cross of Atlantic journeys that brought us to these shores bursting with meanings yet to be explained. Let the nightmare become the dream. *(Brings out two white handkerchiefs from his pockets.)* The touch of a finger and monuments crumble. And yet we have let the wilful peace reign. Through Détente, compromise, complacency. Here is the front line. Cross it and be transformed into a new being with new passions screaming for breath. Release yourselves of your double consciousness. Come and be renewed in the oneness of being. Come and be born anew.

Drumbeat. OMO performs the Dance of the Washing. He waves the handkerchiefs.

Mirror me and with elation unbridled, fondle your most lurid memories. Then let go! Smash the cycle of pain. Now with fear discarded cross over! *(Dances.)* Go forth, go forth!

The CITIZENS sway uncomfortably, trying to copy OMO. It is a joke to them. They feel something in their pockets. To their surprise they bring out white handkerchiefs. The shock soon wears off. They are Brixtonians. Nothing surprises them. They do a mock Morris dance and hit each other with the handkerchiefs.

OMO: Brothers, this is serious.

CITIZEN 1: You said go forth. You're surrendering. Can we cut out the stupid dance?

CITIZEN 2: Bruv. Who are you again?

DONA enters. She is dismayed by what she sees.

OMO: I am the one you prayed would come. I am here and I will never leave you. I will never die. Lastborn's get it easy.

CITIZEN 1: Speak for yourself. I'm a lastborn and all I got was this lousy tee-shirt.

CITIZEN 1 and CITIZEN 2 laugh and high-five each other.

CITIZEN 2: Stop speaking in parables, man. What exactly do you want us to do?

CITIZEN 1: Who are you?

CITIZEN 2: Who are you?

BOTH: *(A la football chant.)* 'Who-are-yer, who-are yer, who-are-yer'…

OMO: *(Stretches out his arms.)* I am the son of/

DONA: Brother Omo! *(To the CITIZENS.)* He's not well, please excuse him. There's nothing more to see. Go!

CITIZENS drift away.

What do you think you're doing?

OMO: They acknowledged me.

DONA: They acknowledged nothing. You are embarrassing The Mission. You cannot go round inferring that you're the messiah.

OMO: They acknowledged me.

DONA: We'll go see Dr Gupta. He'll put you back on your medication. Until then, I don't want you out preaching. You will stay in the bed-sit until I see that you are suitably recovered.

OMO: Anger has a certain beauty, just before it tips over into rage. You're borderline.

DONA: *(Struggles to control herself.)* I am not angry, Brother Omo. I am disappointed in you.

OMO: Don't be. I haven't started the work/

DONA: Don't say another word. I'll fix an appointment with the clinic for tomorrow. I have to run an errand.

OMO: When will you stop running for The Mission and attend to your soul?

DONA: When I become a minister I will help raise the souls of thousands. I'll be able to heal you completely of your sickness. But right now, do not let The Mission hear about this.

OMO: For my sake or for yours, Dona?

Citizens of Brixton set up OMO's bed-sit. MARIA lies on the bed-sit.

DONA: I have asked you to go home.

OMO: Asked or ordered?

DONA: Don't bite the hand that raised you out of bondage.

They stare at each other. DONA exits. OMO takes off his top.

The following day.

The bed-sit. MARIA is in bed sleeping. OMO is looking out through the window.

MARIA stirs.

MARIA: What time is it?

OMO: I didn't mean to wake you. Sorry.

MARIA: What time's Dona coming?

OMO: The people.

MARIA: Oh God.

OMO: They cry for a leader yet they refuse to answer my call.

MARIA: They use you to pass the time with, the latest Jesus freak. And the white hanky. What was that all about?

OMO: It means eternal victory through love and peace.

MARIA: It means different if you keep acting weird.

OMO stretches out his arms and yawns.

Yeah, you see – that Christ complex: I'm not feeling it.

OMO: *(Goes to her.)* Become the sign, Maria. Reveal the divine revelation to me. Let me become who I am.

MARIA: I'll tell you who I am. I'm a woman who's been down on her luck as many times as I've gone down on men. I can't remember how many times I've checked into bad luck rehab. I've been Maria Maudlin for so long don't ask me if I ever had another name. But I'm alive. I'm right here. That's all that counts. I can bear witness that my luck can change. I've snagged my 'messiah'.

They kiss.

When I looked into your eyes I knew. You looked right into my soul. You wanted *me*.

OMO: In you I find purity. I find the beating heart that will rock the foundations of the establishment.

MARIA: It's fun trying to be special but it's a party you should leave early. You soon get bored. You start to wish to be like every other Joe. Before you know it time has passed and you realise the things you have are not the things you really wanted. You start to think if I get another chance, I'd rewrite that script.

OMO: This is your story. To help me fulfil my mission.

MARIA: It's a mission that you've been crap at so far. *(Wraps her arms round him.)* The world's a turbulent place if you don't have an anchor. You'll be mine and I'll be yours.

The alarm clock goes off.

Ah, I don't feel like going into work.

OMO: Don't go then. Stay with me.

MARIA: The day you get a job is the last day I'll be Maria Maudlin. Oh. *(Takes a contraceptive pill from her handbag.)* Force of habit.

OMO: You do not need that, Maria.

MARIA: A girl's got to keep one leg in the real world.

OMO: *(Takes her hand with the pill. Looks straight into her eyes.)* You do not need that. *(Drops the pill and crushes it underfoot.)* This morning after brings a new world for us.

The town hall clock bell rings.

OMO: Alfie!

MARIA: Don't! When I say I want you to be you I mean who you are, not this mirage. I'm as close as I can be to you and still you're not letting me in.

OMO: I am, Maria. You refuse to see me as I am.

MARIA: There's more to you than this. Fine, you don't want to tell me. *(Turns away.)* I have time for a coffee before Miss Watchtower gets here. *(Dresses.)* Make me a mug.

OMO: *(Holds MARIA.)* Don't fear about the new course your life will take.

MARIA: I can't measure up to whatever ideal you've got in your head.

OMO: Say yes you believe me. Then say yes you love me. That's all I ask.

DONA enters.

DONA: Brother Omo, sorry about yesterday. I… *(Sees MARIA.)* You have nothing to say for yourself? The Mission is

washing its hands of you. You have a week's to vacate
the flat. *(Makes to exit. Turns round.)* How does it feel,
fornicating with a 'messiah'? How's it like playing a part in
his sick pantomime…

MARIA: Watch your mouth, choir girl.

DONA: Who was inside you – the Prime Minister? Jesus? Or
the last punter who swore he was going to be with you
for the rest of your life? Just like him, he'll be gone by
tomorrow and you'll be back to what you've always been –
a lonely fading prostitute.

MARIA: How dare you?

DONA: He's not from Brixton. He won't tell anyone where
he's from. He's a litany of impersonations, a con man
who's finally conned himself. A leech like every other
vomit-eating stray dog you've bedded. He's not your ticket
to redemption, Maria.

MARIA: Who are you?

OMO: Maria…

MARIA: My God. You're just another punter.

OMO: Maria…

*OMO approaches MARIA. MARIA holds her hand out. She opens her
handbag, takes out a pill and swallows it. She exits.*

DONA: You're out of here by week end.

*OMO heads after MARIA. DONA blocks his way. She holds out her
hand. OMO hands her the crucifix. He grabs the Caftan and exits.*

DONA beckons to the CITIZENS. They enter and clear the set.

The Street.

*SARAH wheels by. GREG crosses by with his camera. He focuses on
SARAH.*

SARAH: Get that camera out of my face.

GREG: I know you. You're Sarah Green.

SARAH: You deaf?

GREG: *(Lowers the camera.)* Disability is the new black. You
could win the sympathy vote on 'I'm a Celebrity'. Make
some money out of your tragedy.

SARAH glares at him.

Sorry to disturb you, 'English Rose'. *(Exits.)*

MARIA MAUDLIN enters, distraught. SARAH sees her.

SARAH: Hey! Maudlin!

MARIA passes SARAH by, ignoring her.

Don't ignore me!

MARAI: *(Turns round.)* What is it now?

SARAH: Stop desecrating my image!

MARIA: You don't own the flag.

SARAH: You had to copy me. You turned my crowning moment into a cheap freak show.

MARIA: If you'd been sent up on 'Little Britain' you'd be whooping it up, blackface and all.

SARAH: How many more punters can that calcified cunt of yours take?

MARIA: I don't have time for this. My head is in a weird place.

SARAH: It's not in some man's groin.

MARIA: I walked into that one.

SARAH: You can walk. I pass by you in this wheelchair everyday yet you continue mocking me in that house of filth.

MARIA: You know I genuinely felt for you. A Brixton girl makes good and then this happens to you. But life doesn't stop because you meet with tragedy, not even for you, English Rose.

SARAH: Don't call me that you pus pit.

MARIA: That driver who knocked you down, he's going to hell. He let you live.

SARAH rams MARIA with her wheelchair. MARIA slaps her. They glare at each other. Citizens gather to watch. OMO enters.

CITIZEN 1: Hey, it's the 'Christ' of Coldharbour Lane.

CITIZEN 2: You gonna perform a miracle or what?

OMO: Maria! Maria…

MARIA: Don't touch me.

OMO: I love you.

MARIA: I hate you.

OMO: Maria…

MARIA: Get a life! Get a life!

OMO: Maria!

A bell rings.

It is time. Surely it is time. *(To the crowd, desperately.)* You have asked for a miracle, a wonder to take for a sign.

CITIZEN 3: Get on with it! The bookies close in an hour.

GREG enters. He watches the proceedings.

OMO, riddled with uncertainty, grabs SARAH's wheelchair. He pins her shoulders.

SARAH: Let go of me! Let go!

OMO: Drink with me of the communion of blood that has been denied you since the crossing of the middle passage. *(Brings out his handkerchiefs.)*

CITIZEN 1 and CITIZEN 2 find the handkerchiefs have miraculously reappeared in their pockets.

CITIZEN 1: Shit, not the handkerchiefs again.

SARAH: Keep your hands off me!

CITIZEN 2: Not the dance. Please not the dance.

OMO sways.

Ah fuck.

OMO: Only the truth can demolish the old foundation. Only then will you become manumitted in spirit and in body. Only then can we become a union of souls. Wave the handkerchief of freedom. Wave!

SARAH: Get off me you madman! Help! Help!

Citizens wave their handkerchiefs, unserious. SARAH stops struggling, entranced. Citizens pay attention. OMO hands SARAH each end of his handkerchiefs.

OMO: We are waves that will flood the institutions whose buildings grope the sky. We will drown the folded lie. The time has come for the leap across the river! For the river to flow with blood.

CITIZEN 2: Shit! He's Enoch Powell returned as a black man. There is a God after all.

CITIZEN 1: *(Falls to his knees.)* God! Make me white! Make me white!

CITIZEN 2 glares at him. CITIZEN 1 stands up sheepishly.

OMO: Now is the time, Father. Do not forsake me in my appointed hour. To you, Sarah Green I say: get up and walk!

OMO pulls on the handkerchiefs. Slowly, during his speech, SARAH rises.

Break free of the cycle. Throw away your crutches. Claim your birthright of freedom. Believe! Believe! Believe…!

The stage is covered in white light. CITIZENS shield their eyes. The light fades.

SARAH is standing. She takes a tentative step, then another, and another. Uproar.

Citizens wave their handkerchiefs. MARIA looks on in shock. SARAH is dumbfounded. She jumps for joy. OMO is surprised he has performed the miracle. SARAH runs round the stage and exits. All the while GREG looks stunned. He recovers his wits and records with his camera.

OMO: *(Does the Dance of the Washing, enraptured.)* Yes, Father! Yes, Father! Yes, yes, yes!

The town hall bell rings crazily. Citizens dance with OMO. They exit, leaving MARIA MAUDLIN stunned. She walks off. GREG exits after them, recording.

SARAH runs around the stage. She comes to centrestage and jogs on the spot.

SARAH: I can't stop running. I've gone up Coldharbour Lane and up Brixton Hill. I feel as invincible as the day I took that gold medal. The English Rose is back and she smells twice as nice. *(She runs off.)*

DONA, outside Brixton Station, preaching.

CITIZENS rush past her.

DONA: Brother, hear the good news! … Sister, receive the word! Where is everyone rushing to?

GREG dashes in with a camcorder. He approaches DONA.

GREG: *(Sees DONA.)* Where is he?

DONA: Who?

GREG: Your friend, brother, co-conspirator. I saw you together. Omo or whatever his name is.

DONA: Omo is no longer with The Mission.

GREG: Come now. I know what you and your cult are up to.

DONA: I've had enough of you people smearing us.

GREG: I'll find out how you tricked the Brixtonites. I'll find out and I'll expose all of you for the money grabbing charlatans you are.

DONA slaps GREG.

Ow! If you think I'm just going to turn the other cheek/

DONA slaps him on the other cheek. GREG legs it. DONA rages after him.

From the other side of the stage, OMO enters, followed by the Citizens of Brixton. He stands centrestage. They surround him. His caftan is dirty. GREG dashes in with DONA hot on his tail. They stop to take in the scene. GREG records the event on his camcorder.

CITIZEN 1: Omo, please, it's my little boy's schooling. He's not in the right catchment area. I need to buy a house in Dulwich.

OMO: *(Tries to make himself heard.)* Kingdom will rise against kingdom!

CITIZEN 2: The supermarkets are squeezing my margins. I've got a wife and kids to support. I just need to break even and to have spare.

OMO: Son will rise against father!

CITIZEN 3: My hip operation's been postponed again. You don't have a waiting list for your miracles, do you?

OMO: Daughter will rise against mother!

CITIZEN 4: I promised the council I'd keep the noise down but they still want to kick me out of my flat.

CITIZEN 5: A hundred thousand pounds and I'll stop dealing.

CITIZEN 6: If you give me the lottery numbers for Saturday, I'll give ten per cent to your church.

OMO: I have no church.

CITIZEN 6: Make it ten and a half per cent.

OMO: This is not what I'm about.

CITIZEN 5: You're about transforming lives. That's what we want, innit people?

ALL: Yeah!

GREG gets closer in expectation.

OMO: You should have seen the light. We're supposed to march across the river. We're supposed to wipe clean the slate.

CITIZEN 4: Wipe clean the slate? You mean like topple the state?

OMO: My people have heard me!

CITIZEN 3: Hold on cowboy. We didn't plan on a revolution.

CITIZEN 6: That is suicide. Why d'you want to put your life in danger?

CITIZEN 3: You're still black, you know. You ain't getting crucified for nobody. Just be the god of small things.

CITIZEN 6: This is our time.

CITIZEN 4: This is our turn!

ALL: Yeah!

OMO: If you reject my message you deny my Father who has sent me.

CITIZEN 4: Yeah, well, never as good as the first time, innit?

CITIZEN 3: You mad?

CITIZEN 4: I'm just saying, man.

OMO: Now when I offer you the chance to become the acknowledged legislators of your destinies, to shape the world in your own image, you withdraw to the lines of détente? For how long will you be the consumers of your woes? For how long do you choose to remain beasts of England?

CITIZEN 4: Hey! We're not asking for too much.

CITIZEN 5: Ask your man Jesus if he really wanted to have his arse nailed to a cross.

CITIZEN 6: That's right! You ain't the final curtain. I never heard you warning about the End Times.

CITIZEN 5: Not even a parable.

CITIZEN 6: A good life in this world, that's all we want. That's what I'd call a revolution.

ALL: Yeah!

CITIZEN 3: And rims! I want rims!

OMO looks at the citizens. He shakes his head as he makes to depart.

OMO: I cannot pour new wine into old wineskins.

CITIZEN 3: Omo where are you going? Omo!

CITIZEN 4: Truly it is written in The Mail, 'can anything good come out of Brixton?'

The citizens surround him, blocking his way, begging him not to leave.

DONA: Don't beg him! He's a fake! How did you get these people to believe in your heresy?

CITIZEN 5: It isn't hearsay. I saw it with my own eyes.

DONA: Renounce yourself now!

GREG goes closer to her. She shoves him away.

Where is she? Where is Maria Maudlin?

CITIZENS: *(Dreamily.)* Ah…

A patch forms on one of the citizens' trousers. He has wet himself.

DONA: You and that harlot are in collusion. You've duped these poor fools. You will rot in hell right next to her.

CITIZEN 3: Sister. It was not Maria Maudlin.

CITIZEN 4: Yeah, it was the wheelchair woman.

DONA: Sarah Green?

CITIZEN 3: Yeah. The English Rose. She's walking.

DONA: That's a lie.

CITIZEN 4: You'd have seen her for yourself only she got the Forest Gump. She just ran and ran.

OMO: Dona. You can help me prepare them for the new world we shall bring into being.

DONA: He's insane. He's been in the madhouse. He's suffering another episode. It's true. Ask him.

CITIZENS fall silent. They look at OMO. OMO, shaken, looks at DONA and at the CITIZENS. He walks away.

DONA: I knew you wouldn't fall for his falsehood. You're Brixtonians. You've seen and heard it all/

CITIZENS: *(As they run after OMO.)* Omo, please help me, help me! *(They exit after OMO.)*

DONA turns to GREG. GREG cowers, thinking she's going to slap him.

DONA: Help me stop this madness. We can expose him.

GREG: So you really aren't part of his scheme.

DONA: I can't let The Mission find out about this.

GREG: You're on your own, 'sister'. *(Brings out his mobile phone.)* Greg here. Hold on. *(To DONA.)* Don't you have a saviour to crucify?

DONA, exasperated, exits.

GREG: *(On the phone. During the conversation he changes into JASON. He puts on black gloves and dark glasses.)* Jason, it's Greg. *Greg* from… Yes, that Greg. I've got something for you. Yes he's a threat to national security. No he's not got a beard. No he doesn't have a rucksack. This is bigger than that. I'm talking Chartists and Levellers. Yes, the R-word. I want guarantees first. Yes, take your bloody time…

GREG is now JASON.

JASON: *(Covers the phone.)* I remember Greg. Ambitious bastard. Revolution in Brixton? That recessive Norman gene pops up in strange places. It's my job to stop the rabble from storming the Palace – by any means necessary. *(To GREG.)* Greg? Yes. You will get a call from the Secretary after we nullify this threat. *(Hangs up. Dials another number.)* Secretary. It's Jason. Yes sir… First thing I suggest is that we dismantle the town hall bell… *(Covers the phone. To the audience, menacingly.)* For my ears only.

The gentleman's club.

MARIA, dazed. Light up on SARAH running on the spot, draped in the Union Jack, her gold medal around her neck, in a different time and place. MARIA crumbles to the floor weeping. She falls asleep.

SARAH stops running. She crosses into MARIA's space and covers her with the Union Jack.

Brixton High Street.

Citizens running in different directions calling out OMO's name. They run off in different directions, leaving behind CITIZENS 1 and 2.

CITIZEN 1: *(Huffs.)* You sure he's not in the Barrier Block?

CITIZEN 2: *(Testily.)* We're both coming from there, aren't we?

CITIZEN 1: Man, I got to catch my breath. *(Sits down.)*

CITIZEN 2: He'll be out of miracles by the time we find him.

CITIZEN 1: I'm not Sarah Green. I can't keep running all over Brixton. He's the real deal, man. He's here to stay.

CITIZEN 2: So was Windows 95.

CITIZEN 1: Give me a few minutes.

CITIZEN 2: *(Sits down.)* Where's your beads?

CITIZEN 1: *(Looks down at his chest.)* Ha! They must have come off when we was running after Omo.

CITIZEN 2: He might be in the Satay Bar. *(Stands up.)* Come on. It's only up the road. *(Holds out his hand. Pulls up CITIZEN 1.)*

CITIZEN 1: So now you've seen what he can do, what are you going to ask him for? And please don't say world peace.

CITIZEN 2: *(Pause.)* I don't know.

Windrush Square. Night.

ROBBIE is sleeping on a bench, his hand down his trousers enjoying a dream.

OMO enters, with a stick. He takes off his caftan and proceeds to flagellate himself.

ROBBIE: *(In his sleep.)* Yes Baby, I've been a naughty boy… *(Stirs. Sees OMO.)* Hey! *(Takes the stick off OMO. Inspects OMO's back.)* Reasonable chastisement, that's what the law states, yeah.

OMO: What's the time?

ROBBIE: I don't know. The town hall clock stopped working since that stunt you pulled with Sarah. That was some serious shit.

OMO: I made a mistake. I thought Maria was the sign.

ROBBIE: Don't beat yourself up about it.

OMO: I am not worthy.

ROBBIE: Come on. You've got the whole of Brixton on your side. People don't care that you're loopy.

OMO: They are in so deep. They do not recognise their collaboration in their own oppression.

ROBBIE: Can you blame them? Omo, ours is a country with a history of failed revolutions, of reforms pawned off as radical change. Co-optation has been the order from day one. The people realised that ages ago. Since then they've opted for what they can get. They're like the unions. They've become an interest group holding out for a bigger cut of the pie.

OMO: Maria told me she was not ready. I should have waited. The people, they forced me to perform a wonder.

ROBBIE: OK so you fucked up. Take it on the chin and move on.

OMO: And now the bell has stopped ringing.

ROBBIE: Take the time off, man. *(Makes OMO sit down.)* That Mission girl said nasty stuff about you. Is it true?

OMO: You don't go telling people you were abandoned in a dustbin.

OMO waits for ROBBIE to respond. ROBBIE is silent.

Not many people know how to respond to that. I got adopted by a Nigerian couple. They'd lost three kids, one after the other. They believed it was the same child being reincarnated, crossing between the spirit world and here. And then they stopped having kids. They went to this African church and the pastor told them I was their child returned through another woman. They gave me the bangles and this pendant (*Reveals the pendant.*) to prevent me from returning to the spirit world. (*Shows his tattoo.*) And if I did die they gave me this tattoo so they'd know it was me back again. After I survived a few life-threatening scrapes my father said I could never die so long as I wore my protection. Since then I've seen myself as special.

Everything I did pointed towards doing something great in my life. I took off my shirt during PE, the teacher saw the scar. She called social services and I got taken off them. Until I became a man I was being pushed from one home to the other. The only place I felt I belonged to was here. Here where I was left to die.

ROBBIE: So what's all that about you impersonating people?

OMO: My parents told me I could be anything. I took it literally when I got taken away from them. Then I thought it could be the spirits manifesting in me in different voices.

ROBBIE: But you're not a reincarnation.

OMO: Once in a while I feel something trying to pull me out of this world. It hasn't happened for a while. I love this world. I love Maria.

ROBBIE: Tell her the truth. I'm sure she'll believe you.

OMO: And what do I tell the people of Brixton?

ROBBIE: Tell them you are the Christ of the End Times. And that the fire and brimstone arrives tomorrow. They'll forget about their mortgages and their new cars.

OMO: Fire and brimstone. That is so old school.

ROBBIE: It works.

OMO: If I convince the Brixtonians, will you stand beside me?

ROBBIE: Why not? Giro doesn't go that far in this world anyway. So long as you don't take your rock off.

OMO: When the bell rings again, you will know it is time.

ROBBIE: Obviously you know nothing about council maintenance. Clear off. Now! Your peeps are waiting and man needs to dream.

OMO leaves.

ROBBIE: Omo!

OMO turns round.

You got a pound?

They smile.

Citizens of Brixton rush round looking for OMO. They set up the gentleman's club and continue to look for OMO. They exit. SARAH runs in and jogs on the spot, centrestage.

SARAH: I haven't heard the bell ring yet. Where's Omo to give me the word? In the beginning was the Word, right? The people are still scratching around, looking for their own little patch of Albion. Soon the scales will fall from their eyes. They will see the New Jerusalem on the horizon and raise a mighty shout! For Brixton! For England! For Britain!

SARAH runs out.

The gentleman's club.

MARIA wakes up. JASON enters, unnoticed by MARIA. He is in the right place. He brings out his PDA and matches a photo to MARIA.

MARIA: Who are you?

JASON: Where can I find Omo?

MARIA: What do you want with him?

JASON: Where is he?

MARIA: I don't know.

JASON: *(Brings out a knife.)* Where is Omo?

MARIA: I don't know! I don't know!

JASON stabs her to death. He snatches the flag off her to prevent her blood from soaking it. He folds it neatly, puts it away and exits.

By the station.

DONA, with a bell.

DONA: The elders have withheld my promotion subject to an inquiry. I got this bell. I thought, if I'd ring it I'd put the genie back into his bottle. This would turn out to be a bad dream. I'm too afraid to ring it. Tell me, what am I supposed to do in a situation like this? Show me a sign. Please.

SARAH runs by.

DONA: Sarah?

SARAH stops. DONA cannot believe her eyes.

DONA: *(Stammers.)* You know you can never compete again. They'll test you for every drug under the sun. You will test positive for every one of them.

SARAH: Don't be afraid, Dona.

DONA: I'm not afraid.

SARAH: *(Holds DONA's face.)* It's all right. Everything will be all right. Believe. That's all you have to do. The people will understand. They will come out for the crossing of the river. *(Takes DONA's bell and runs off.)* They will come out and we will shake the city to its foundation! Say the word! Say the word!

DONA: *(Shakes violently, vomits. Lets out a scream.)* I believe! I believe! I believe! *(Falls to the ground, shaking.)*

JASON runs in.

JASON: That was Sarah Green? *(Shakes DONA.)* Hey!

DONA: I believe! I believe!

JASON shoves her aside. He makes to run after SARAH. He turns round. He looks into his PDA and recognises DONA.

JASON: Dona.

DONA: I believe.

JASON: Where is Omo?

DONA: I believe.

JASON: *(Reaches for his knife.)* Where is Omo?

SARAH runs across ringing the bell.

SARAH: Come out for the crossing of the river! Shake off the wilful peace! *(Stands on one side of the stage.)* The word is coming!

SARAH exits. JASON runs after her.

DONA: *(Stops shaking, faces the audience.)* Believe.

The gentleman's club, on one half of the stage. OMO cradles MARIA's lifeless body.

Brixton High Street on the other half of the stage.

OMO: Maria… Maria! *(Takes off his rock pendant and the ankle bracelet. He puts them on MARIA. He puts two handkerchiefs over her.)*

Music.

Blessed mother, bridge between worlds, you cause joy to reign in the kingdoms. The seed on earth is planted. There will be no more painful returns. Your journey is not at an end. Stand up and dance. Ignite the rhythm to drive your passion for life. Get up and dance a new dance! Dance for joy. Dance for life. Dance for the future.

Slowly, MARIA rises. She picks up the handkerchiefs and dances the Dance of The Washing. OMO kisses her feet. The baton has been passed.

SARAH runs by. JASON runs after her with a hammer. He stops to catch his breath.

SARAH runs past him. He trips her. He drags her offstage.

OMO: You have wept your last tears – Mother.

The sound of a heartbeat. MARIA touches her stomach. She stands up. They kiss.

Blinding light bathes them both.

OMO: Tell the world! Tell the world!

MARIA dances off.

JASON enters, cleaning his bloody hands clinically. He walks across to OMO.

OMO: I know what to tell the people. We shall tear down the City brick by brick. We shall rip every banknote to pieces. We shall melt every coin. We shall reclaim the land! We shall burn every deed, every leasehold. We shall dig up every gate in our path. There will be an outpouring of freedom the likes of which this nation has never seen. *(Turns to JASON.)* The time has come. Alfie will ring his bell and all who have ears will hear.

JASON: The bell is out of commission. Health and safety.

OMO: Sh!

Faintly, in the distance the sound of a town hall bell.

OMO: You hear it?

The bell gets louder. JASON brings out his knife. OMO looks at him and smiles.

OMO: My Father has said it: I will not die. Lastborns get it…

JASON stabs him. OMO smiles curiously at him. JASON stabs him again and again. OMO dies. JASON photographs him with his PDA. He removes OMO's pendant and drags his body off stage.

Sound of the bell getting louder.

Windrush Square.

DONA, MARIA, cleaning up a bloodied SARAH. She is back in the wheelchair, her body shattered.

DONA: I found her like this.

MARIA: Why didn't you take her to a hospital?

DONA: You try.

MARIA: Dona, we can't find Omo. I'm taking you to a doctor.

MARIA makes to wheel DONA away. DONA resists with every fibre of her broken body.

MARIA: You'll hurt yourself… All right! All right, Sarah.

DONA: I thought Omo was with you.

MARIA: I remember dancing… Oh my God. *(Feels her body for the stab wounds. Dazed.)*

DONA: What is it, Maria? Maria!

SARAH moans. The bell gets louder. The sound of people approaching. They chant:

CITIZENS: Where is Omo? Where is Omo?

MARIA snaps out of her daze. She grabs SARAH's wheelchair.

MARIA: We've got to get Sarah out of here.

SARAH resists.

Quickly! Before people see her.

DONA: Let them see her.

MARIA: I'm not having you let people think Omo was a lie.

DONA: Believe, Maria.

MARIA looks surprised at DONA. DONA smiles.

DONA: This is happening for a reason. When Omo comes he'll reveal all to us.

CITIZENS enter.

CITIZENS: *(Chant.)* Where is Omo? Where is Omo?

CITIZEN 1: Maria! Where's Omo?

MARIA: I don't know where he is.

JASON appears. He stands at the back. He is shocked to see MARIA alive.

CITIZEN 2: What do you mean you don't know?

CITIZEN 3: *(Sees SARAH.)* Shit! Sarah! What happened to you?

Unrest in the crowd. JASON inches forward to MARIA.

CITIZEN 4: *(To DONA.)* Your people have done this!

DONA: I'm no longer with The Mission.

CITIZEN 4: Liar!

CITIZEN 3: Lay hands on her!

CITIZENS 1 and 2 try to help DONA.

CITIZEN 1: Easy bruv!

CITIZEN 2: Calm down! Everybody calm down.

CITIZEN 3: Get the fuck off!

CITIZENS 1 and 2 get shoved aside.

JASON stops. He smiles.

SARAH comes between the CITIZENS and DONA.

MARIA: Stop! This is what they want! To fracture us into pieces, to stem the wave.

CITIZEN 3: Who are 'they'?

MARIA: You are 'they'! You who know the truth but refuse to act upon it, you the slaves of self-hatred and complacency. Grin and bear it!

CITIZEN 4: Fuck off with that crap! I want my miracle.

The crowd yell at them. MARIA looks in askance at DONA. She sees JASON and is shaken. JASON raises OMO's pendant for MARIA and DONA to see. MARIA falters. DONA holds MARIA up.

CITIZENS: Bring out Omo!

DONA: He has gone on ahead!

CITIZEN 6: You lie!

JASON laughs.

DONA: He has crossed to the other side.

CITIZEN 1: You mean he's crossed the river?

ROBBIE enters.

ROBBIE: What are you peeps still doing here?

SARAH raises her handkerchief. She waves it furiously as she rocks back and forth.

The bell rings louder.

SARAH: *(Struggles with her speech.)* Shake off the wilful peace! Shake off the wilful peace!

CITIZENS 1 and 2 join in the refrain, waving their handkerchiefs.

DONA: Shake off the wilful peace!

DONA holds up MARIA. She encourages her to join in.

ROBBIE: You people deaf? Shake off the wilful peace!

CITIZENS: *(Slowly they begin to wave their handkerchiefs.)* Shake off the wilful peace.

JASON brings out his mobile phone and phones.

The chant of the CITIZENS gets louder. JASON heads for MARIA.

MARIA: Across the river!

The crowd surges forward. JASON is knocked to the ground. He is trampled to death. White handkerchiefs fall from the sky, carpeting the stage.

Soundscape: marching turns to rioting. Gunshots.

Windrush Square. A year later. Winter. Snow covers the ground.

ROBBIE: We haven't gained so much to lose it all by being careless, so I'll say this for the last time. Check with our doctors before you take any medicine. Infiltrators, traitors, they're all in the game. The enemy will throw whatever he's got at us. One year is a drop in the ocean of history. We've done so well to come this far. And are we backing down?

CITIZENS: No!

SARAH is wheeled in by DONA.

ROBBIE: So keep on being your brother's keeper. Keep looking out for one another. The journey is long but we knew that when we set foot on the road. There ain't no miracles in this world.

CITIZEN 1: I'd still like a bit of KFC every now and again though.

CITIZEN 2: When's the heating coming back on?

ROBBIE: Our engineers are working on it. The heating, the electricity, the water. We took enough equipment before we lost Battersea. The Tulse Hill power station will soon be online. Don't you worry about it. This is us saying and doing. This is us staking our claim. And aren't you proud?

CITIZENS: Yeah!

ROBBIE: I thought I heard you say that.

DONA: Say it, Robbie!

SARAH cheers.

ROBBIE continues addressing the crowd.

DONA: It's almost 3.

SARAH shakes her head.

DONA: Okay, we'll stay a little while longer. The therapist will go mad if you're late again.

MARIA enters, pushing a pram, a rifle slung round her shoulder.

DONA: Hi, Maria.

MARIA: Hi Dona, hi Sarah.

DONA: How's junior?

MARIA: As sweet as ever.

DONA: Oh, that birthmark's getting uglier by the day. What did the GP say?

SARAH gestures to MARIA. MARIA takes the baby out and hands him to SARAH. There is a bracelet around the baby's ankle.

MARIA: I haven't been.

DONA: Maria!

MARIA: It's fine. I know what it is.

ROBBIE: … I ask you once again. What will send our society back to square one?

CITIZENS: Complacency!

ROBBIE: I thought I heard you say that.

DONA: Robbie's on form today.

MARIA: Is he ever.

CITIZEN 2: Is it true the Manchester crew have captured Cheshire?

ROBBIE: Our friends in the North aren't the only ones making gains. Liverpool, Newcastle, Leeds, Nottingham,

Birmingham and Glasgow, our units have all made gains. We've made up for losses in Stoke and Edinburgh.

CITIZEN 1: I hear we took a beating in Llanelli.

ROBBIE: We're getting more Welsh speakers to translate the road signs. You live and you learn. Big up to our leader who leads from the front, Commander Maudlin, just returned from leading A section to reclaim Elephant and Castle.

CITIZENS cheer.

ROBBIE: Now she's off to help D section hold Waterloo Bridge. Commander Maudlin, I salute your indefatigable spirit.

CITIZENS cheer.

DONA: You be careful.

MARIA: I will. *(To the baby.)* Won't I, Babatunde?[1]

A bell rings.

The End.

---

1   Yoruba, meaning the father returns.

THE HOUNDING OF DAVID OLUWALE

Adapted from
'Nationality: Wog. The Hounding of David Oluwale'
By Kester Aspden

*The Hounding of David Oluwale w*as produced by Eclipse Theatre. It was first performed on 31 January 2009 at the Courtyard Theatre, West Yorkshire Playhouse, Leeds, with the following cast:

CHIKE / JONES	Howard Charles
PERKINS	Ryan Early
DAVID OLUWALE	Daniel Francis
KITCHING	Steve Jackson
ELLERKER	Luke Jardine
KAYODE / ADE	Richard Pepple
ALICE / PATIENCE	Clare Perkins
JANET / MEG	Laura Power

Additional characters played by members of the ensemble.

Director, Dawn Walton
Designer, Emma Wee
Lighting Designer, Johanna Town
Sound Designer, Mic Pool
Movement Director, Stephen Medlin
Dialect Coach, Neil Swain
Casting Director, Julia Horan CDG
Lindy Hop Instructor, Jeanefer Jean Charles
Fight Director, Kate Waters
Dramaturg, Alex Chisholm
Assistant Director, Simeilia Hodge-Dallaway
Assistant Director, Madeleine O'Reilly

Characters

David Oluwole (Oluwale)

King Edward Hotel Waiter/Waitress

DCS John Perkins

Hotel Customer

Sergeant Ken Kitching

Hostel Warden

Inspector Geoffrey Ellerker

Frank

PC Jones

WPC Meg Harris

Alice

Sergeant Harwood

Kayode

Nurse Allen

Chike

Nurse Patience

Ade

Baba Tailor

Chief Superintendent

Park Keeper

Aldermen (1 Labour, 1 Conservative)

Janet

Magistrate/Judge

Sheila

Young Men 1 and 2

DJ

Psychiatrist

Barman

Unemployed Young Man

Nurse

Court Foreperson

Probation Officer

Citizens Advice Officer

Sailor

Policemen, Market traders, Vagrants Frogman, Passers-by

Note
A / indicates an interruption.

Act One

SCENE ONE

May 1969. The waterfront. River Aire's polluted waves lap at the filthy shore. POLICEMAN stands over a body in a zipped up body bag. FROGMAN puts items from a wet duffel bag into an evidence bag. He looks around impatiently and lets a soggy piece of paper fall to the ground.

POLICEMAN: Easy! Evidence, that is.

FROGMAN: *(Puts it in the evidence bag.)* Smithy driving. Slower than a blind tortoise.

POLICEMAN: What's the hurry?

FROGMAN: Promised the wife an evening out. Start late shift tomorrer.

POLICEMAN opens the body bag. Noxious gases release into the air.

POLICEMAN: Aw!

FROGMAN: Worr you go and do that for?

POLICEMAN: *(Scrutinises the body.)* Coroner'll have a right job making him out.

FROGMAN: You know him. Coloured dosser used to hang around city centre. Regular customer when I were at Millgarth.

POLICEMAN: By God. It is. Poor old Uggy.

FROGMAN: I always called him George.

POLICEMAN: What was his real name?

FROGMAN: David. David Allywally, Allywalla…

POLICEMAN rummages through the evidence bag. He picks out a bible with documents inside it.

POLICEMAN: *(Reads a document. Attempts to pronounce DAVID's surname.)* David… *(Thinks better of it. Brings out his notebook, inspects the body.)* Knew him well then?

FROGMAN: Other officers dealt with him mostly. Help get me gear ter roadside.

POLICEMAN: *(Points to the body's head.)* See that bruise?

FROGMAN: Banged his head on way in.

POLICEMAN: *(Makes notes as he surveys the body.)* CID might want to have a look.

FROGMAN: He fell in! Probably drunk. CID.

POLICEMAN: See this other bruise here/

FROGMAN: Coroner'll see to it now pack it in, will yer! (*As he exits, angrily.*) Smithy! Where are yer, yer bastard?

POLICEMAN puts away his notebook and returns the documents to the evidence bag. He rummages through the bag. He holds up a rosary.

PERKINS enters.

PERKINS: What made you think the bump on his head was suspicious?

POLICEMAN: (*Puts back the rosary into the evidence bag.*) I've dealt with a drowning before, sir. He couldn't have got those bumps just by falling in. *(Exits.)*

DAVID sits up.

DAVID: It's not a good idea to disturb the dead. *(Gets out of the body bag.)*

PERKINS: From what I gleaned from your file you weren't one to let things go.

DAVID: You've been poking through my file.

PERKINS: I'm Detective Chief Superintendent John Perkins, from Scotland Yard.

PERKINS proffers his hand. DAVID doesn't shake it. PERKINS retracts his hand.

PERKINS: I'm heading the investigation into your…your unfortunate incident.

DAVID: You're not joking? I knew they would not forget me! Man! *(Scrutinizes PERKINS.)* You're not from here.

PERKINS: No.

DAVID: Do you have any connection to Leeds?

PERKINS: No.

DAVID: *(Disappointed.)* I wanted a Loiner.

PERKINS: I was called in by the Chief Constable himself.

DAVID: The Chief Constable himself!

PERKINS: It's procedure. To avoid a conflict of interest.

DAVID: I see.

PERKINS: And the fact that being a foreigner you might not get justice.

DAVID: Do you know the roughest pub in Leeds?

PERKINS: No.

DAVID: Do you know which tailor sews the finest suits? Which bakery bakes the tastiest cakes? Do you know the best place for fish and chips?

PERKINS: No.

DAVID: Can you tell Leeds from Bradford, or Leeds from Sheffield?

PERKINS: Northerners all sound the same to me.

DAVID: That makes you the only foreigner here.

Pause.

PERKINS: I'd like to know about your time in Leeds, to give me a picture of you as a person.

DAVID: You have your files.

PERKINS: There's not enough in them to go on.

DAVID: The people will tell you all you need to know about me.

PERKINS: I'd rather ask you.

DAVID: The big guns called you. That means they have accepted me as their own. They like straightforwardness here. Get off on the right foot with them and they will open up to you. It's the only way you can get to the truth of my, what did you call it, 'unfortunate incident'.

SCENE TWO

PERKINS in his office. He is under the desk. There are a load of files on his desk.

CHIEF CONSTABLE enters.

CHIEF CONSTABLE: DCS Perkins. DCS Perkins?

PERKINS: *(Comes out from under the table.)* Good afternoon, Chief Constable.

CHIEF CONSTABLE: What on earth are you doing under the desk?

PERKINS: Looking for bugs.

CHIEF CONSTABLE: You mean bugging devices? You're joking, aren't you?

PERKINS: You can't be too careful. What can I do for you?

CHIEF CONSTABLE: I know how hard it must be, being out of station for so long. You'd make life easy for yourself if you socialised with my officers. Get to know them, that sort of stuff.

PERKINS: To be honest I'm not the pub type.

CHIEF CONSTABLE: *(Jokily.)* How did you make DCS?

PERKINS: By doing my job.

CHIEF CONSTABLE: A sense of humour wouldn't hurt either.

PERKINS: Besides, I might have to question the officers.

CHIEF CONSTABLE: How far along are you with your investigation?

PERKINS: *(Reads from a file.)* After looking into the activities of the Group Three shift of Millgarth Station, Inspector Geoff Ellerker and Sergeant Ken Kitching are my two main suspects.

CHIEF CONSTABLE: So you'll be formally charging them.

PERKINS: I'll be appealing for witnesses to come forward with information relating to the eighteenth of April, nineteen sixty-nine when David Oluwale was last seen alive.

CHIEF CONSTABLE: You've interviewed half of Leeds already.

PERKINS: I'll need to talk to the Millgarth officers again.

CHIEF CONSTABLE: How much longer is your investigation going to take?

PERKINS: Is there a problem?

CHIEF CONSTABLE: City Police is going through a rough patch. I don't want anything that will further damage the trust that our citizens place in us. It doesn't help when David Oluwale's face is on the front page every day.

PERKINS: I didn't come here to take part in a popularity contest.

CHIEF CONSTABLE: Presenting a good image is vital to our work. You're police. You understand what we have to do to get the job done. Sometimes an officer might overstep the boundary in the course of carrying out his duty.

PERKINS: But if overstepping the boundary involves getting a man killed/

CHIEF CONSTABLE: I am not condoning such actions. I am talking about us maintaining the people's respect to do our job. I don't have to tell you how hard it is to regain once you've lost it.

PERKINS: I thought Yorkshire men were known for straight talking.

CHIEF CONSTABLE: All right then. None of us here's in favour of the claptrap coming out of Home Office about merging us with West Riding and Bradford. Any likelihood of more mud being slung at us won't help our case. It might mean very little to you but this city takes pride in its own. I'm asking you to do your bit as a policeman in helping us get the best outcome for this investigation.

PERKINS: I assume the best outcome would be getting the truth.

CHIEF CONSTABLE: I'm not saying otherwise. After all it was one of ours who blew the whistle in the first place.

PERKINS: The new lad.

CHIEF CONSTABLE: He's still one of ours. I brought in Scotland Yard. I didn't have to but I did. And it's not for you to make it look like we're a bunch of thugs who take the law into our hands. What you will find are two bad apples. I don't wish to keep pressing the matter but I need you to understand that there is something bigger at stake here. I wonder if London would have batted an eyelid if it didn't involve a coloured man. We shouldn't fall into the hands of the politicians and their agendas. We do that and God knows where all this tinkering will lead to.

PERKINS: You'll excuse me if I don't care about your politics.

CHIEF CONSTABLE: The higher up you go the more you'll find everything is politics.

PERKINS: I'm not naïve. A man died. That's all that counts in this investigation.

CHIEF CONSTABLE: I have to look at the big picture. I'd ask you to do the same. Think of the consequences, if it's worth it for a man like David Oluwale. For all our sakes.

CHIEF CONSTABLE exits.

DAVID enters.

DAVID: What is there to sharing a few pints?

PERKINS: I forgot to mention. I'm not good at making new friends.

DAVID: And all these files. You should have enough facts to find out what happened.

PERKINS: Facts yes: when last you signed on, your spells in prison, your court appearances.

DAVID: What about your witness statements?

PERKINS: You heard the Chief Constable. You're the wrong man.

DAVID: He didn't say that.

PERKINS: He implied it.

DAVID: You implied it. I know my people.

PERKINS hands DAVID a paper from a file. DAVID opens and reads it.

DAVID: He's talking rubbish.

PERKINS hands him another paper from the file.

DAVID: *(Reads.)* I never did that.

PERKINS: That's you, David. That's you in ten, fifty, a hundred years' time.

DAVID: You picked these ones on purpose. *(Picks a file. Reads from it. Drops it.)* That is not me. That is not me!

PERKINS: This is all I have to go on.

DAVID: You can't!

PERKINS: Then you tell me.

Pause.

DAVID: When you're young, you dreams about your future. Your life is like a movie and you are the hero.

SCENE THREE

August 1949. The cargo hold of the Temple Bar filled with sacks of groundnuts, on the Atlantic Ocean. A sailor shines his torch over the pile. From offstage, someone shouts his name: 'Sam!' The sailor exits. Above the pile of groundnuts, DAVID appears cautiously, then ADE, and finally CHIKE. They sigh with relief and clamber on top of the groundnuts.

ADE: *(Whispers.)* You think this is one of your stupid films?

DAVID: *(Whispers.)* I didn't mean to shout. What's your problem?

ADE: Your bad head that will let them discover us is my problem.

DAVID: There is no one-eyed sailor on this ship.

CHIKE laughs quietly.

DAVID: *Abi,*[1] Chike? You must have bad head to be caught by a one-eyed man.

ADE: When they catch us and throw us overboard the sharks will decide which one of us has bad head.

DAVID: *Ade*! Ah-ah. *Pata-pata*[2] they will make us wash the deck.

ADE: The British Government has decreed that captains must not bring in stowaways. *(Signals to CHIKE to join in the con.)* Chike, am I lying?

CHIKE: *(Nods earnestly.)* Not at all, my brother.

DAVID: *(Brings out his British Travel Certificate.)* This Travel Certificate gives me the right to enter the UK. *(Shows him a page.)* What does it say? I am a British subject.

ADE: All the more reason why they must feed us to the sharks.

DAVID: My British Travel Certificate/

ADE: Will be their appetizer. So when next you describe your Yankee films, leave out the sound effects. OK? *OK*?

DAVID: *(Subdued.)* OK.

ADE and CHIKE laugh at DAVID.

DAVID: I knew you were lying! I did!

ADE: Sh!

---

1   Not so?
2   The most they can do

Wary silence. CHIKE gestures 'shall we eat?' The other two give him the thumbs up. CHIKE disappears behind the groundnut stack while DAVID gets their bowls. CHIKE returns with a bag half full of gari.

CHIKE: We have to manage the *gari.*

ADE: Let us agree: one cup a day as from today.

CHIKE brings out an empty milk tin from the bag to measure the gari into the bowls.

DAVID: Wait, oh. One cup each or one cup between the three of us?

CHIKE: One between the three of us.

DAVID: We will die before we reach Hull!

ADE: You. They can set trap for you with food.

CHIKE: *(Measures out the gari.) Nna,*[3] David. What will you do when you get to UK?

DAVID: I'm going to become an engineer.

ADE: You are a dreamer. You did not complete your School Cert. How are you going to become an engineer?

DAVID: I will save money and go to Cambridge.

ADE: It is not your kind that goes to Cambridge. The scholarship boys have connections.

DAVID: I know people.

ADE: Who do you know?

DAVID: Baba *Isale*, my local butcher.

DAVID and CHIKE laugh.

ADE: You guys are not serious.

Footsteps. They dive behind the stack. The sailor returns with a hosepipe and focuses it on the groundnuts. Smoke billows out of the hosepipe. Coughing, DAVID, ADE and CHIKE raise their hands as they come out of their hiding place. They walk across the stage trying to see through the smoke, which turns into smog, onto the court dock. DAVID, ADE and CHIKE stand before the MAGISTRATE.

MAGISTRATE: The law prevents me from repatriating you. I sentence you each to twenty-eight days in prison. *(Bangs his gavel.)*

---

3   Hey

ADE and CHIKE exit.

PERKINS enters.

DAVID: We served the twenty-eight days in Armley Prison. After we came out I decided to stay in Leeds. Chike had friends there. I could settle in quickly.

SCENE FOUR

Leeds. KAYODE's room.

DAVID and CHIKE enter. DAVID is with his suitcase.

CHIKE: This is David aka Yankee. David, Kayode, my landlord's son in Lagos.

KAYODE: *(Shakes DAVID's hand.)* David, you are welcome. You don't look American to me.

DAVID: *(Turns to show KAYODE his back pockets.)* This is Yankee-style trousers. They have two back pockets.

KAYODE: *(Unimpressed.)* Have a seat. Some tea?

DAVID: Yes, please.

DAVID sees a photo album on the table. He flicks through it.

KAYODE: *(Puts on the kettle.)* You will like this house. All the tenants are African. You've seen your room? *(Comes over to DAVID.)*

DAVID: It's OK.

KAYODE: How are you finding the UK so far?

DAVID: The cold is too much.

KAYODE: My first winter here, I thought I was going to die. *(Points to a photo in the album.)* I ran out of paraffin that day. I wore two leggings and two jumpers underneath my suit.

CHIKE: I remember the first letter you wrote me. It was covered in tear stains.

Kayode: I was homesick. Your turn will come.

DAVID: Strong men don't weep.

KAYODE: So you are a strong man, eh?

DAVID: Yes, like John Wayne.

The kettle whistles. KAYODE makes the tea.

KAYODE: Chike tells me you trained as a tailor. You're in the right place. Leeds is the city of cloth. *(Brings the tea.)*

DAVID: I'm working for Grimshaw Tailors near the market.

CHIKE: Ah, I thought you were at Harrison's?

DAVID: He was using me like an apprentice. Until I left I didn't touch a needle.

KAYODE: Before *oyinbo*[4] allows you near his machine you will work tire[5]. Even then he will keep an eye on you.

DAVID: It is looking the same with Grimshaw.

KAYODE: You are lucky. We that came here before you, we know what we suffered just to get a roof over our heads. Look at you with your own room and when did you arrive? All you have to do now is earn your money.

CHIKE: It's what I've been telling him.

KAYODE: You are a stranger in another man's country. Don't forget that. Gallivanting from job to job will only get you a reputation. Nobody will employ you.

DAVID: Have you ever been to Bradford?

KAYODE: Why do you want to know?

DAVID: I want to check the place out.

CHIKE: You should have said. I would have told Ade about the room instead. Who do you know in Bradford?

KAYODE: You newcomers, looking for streets paved with gold. You think that I did not have the same dreams? Or you think you are better than we that you met here?

CHIKE: Tell him, Kayode.

DAVID: But *oyinbo* in our country, they do whatever they please.

KAYODE: You're comparing your situation with theirs?

DAVID: *(Stands up.)* Look at us, in the UK! *(Points outside the window.)* The centre of the world and we want to tie ourselves down. What will you tell people when you return home and they ask, 'what did you bring for me?' You will

---

4   the white man
5   forever

tell them stories? Or do you want to flash sterling in their faces and say I went and I conquered?

KAYODE: You are still dreaming.

CHIKE: Give Grimshaw's a few weeks. At least a month. Yankee!

DAVID: I'll try. *(Looks out of window.)*

PERKINS enters.

DAVID: I did try. But I was nothing more than a labourer heaving bolts of cloth from the market to the shop. I soon left for Bradford. Before I knew it I was back in Leeds.

PERKINS: Why did you leave Bradford?

SCENE FIVE

1950. Night. The Mecca Dance Hall. Music plays. A YOUNG LOCAL by the bar caresses his pint. He sees a woman. He approaches her. She rebuffs him. He returns to the bar.

DAVID, CHIKE and ADE are at a table.

DAVID: The factory floor was full of idiots. You guys wear suit to work. Does that make you arrogant? When I brought out *The Times* to read it was as if I had stabbed someone.

CHIKE: That is how it is here, Yankee.

DAVID: I beg. *Ehen[6]*, after I left Bradford I said OK let me try Sheffield, maybe there is better for me there.

CHIKE: How was it?

DAVID: It was worse! And their girls! Hard as stainless steel, man. They won't give you face no matter how slick your chat is. Even when I posed with my Yankee trousers! They lack sophistication.

ADE: No be you carry your head go Bradford?

DAVID: *Jo.[7]* Are they taking people at your place?

CHIKE: Come round on Monday. They will need a reference from your last job.

DAVID scratches his head sheepishly.

CHIKE: What?

6   In this context, 'Where was I?'
7   Please.

DAVID: *(Hesitates.)* I fell into small trouble in Sheffield. Man don get criminal record.

CHIKE: David!

ADE: Wetin[8] you do?

DAVID: *(Whispers.)* You know say man dey smoke cannabis.

CHIKE searches DAVID'S trouser pocket closest to him.

DAVID: Wetin now?

CHIKE brings out a small bag of cannabis from DAVID's trouser pocket.

DAVID: *(Snatches it back.)* It's for my personal use.

ADE: Shut up!

They continue arguing.

JANET enters and sits at a table. DAVID and his friends clock her. YOUNG MAN dances badly over to her.

JANET: No thanks.

DAVID and his friends laugh out loud as YOUNG MAN returns to his spot. YOUNG MAN glares at them.

DAVID: Guys. Which one are you going for?

CHIKE: I'm OK.

DAVID: Ade?

ADE: *(Looks at WOMAN then at JANET. Points to JANET.)* That one.

DAVID: I saw her first.

ADE: Too late. I've claimed her. *Mo gbe'se le.[9] (Heads for JANET.)*

DAVID: Wait! You cannot toast her empty-handed.

ADE: *Shebi[10]* I will ask her what she wants to drink first.

DAVID: She's not a Sheffield girl. Leeds women like men who show initiative.

ADE: Chike. Help me get a gin and lime.

CHIKE: I'm not your houseboy.

ADE: *(Tentative.)* Watch David for me. Don't let him toast her.

---

8   What did
9   She's mine.
10   But

CHIKE: *(To DAVID.)* You are under arrest. *Oya[11]*, Ade, before someone else claims her.

ADE goes to the bar. DAVID and CHIKE run over to JANET. YOUNG MAN refuses to give way to ADE. He moves to another side of the bar to be served by the barman.

DAVID: Fine lady like you on your own? Something is wrong with this picture.

JANET: I'm expecting me girlfriend.

DAVID: Oh. I didn't know you were, you were…

JANET: I'm not that way inclined.

DAVID: You turned down that guy.

JANET: Not my type.

CHIKE: Please don't mind my friend. He is slow.

DAVID: May I know your name?

JANET: Janet.

DAVID: Nice to meet you, Janet. I'm David.

CHIKE: Chike is my name.

JANET: Nice to meet you. Where are you from?

DAVID: Nigeria, where the cocoa comes from.

CHIKE: And the groundnuts.

JANET: The what?

DAVID: Don't mind my friend. He is very, very slow. He meant peanuts.

JANET: Oh.

ADE returns with the drink to see DAVID and CHIKE with JANET.

DAVID: What took you? *(Takes the drinks from ADE.)* For you.

JANET: Ooh, ta. *(Takes a sip.)* How did you know?

DAVID: I can read people's minds.

JANET: That black magic stuff isn't real is it?

DAVID: *(Closes his eyes and waves his hands.)* Right now, the music will change and you and I will dance to the next song.

---

11   In this contex, 'quick'

The music changes. DAVID offers his hand to JANET. They dance. CHIKE and ADE rush to the other woman. CHIKE gets to her first. She accepts his offer of a dance.

DAVID and JANET dance near ADE. DAVID gives him teasing looks.

DAVID: So, Janet. Where do you live?

JANET: Not too far from here. I've just moved in.

DAVID: Your accent. You're from Sheffield.

JANET: Yes.

ADE hears this and moves in.

ADE: May I?

DAVID: Don't disturb us, my friend.

ADE: Janet, has David told you what he thinks of Sheffield girls?

DAVID relinquishes JANET to ADE.

The next song playing is a jive number. DAVID dances by himself. He becomes the centre of attention. People clap and cheer, except for YOUNG MAN. DAVID reclaims JANET from ADE. The song ends. DAVID and his friends return to their seats.

JANET: Where did you learn to dance like that?

DAVID: Dancing is in my blood. Another drink?

JANET: Yes please.

DAVID and ADE head for the bar. CHIKE heads for the toilet. YOUNG MAN heads for the exit. He deliberately barges into DAVID. DAVID reacts. ADE pulls him away.

YOUNG MAN: *(To JANET.)* Whore.

JANET: Excuse me?

YOUNG MAN: Not good enough for yer, yer go dancing with them sambos.

DAVID: Is this idiot disturbing you?

YOUNG MAN: Bog off back to yer jungle, monkey.

DAVID: Your father is a monkey.

YOUNG MAN: Sambo!

DAVID: Honkie!

YOUNG MAN: Wog!

DJ: Hey! None of that in here.

They stand down. YOUNG MAN exits.

DJ: Oh, the tension, and so near to closing. I've got just the right song to calm you down.

Soft music. People dance.

JANET: Thanks for standing up for us. It were… It were chivalrous.

DAVID: I can show you some more chivalry, just you and me at my place.

JANET takes his hand. They exit. Everyone else keeps dancing until the music dies out.

DJ: See you all next Friday. Goodnight!

DAVID: What a night it was. Janet and I, we… We began to see each other.

SCENE SIX

Afternoon. JANET, in a textile worker's uniform sits on a bench in the city centre. DAVID, in his work overalls, enters with sandwiches. He hands her one. They eat.

Passers-by stare at them.

DAVID: *(To a staring passerby.)* What? You've never seen a man with a woman before?

PASSERBY hurries off.

They continue eating. JANET brushes crumbs off DAVID's lap. DAVID deliberately shakes crumbs all over his crotch area.

JANET: Cheeky. That's you all over.

DAVID: That's the only way to live.

JANET: Oh yeah?

DAVID: Oh yeah.

JANET: I'm not surprised. Takes that kind of man to leave yer country and come all the way here. Must be like starting all over again. What's it like, Nigeria?

DAVID: It's a lovely place.

JANET: Do you like live with lions and elephants?

DAVID: We don't live in a jungle.

JANET: I'm only asking. I don't know about these things. You must miss home.

DAVID: Very much. Do you miss home?

JANET: Sheffield is only down the road.

DAVID: Do you miss it?

JANET: I visit me Mam every month.

DAVID: I miss my mother most of all.

JANET: Bet she's dead proud of you.

DAVID: When I become an engineer, she will be even prouder.

JANET: You want to be an engineer?

DAVID: It's a big man's job in Nigeria. After I qualify I will go back and build houses just like the big town houses here. The biggest I will build for my mother.

JANET: Sounds like you've got your life all sorted.

DAVID: What of you?

JANET: Me? Oh, don't know. Have a family. Wouldn't mind having a house with a garden. What more can a girl like me ask for?

DAVID: How do you mean, a girl like you?

JANET: You know, a girl like me.

DAVID: Your background has nothing to do with it. If you want something, you work towards it.

JANET: I wish it were that easy.

DAVID: You British. Everything is class, class, class. Africans don't behave like that.

A group of African students pass by.

DAVID: Hey my brothers! How una dey?[12]

They look at his overalls, ignore him and walk on.

DAVID: *(Shouts at them.)* We shall all meet at Apapa[13]! Idiots! … They've stayed here too long.

JANET: You've got an answer for everything.

A passerby stares at them.

---

12   How are you?
13   Apapa Port: the place where ships sailing to Nigeria docked.

DAVID: If this is too much for you, we can stop meeting in public.

JANET: *(To the passerby.)* What are you staring at?

PASSERBY hurries off.

JANET: *(Stands up.)* Same time tomorrow then?

DAVID: *(Holds her hand.)* You know, behind every successful man is a woman as strong as stainless steel.

PERKINS enters.

DAVID: Janet was strong but she knew the society she came from. She tried to help me blend in. Keep your head down. Don't make a fuss. I soon got used to living that way. I got a job in the slaughterhouse in the market. I saw my friends on Friday nights at the dance hall. When I could afford it I took Janet to the movies on Saturdays. I couldn't have asked for more.

SCENE SEVEN

1953. Afternoon. King Edward Hotel.

DAVID sits at a table, smoking a cigarette. A customer sits at another table. The hotel staff decorate the hall with banners for Princess Elizabeth's coronation. There are small Union Jack flags on the table. DAVID playfully waves one.

WAITRESS serves DAVID a cup of tea. DAVID pays for it.

DAVID: Happy coronation!

WAITRESS: And to you.

DAVID: Long live the Queen. Fine woman.

Another customer enters. WAITRESS takes her order. WAITER enters. WAITRESS takes off her apron as she gives WAITER the order for the customer's table and exits. WAITER is about to go to the kitchen when DAVID catches his attention and orders another tea. WAITER takes DAVID's order and exits to kitchen. DAVID drinks up the first cup of tea just as WAITER enters and serves DAVID a fresh cup. DAVID pays for it. DAVID finishes his tea and heads for the door. WAITER sees him leaving and runs after him.

WAITER: Ay up! Yer haven't paid for yer tea!

DAVID: I paid you.

WAITER: For other one.

DAVID: I paid the waitress.

WAITER: No yer didn't.

DAVID: I did.

WAITER: No yer didn't.

DAVID: How long have I been coming here that today I wouldn't pay for my tea?

WAITER: Pay up.

DAVID: Don't spoil the coronation for us.

WAITER: That's got nowt to do wi' you not paying for yer tea.

DAVID: It's a simple misunderstanding. Ask your colleague. She will tell you.

WAITER: She's not here is she?

DAVID: You are saying that I deliberately refused to pay?

WAITER: Aren't you a bright one?

DAVID: Mister Man, if this is a joke stop it right now.

WAITER: Who says I'm joking wi' yer?

DAVID: God save the Queen. (*Makes to leave.*)

WAITER blocks his way.

CUSTOMER waves to catch someone's attention. PC enters. He stands to the other side of DAVID.

DAVID: *(Heatedly.)* Don't let me be angry with you, oh.

WAITER: Or what?

PC: What's up?

WAITER: He won't pay for his tea.

DAVID: Officer, don't mind him. I've paid him.

WAITER: No you haven't.

DAVID: I mean the waitress.

WAITER: He's lying.

DAVID: You are the bloody liar!

PC: Calm down! *(Steps closer to DAVID.)*

DAVID: *(Sways, feeling trapped.)* Let us get his colleague then I can be on my way. I'm sure you have better things to do.

PC: You telling me how to do my job?

DAVID: How can I tell you how to do your job?

PC: Stand still. Stand still I said.

DAVID: I can move about if I like.

PC: Look at me when I talk to you.

DAVID: You are holding me here against my will!

PC: Don't raise your voice to me.

DAVID: I'm not shouting.

PC: I said do not raise your voice.

WAITER: He was ready to tear up the place afore you came along.

DAVID: You lying bastard!

PC: *(Gets hold of him.)* We'll sort this out down the station.

DAVID: Don't touch me! Do not touch me!

PC: I'm arresting you/

DAVID: Leave me alone! Leave me!

They struggle. POLICEMAN hits him over the head with his truncheon. DAVID falls to the ground.

As PERKINS talks, NURSE 1 and NURSE 2 wheel in a trolley. They put DAVID on it.

PERKINS: David Oluwale was charged with disorderly conduct and with assaulting a police officer. He was sentenced to two months in Armley Prison. The prison medical officer's report states that David began to act in a strange manner which prompted his admission into St. James's Hospital Psychiatric Unit. According to his attending psychiatrist, David Oluwale appeared 'apprehensive, noisy, and frightened without cause.' He behaved in a childish manner and would weep when talking of his fears. David Oluwale was transferred to Menston Asylum where he was diagnosed with schizophrenia.

SCENE EIGHT

Menston Hospital.

NURSE 1 injects DAVID with insulin. Next the nurses put electrodes to his temple and apply electric shock treatment to him. PERKINS covers DAVID with a Yoruba wrapper as he falls into a stupor.

DAVID at home, asleep. ALICE enters with her shopping.

ALICE: Ah. The man of the house! Sorry! I didn't know you were sleeping.

DAVID: It's OK *Maa'mi.*

ALICE: My big man has been working hard.

DAVID goes to help her.

ALICE: Don't worry. Go back to bed.

DAVID: There is something I/

ALICE: *(Happily.)* I bought enough food for the week, even at the inflated prices. *(Points to a bag.)* You should have seen *Baba Eleran's*[14] face when I paid him for the meat. He thought I'd ask for credit. What shall I cook for you? *Amala* with *gbegiri* soup and plenty of meat for my big man.

DAVID: Yes, *Maa'mi.*

ALICE: Tomorrow I will pay the produce guild my dues. Once I sell off my provisions I will start selling yams. I know a village where I can get them cheap.

DAVID: *Maa'mi/*

ALICE: In no time I will make profit then I can pay back all the money I owe.

David: *Maa'mi*! I want to go to UK.

ALICE: Excuse me?

DAVID: I want to go to UK.

ALICE: You talk as if you are going down the road. Or did you not say you want to go to UK?

DAVID: Yes, *Maa'mi.*

ALICE: Put the water on the fire.

DAVID: Nothing is happening for me here. My youth is running away from me.

---

14   The butcher.

ALICE: It's because your father is no longer with us. He would have taught you that to become a man takes a lifetime… Things are looking up for you. You will waste your effort to start over again.

DAVID: I do nothing but cut grass and fetch tennis balls all day.

ALICE: If not for your impatience you could have qualified as a tailor. If I do this yam business I will be able to afford your school fees and you can return to school. Isn't that what you want?

DAVID: I have to seize my chance. My friends are planning to go once they raise money for their travel.

ALICE: It is only you and me, David. How can I let you go that far? Even when you're late from the cinema it is not long before I come looking for you.

DAVID: Yes – with a slipper.

ALICE: I'm not joking!

DAVID: I have to come out from your wrapper. I can send you money. When I return it will be as somebody. Imagine, David Oluwole, in *The African Cowboy*, co-starring John Wayne.

ALICE: Is this the foolish dream that is making you run to the UK? And you think I will let you go? No way!

DAVID: *Maa'mi.* I will behave myself when I get there. Trust me.

ALICE: You never stay in one place. How can I help you if you get into trouble?

DAVID: I will stick with my friends.

ALICE: There are those who have gone and have never returned. As soon as they reach overseas they forget us.

DAVID: How can I forget my mother?

ALICE: I know people it has happened to.

DAVID: I have only you. This is my home. I cannot leave without your blessing.

ALICE: I will think about it. *(Exits.)*

    DAVID returns to the bed in Menston.

    PERKINS enters.

DAVID: My mother was right to worry. If she sent me down the street I'd have travelled half of Lagos. I could never stay in one place. The grass was always greener elsewhere. And the grass was greenest in the UK. That was what we were taught in school. I was nineteen when I boarded the ship to seek my destiny. The head is the seat of one's destiny, you know.

The nurses enter.

PERKINS: How long were you in Menston for?

DAVID: Eight/

The nurses remove DAVID off the trolley and exit with it.

PERKINS: Eight months?

DAVID: Eight years.

PERKINS: Eight years?

DAVID: Eight long years of shock therapy and insulin injections. Eight years of bad food and small talk with my fellow inmates. To me, Menston was a prison.

NURSE enters with DAVID's briefcase. He hands it to DAVID.

DAVID: *(Relieved.)* I thought they'd never let me out.

SCENE NINE

1961.

Enoch Powell: Care in the Community: The Water Tower Speech.

VOICE: I now present to you the Minister for Health, Mr Enoch Powell.

Applause.

POWELL: '… The theme of your Conference this year is an integrated service for mental disorders…in fifteen years time there may well be needed not more than half as many places in hospitals for mental illness as there are today… Few ought to be in great isolated institutions or clumps of institutions… The pattern of provision in the community…'

A derelict street. A worker goes around painting 'x's' on the doors.

DAVID: Excuse me. I can't find my house.

WORKER: This whole street's marked for demolition.

DAVID: Did Janet tell you where she went?

WORKER: Don't know any Janet.

DAVID: Where did you put my belongings? Please tell me where they are.

WORKER exits.

DAVID: Where do I sleep tonight?

SCENE TEN

A shelter for the homeless. DAVID, led by HOSTEL WARDEN, enters with bed sheets. The sounds in the rooms around can be heard.

FRANK, a homeless man, is lying on one of the beds.

WARDEN: Frank, meet your new room-mate.

FRANK: I'm not sharing my room with a wog!

WARDEN: *(To DAVID.)* You'll get a meal and a hot bath. Look like you need both.

FRANK: I said I'm not sharing with a, with him! He smells! *(Picks up his bag.)*

WARDEN: Frank!

FRANK exits.

WARDEN: S'all yours for now.

DAVID: Warden. Can you tell the people next door to keep it quiet?

WARDEN: This is a hostel, not a hotel.

WARDEN exits. The noises in the other rooms get louder. It morphs into the sound of demolition work. DAVID covers his ears with the pillow. He stands up, takes his briefcase and walks out.

SCENE ELEVEN

Leeds City Council.

ALDERMAN, wearing a red rosette, underneath a projection of the Leeds Coat of Arms. Around him the demolition of buildings.

ALDERMAN: Members of Leeds City Council, history conspires that a Labour-run council closes the era of our great industries and with it the associated soot and grime. Imagine if you will a citadel of the new economy, its beacon guiding all and sundry to a land of opportunity, a paradise of shops and high rises and leading to that citadel a ring road more laden with promise than the Silk Road. Gentlemen, I present to you…

The coat of arms gives way to a projection of the inner ring road.

ALDERMAN: … Britain's first urban motorway. All roads lead to Leeds. Follow me on the path to prosperity for one and all.

Applause.

Workers and people pass by. DAVID is alone, confused. Night falls. DAVID scouts around for old newspapers. He throws some away until he finds The Times *and puts it on the floor. He covers himself with the rest of the newspaper. He uses his briefcase as a pillow. As it gets darker from all corners vagrants appear and bed down.*

PROBATIONER JONES enters.

JONES: *(To the vagrants.)* On your way.

The vagrants leave. DAVID remains, sleeping. JONES nudges DAVID with his truncheon. DAVID stirs. JONES is surprised when he realises DAVID is black.

JONES: What you doing here?

DAVID: I'm sleeping.

JONES: You what?

DAVID: Sleeping. Sleeping.

JONES: You been drinking?

DAVID: No, I've not been drinking.

JONES: *(Brings out his duty book.)* Name.

DAVID: David Oluwole.

JONES: What?

DAVID: David.

JONES: Your surname.

DAVID: Oluwole. O, L, U/

JONES: *(Gives up.)* Address.

DAVID: I used to live nearby. Just round the corner/

JONES: If you're homeless you go to a shelter.

DAVID: Sincerely I'm fine here.

JONES: You go to a shelter or I arrest you for vagrancy.

DAVID: But this is my home.

JONES: I'll not tell you again.

> *DAVID folds the newspaper neatly and puts it into his briefcase. He shuffles off.*

JONES: Hey! *(Points in the opposite direction.)* Shelter's that way.

DAVID: I will try another shelter.

JONES: And where is this other shelter?

> *DAVID turns round and exits.*

> *JONES looks around at the empty streets with pride. He exits.*

> *The vagrants return and bed down to sleep. SERGEANT KITCHING enters. He kicks one of the vagrants. They all dash off. JONES dashes in. KITCHING glares at JONES who looks apologetic. KITCHING exits, followed quickly by JONES.*

SCENE TWELVE

Millgarth Police Station.

Desk Sergeant HARWOOD and WPC MEG HARRIS go through paperwork at the counter.

KITCHING and PROBATIONER JONES enter.

KITCHING: *(To JONES.)* Let that be the last time.

HARWOOD: What's Jones done now, Kitching?

KITCHING: Keeps playing Padre with dossers down market. *(To JONES.)* Stick me in for oh three hundred hours on Headrow.

JONES: But we weren't on Headrow at oh three…

> *JONES wilts under the glare of KITCHING and HARWOOD. He jots into his duty-book.*

HARWOOD: Supposed to be learning Probationer here the ropes.

KITCHING: You in, Harwood?

HARWOOD: Ellerker'll soon drop by.

KITCHING: You're out, then. Meg, make us a tea, love.

MEG exits to the mess room.

HARWOOD: Give me a minute.

KITCHING and JONES exit to mess room. KITCHING sits down. JONES sits down next to him. KITCHING glares at him. JONES moves to the opposite end of the table. MEG brings KITCHING his tea.

KITCHING: *(Brings out a pack of cards.)* Ta, love.

MEG goes back to the counter.

HARWOOD: Make us a cuppa, will you?

MEG: You could have asked when I made one for Sergeant Kitching.

HARWOOD: I'm asking you now.

MEG returns to the mess room behind HARWOOD. HARWOOD draws up a chair next to KITCHING.

HARWOOD: Hurry up. Can't leave the counter unattended.

MEG puts the tea down in front of him with a bang. KITCHING and HARWOOD cheer. JONES wants to ask her for a tea. He thinks better of it.

HARWOOD: What are we playing?

KITCHING: Hearts. *(Shuffles the cards.)*

JONES looks eagerly at KITCHING. KITCHING nods. JONES draws up his chair.

HARWOOD: 'Golden Boy'[15] did it fer us again o'er the weekend. Reckon we'll be champions this year… You said he wasn't worth six thousand pounds.

KITCHING: No Welshman's worth six thousand pounds.

HARWOOD: That's why your lot are in second division.

KITCHING: Give us next year. Hunslet will rise again.

HARWOOD: Well this year it'll be us in final. Bet my life on it.

They keep playing.

HARWOOD: You were right. Johnson's taken over desk duties at Ireland Wood.

KITCHING: Told yer.

HARWOOD: Just because he refused to ride in the Panda car?

15   Nickname of Lewis Jones. Leeds Rugby League star.

KITCHING: Twenty-five years on the beat, behind a bleeding desk.

HARWOOD: He should've just gone with it.

KITCHING: Don't matter anyhow.

HARWOOD: The Panda's not so bad. Get round your pub crawl quicker.

KITCHING: This isn't Z Cars, Harwood. D'you remember Johnson ever needing a bloody Home Office order ter bring in the Houlihan boys? Single-handed he took on the three of 'em. Or 'Rugger' Harris? Elland Road was dead quiet when he were on duty. Pansy here couldn't clear the market of vagrants. PC Wigton, half your size, would've emptied dark arches just by waving his cape back in day. Look at him, Harwood, that's the face of new police. That's who they'll be replacing us with. A bloody social worker. Get us a refill! S'all you're good for.

JONES goes to get the tea.

KITCHING and HARWOOD continue playing.

HARWOOD: I take it you're not keen on our high flying Inspector Ellerker then?

KITCHING: How d'you think he made inspector so fast? These sodding grammar school boys climbing up their mentor's school tie.

HARWOOD: Heard he did all right at CID.

KITCHING: What's he know about real policing?

HARWOOD: You'll have plenty of time to put him straight, won't you?

KITCHING: He's not pushing me around in me own station.

HARWOOD: You'll do as you're told. Chain of command.

KITCHING: I'll tell him where to stick his chain of command.

INSPECTOR ELLERKER enters.

MEG: Good evening, sir.

ELLERKER: Where's Sergeant Harwood?

MEG: He's in the mess room.

ELLERKER: Have you heard from Sergeant Kitching?

MEG: He's in there too.

ELLERKER goes into the mess room. KITCHING and HARWOOD stand up.

KITCHING: Evening sir.

HARWOOD: Evening sir.

ELLERKER: Why aren't you out on patrol, Sergeant?

KITCHING: Just dropping by.

HARWOOD: That's right, sir. They were/

ELLERKER: Aren't you supposed to be at the counter, Sergeant Harwood?

HARWOOD goes to the counter.

ELLERKER: I'm checking the points. I see my officers on duty but my Sergeant's nowhere to be found because he's back at the station with his feet up. What if your attention was needed?

KITCHING: They know where to find me, sir.

ELLERKER: They know where to find you.

KITCHING: Yes.

ELLERKER: And where would Probationer Jones's duty-book have put you – on Call Lane or here?

KITCHING: I'm always where I should be.

ELLERKER: Your old inspector may have tolerated your slackness but I won't. Things are going to change around here whether you like it or not. Am I clear?

KITCHING: *(Picks up his helmet.)* Yes, sir.

ELLERKER: I expect you as the senior sergeant to set an example and to help the men adjust. They seem to respect you, only God knows why.

KITCHING: They know where they stand with me.

ELLERKER: What are you inferring?

KITCHING: Just making a point.

ELLERKER: What is your point?

KITCHING: The men don't really know you. You're their inspector, yes. But take yesterday's parade for instance. You were all nice and friendly.

ELLERKER: What's wrong with that?

KITCHING: Nothing. But take the day before.

ELLERKER: Some of the men were slacking. They needed to be told.

KITCHING: You can't be mates with them one minute and a sergeant-major the next.

ELLERKER: I'm still getting to know the group.

KITCHING: You want to be up to your eyes with their personal problems?

ELLERKER: I wouldn't be much of a leader if I didn't know my own men.

KITCHING: Gain their respect. That's all you need. *(Makes to leave.)*

ELLERKER: Sergeant! How do you suggest I do that?

KITCHING: How about we make a stop at the Irish Club?

ELLERKER: I don't drink.

KITCHING: You don't drink! Well, that needs fixing. What say we work on it tonight?

SCENE THIRTEEN

DAVID sitting on bench with PERKINS.

DAVID: I went to Sheffield to look for Janet but I could not find her. When I came back to Leeds I tried staying at a shelter but it was either they didn't like the way I looked or I got into a fight with a resident. Once in a while I found work so I was able to rent a room on and off. The market was my favourite place. The traders would give me leftovers. I'd go down to the Tavern to have a pint and listen to music on the jukebox. *(Feels his pockets.)* That became my regular day.

PERKINS: What about your old friends?

DAVID: I don't recall any of them coming to see me in Menston.

PERKINS: So you never caught up with them after you came out?

DAVID: Not as much as before. They helped me whenever they could.

KAYODE enters.

KAYODE: David? David.

DAVID: Ah, Kayode. How are you? How is your family?

KAYODE: Fine, fine. Shouldn't you be at work?

DAVID: I'm on my break.

KAYODE: This is very far from the foundry.

DAVID: I just want to be by myself. Thanks for getting me the job.

KAYODE: So what time is your break over?

DAVID: Soon.

KAYODE: When is soon?

DAVID: Ah, Kayode, you have become policeman?

KAYODE: If you are not working how are you going to rent lodgings?

DAVID: Did I say I am not working?

KAYODE: Chike said last week you spent a night in his house.

DAVID: *Ehen*?

KAYODE: And that you spent the night before at Ade's.

DAVID: Is it a crime to stay at my friends?

KAYODE: David, I spoke to your supervisor yesterday. He said he fired you for fighting with your co-worker.

DAVID: You know? Then why are you querying me as if I'm a small child?

KAYODE: I had to beg him to take you.

DAVID: Have I not thanked you already, or you want me to prostrate?

KAYODE: It's my fault. I was concerned for your welfare.

DAVID: Kayode! I'm trying. It's not been easy. Everything has changed. Don't be annoyed. Kayus-Daddy! Stay in one place! Don't go to Bradford! Do your work! You are a good friend. God will send you your own helper.

KAYODE: Amen.

DAVID: What of the children?

KAYODE: They always ask when next is Uncle David coming to play with us.

DAVID: I miss them too.

KAYODE: Do you have a place to stay tonight?

DAVID: Yes, in a shelter. Until I get another room.

KAYODE: Oh, OK. *(Brings out money.)* A token, for a meal.

DAVID: Kayode!

KAYODE: Take! *(Pushes the money into DAVID's hand.)*

DAVID: This is too much! *(Returns most of it.)* Give to the children.

KAYODE: David…

DAVID: *(Presses the money into KAYODE's hand.)* Buy something nice for them. Say it is from their Uncle David. I will come and play with them soon.

KAYODE holds on to DAVID's hand.

KAYODE: Spend tonight with us.

DAVID: I'll lose my bed. In fact I must go there now before they give it to someone else. *(Stands up.)*

KAYODE: You're sure?

DAVID: If you can help me get another job…

KAYODE: I'll see what I can do. Take care, David.

DAVID exits.

PERKINS: Guilt is a bastard.

KAYODE: Pardon me?

PERKINS: How come you never visited him in Menston?

KAYODE: I had responsibilities.

PERKINS: That's your excuse for not visiting him once in eight years.

KAYODE: You've no idea what it was like for us back then, the struggles just to do the things that you take for granted. I told him not to get into trouble.

PERKINS: I see. It's David's fault. He had it coming/

KAYODE: That's not what I meant!

PERKINS: Why didn't you contact his mother?

KAYODE: And tell her what? That her son has gone soft in the head? I did my best for him when he came out. We all did. David was not the same person but he still had his pride. I couldn't take that away from him. I wished I could have helped him more but what else could I have done?

PERKINS: You'll never know now, will you?

KAYODE walks off, he turns to look at PERKINS who is staring at him. KAYODE puts his head down and exits.

SCENE FOURTEEN

1965, Woodhouse Moor.

DAVID enters and prepares to lie down.

DAVID: It was getting tougher for me to find a place to bed down on the city outskirts. You want to see the police harassing us. The parks were easier. They did not come around so often to move me on. I felt lonely after being in the market. I couldn't wait for morning. (*Lies down.*)

ALICE enters.

ALICE: You didn't write.

DAVID: *Maa'mi*!

ALICE: You promised you wouldn't be like those ones who forget.

ALICE walks off.

DAVID: *Maa'mi* where are you going? *Maa'mi* wait!

ALICE exits.

DAVID: *(Gathers his newspapers into his brief case.)* I'm coming. I'm coming. *Maa'mi*! (*He runs around in different directions. She is gone. He returns to his place.*) I will wait for you here!

POLICEMAN enters.

POLICEMAN: Can't lay here, Uggy.

DAVID: I must wait for her here. She is coming back.

POLICEMAN: Come on.

DAVID: *Maa'mi* will be angry if I move from here.

POLICEMAN: *(Grabs him.)* Up.

DAVID bites his finger.

POLICEMAN: Ow!

POLICEMAN grabs DAVID and hands him over to NURSE ALLEN.

SCENE FIFTEEN

1965, High Royds Hospital.

NURSE ALLEN walks DAVID in to the ward.

PERKINS enters.

DAVID: After the incident with the PC I was taken to High Royds Hospital. The place looked familiar, then I realised it was Menston. They had changed the name. The memories of my last visit flooded back. It took me a while to settle down. Things were not as bad as my first time there. There was no more electro-convulsive therapy, no more insulin injection. Some things change for the better, even if they change only a little.

ALLEN: He was a handful. Built like a miniature Mister Universe; strong as one too. He had this great big set of teeth and he'd bite you if you tried to make him do anything he didn't want to.

PERKINS: Anything like what?

ALLEN: You know, like take his medication, eat his food, go to bed.

PERKINS: You mean he didn't like being bossed around.

ALLEN: We keep patients to a regimen for their own good. He behaved like he was still back in the jungle.

PERKINS: You don't think his stay here helped?

ALLEN: Coloureds can't cope with our way of life. They don't respond to modern treatment because they can't.

PERKINS: Is that your considered opinion?

ALLEN: Call a spade a spade. Ask the other nurses. They'll tell you no different.

PERKINS: How many coloured patients had you looked after before David Oluwale?

ALLEN: None.

PERKINS: And how many now?

ALLEN: We get a few West Indians and African students. Which proves my point. Heard some rot about family pressures. They always come up with excuses. Look what's happened with the Pakis in Burley.

PERKINS: Was there no other diagnosis besides schizophrenia?

ALLEN: Schizophrenia is always the diagnosis for them. Shove a few pills of Largactil down their throats, that'll keep 'em peaceful for a few hours.

PERKINS: And that's what you treated David for?

ALLEN: Yes.

PERKINS: Thanks Mister Allen.

ALLEN: I've been following the case in the papers. It's a sad day when the police turn on their own. I know what it's like having to deal with dregs every day. It isn't pleasant. Loads of decent people have been denied justice. And you're bringing down two of your own for an animal like him.

Light on DAVID and PATIENCE, a Nigerian nurse.

PATIENCE: David, how are you feeling today?

DAVID: I'm fine, Patience. How are you?

PATIENCE: I'm fine, thank you.

DAVID: Tell me. How did you get this work? I don't know, maybe I too can be a nurse.

PATIENCE: You have to train at nursing school first.

DAVID: I was going to be an engineer. I was going to train at Cambridge. I'm thinking the university here is better. I don't want to go too far.

PATIENCE: When you are discharged, you can plan for it.

DAVID: Or am I too old to go to university?

PATIENCE: You can never be too old, David.

DAVID: You are just saying that.

PATIENCE: My sister's right hand couldn't touch her left ear until two years after she should have started primary school. She is now an accountant.

DAVID touches his left ear with his right hand. They laugh.

DAVID: Eh, I need a favour from you.

PATIENCE: Yes?

ALLEN enters.

ALLEN: Haven't you got anything better to do than gossip with the patients?

PATIENCE: I'm coming.

ALLEN: Quick.

PATIENCE: *(Steely.)* I said I'm coming.

ALLEN exits.

PATIENCE: What can I do for you, David?

DAVID: Can you help me write a letter to my mother? She will be worried that all this time she has not heard from me.

PATIENCE: *(Gets out her notebook.)* What is the address?

DAVID: Yaba.

PATIENCE: Where in Yaba?

DAVID: You know Lagos?

PATIENCE: Not very well. I'll write the letter for you. You'll remember the address later.

DAVID: OK… *Maa'mi.* Since the time I last saw you I've tried to keep out of trouble. Once I get a job I will send you money like I promised. Your son, David.

PATIENCE: When last did you see your mother?

DAVID: Ehn?

PATIENCE: You said 'since the time I last saw you'. I thought you hadn't been home since you arrived.

DAVID: Oh. You know how we talk now.

PATIENCE: I know but don't talk like that with the other staff. They will keep you here.

DAVID: Ah, OK, thank you, Patience.

PATIENCE: Try and remember the address and I will post the letter for you.

DAVID: God will keep you.

PATIENCE exits.

DAVID: I never remembered the address. Patience tried to locate her anyway but by the time I left she was unsuccessful. I stayed in High Royds for two years.

ALLEN enters with DAVID's suitcase. He dumps DAVID's briefcase in front of him and exits.

SCENE SIXTEEN

1967. The city centre. Buildings going up. ALDERMAN appears with a blue rosette.

ALDERMAN: The old council leader will claim he initiated our great city's regeneration. But like all things Labour, he was good only for blowing things down. For all his huff and puff Leeds remains the epitome of Northern misery. It's for this reason Westminster continues to dabble in our affairs. Let me say this: Westminster, keep out! Vision is what the former council leader lacked. Vision is what I bring to what I call 'Project Leeds'. 'Project Leeds' is a long-term programme that will place us at the heart of the service sector.

The backdrop changes to an artist's impression of Leeds City Centre.

ALDERMAN: Creating easy access will turn our city centre into a shopper's paradise the likes of which this country has never seen. So come on. Let's get Leeds moving!

Night. VAGRANTS crawl out of the city, finding places to bed down on the street. Suddenly the peace is shattered by the sound of loud drunken singing of the 'Leeds Calypso', followed by the chant of 'Leeds, Leeds, Leeds…'

The VAGRANTS stir.

VAGRANT 1: Shurrup, you hooligans!

The chanting gets closer.

VAGRANT 1: I'll call the police!

The chanting draws closer still. VAGRANT 1 gets up and marches in the direction of the chanting. Recognition of the culprits turns his anger into terror. He gathers his belongings and runs off.

VAGRANT 2: Who is it, Jimmy?

The remaining vagrants seek out the chanters. They run off.

KITCHING and ELLERKER enter, drunk.

ELLERKER: Didn't know you were a fan.

KITCHING: Only when I'm knocking heads of their hooligans.

ELLERKER: Throw your weight behind a team that's on the up. One game with your face to the pitch, you'll be a convert.

KITCHING: Hunslet! Say it with me!

ELLERKER: Lily white's the way to go, Kitching. I'm telling you.

KITCHING: Any team that abandons the city's colours is not worthy of my support.

ELLERKER: You'll see. In fifty years from now United will still be pride of the city. Your Hunslet will be nowt but a muddy memory.

KITCHING: Sh! D'yer hear that?

ELLERKER: It's only a rat. Back to the station.

KITCHING: *(Brings out his baton.)* Halt, police! Stay where you are!

ELLERKER confused, at first, finds his bearings, exits.

KITCHING crashes into a stand and falls asleep.

SCENE SEVENTEEN

April 1968. The city centre.

DAVID, in a hotel doorway.

DAVID: I tried a number of jobs. I didn't stay in them long enough to rent a room. People were getting meaner. I was called dirty names more than when I first arrived. It was getting harder to sleep rough. Even the friendly police had a sharp tone to their voices. It made no difference whether I slept in the city centre or on the outskirts. During the cold months the best place to stay was where you had big doorways.

KITCHING and JONES enter.

KITCHING: And?

JONES: I told them if I came round again and found them there, I'd shove my stick up their arses.

KITCHING: Well?

JONES: Not a dosser in sight, Sarge.

KITCHING: How'd you feel?

JONES: I don't know Sarge.

KITCHING: You don't know? Should be bloody proud. *(Sees DAVID.)*

JONES: Oh, it's only Uggy.

KITCHING: You know him?

JONES: I've moved him on a couple of times.

KITCHING: *(Prods DAVID with his foot.)* Get up.

DAVID: I'm sleeping.

> *KITCHING pulls him up. Recoils from the smell. Rummages through DAVID's briefcase.*

DAVID: I've done nothing wrong.

KITCHING: Where'd you steal the briefcase?

DAVID: I did not steal it. It is mine.

KITCHING: Name.

DAVID: I can't sleep in the parks. I can't sleep in the market/

KITCHING: Name!

DAVID: Since when is sleeping a crime?

KITCHING: I asked you a question.

DAVID: *(To JONES.)* You know me. Please…

JONES: Sarge…

KITCHING: *(Turns DAVID round and handcuffs him.)* We'll do this at the station.

DAVID: My name is David! David Oluwole.

End of Act One.

Act Two

1948. Lagos. The market. DAVID, with a bag of thread with CHIKE. BABA TAILOR waits impatiently in his shop. There is a parcel of clothes beside him.

DAVID: Sheriff kidnaps 'Actor's' girlfriend. 'Actor' gathers his gang and they go to the castle to rescue her.

CHIKE: Wait. The sheriff has a castle.

DAVID: It's the king's castle.

CHIKE: There's a king?

DAVID: The King wants to marry Actor's girlfriend by force. So Actor rides on his horse 'kutuwe-kutuwe'[16] through the forest and they break into the castle, firing arrow, 'fiah, fiah'…

CHIKE: The King has Indians fighting for him.

DAVID: No.

Chike: The Indians are with Actor's gang!

DAVID: There are no Indians in this film! *Jo!*[17] Actor and Sheriff fight with sword/

CHIKE: Which kind of cowboy film is this?

DAVID: It is not cowboy film. It is Robin Hood.

CHIKE: Why didn't you say so? You think I don't know who Robin Hood is? Calling him 'Actor, Actor'.

DAVID: You used to sleep during literature class.

They wrestle playfully. BABA TAILOR hears them and approaches them. CHIKE sees him and dashes off. BABA TAILOR picks up the bag of thread.

DAVID: Don't run! Come back! Let me beat you finish!

BABA TAILOR whacks DAVID's head. He returns to his shop. DAVID follows him.

---

16   clip-clop
17   Please! As in, 'let me finish'.

BABA TAILOR: Simply to go across the market to buy thread you spend the whole day. You come back, you start playing with your useless friends.

DAVID: I'm sorry, Baba.

BABA TAILOR: Sorry for yourself. Take these clothes to Chief!

DAVID: You promised me I would get my first sewing job by month end, that I would no longer be running errands.

BABA TAILOR: Are you taking those clothes?

DAVID: I was here before your nephew. He doesn't pay fees.

BABA TAILOR: Your mother owes me three months arrears.

DAVID: Because you kept me here longer than I should be/

BABA TAILOR: David, you are calling me a thief? *Kia,*[18] get out of my shop. Get out! And don't come back.

ALICE's provisions stall in another part of the market. Customers come by. They haggle over the price then depart without buying anything. ALICE is depressed.

DAVID enters.

ALICE: David. You've finished work already?

DAVID: *Maa'mi.* I have left Baba Tailor.

ALICE picks up her slipper.

DAVID: The man is using me!

ALICE: It is the man's business. He is not going to promote you over his flesh and blood. You are going back.

DAVID: I've learned all I need to know.

ALICE: And how will you set yourself up without a certificate of apprenticeship?

DAVID: I'm not going back.

ALICE raises her slipper to hit him.

ENGLISHWOMAN passes by. The traders beckon to her.

TRADERS: Madam! Madam! Buy from me! Madam! Madam!

ALICE: Madam! Buy from me! Madam!

ENGLISHWOMAN buys food stuff from a produce stall.

ALICE: See. *Oyinbo* forces the traders to sell at controlled price, they hoard their goods and now it is only *oyinbo* who can

18 Quick

afford to buy at inflated prices. I want to go into food trade. How can I when the money I would have used to pay the guild fees I've spent it on your apprenticeship. And now you want to throw it away?

ENGLISHWOMAN exits.

DAVID: You always say that I should fight for my right.

ALICE: But you must pick your battles. Courage without wisdom is foolhardiness. (*To the trader next to her.*) Mama! Watch my stall for me.

They walk over to BABA TAILOR's stall. BABA TAILOR is reading a telegram.

ALICE: (*Curtseys.*) Baba, oh.

BABA TAILOR: Ah, Mama David. How are you?

ALICE: We are fine, thank you, Baba. (*Sees the telegram. Worried.*) Hope no problem?

BABA TAILOR: Ah, no, oh. My son is well. He wanted me to know that he has sent me two pounds through his friend.

ALICE: May God give him good health to continue providing for you.

BABA TAILOR: Amen.

ALICE: (*Kneels.*) Baba, I've come because of David. (*Shoves DAVID forward.*) He realises how badly he has offended you. (*To DAVID.*) Oya, do bale![19]

DAVID: (*Prostrates.*) I'm sorry, Baba.

BABA TAILOR: Get up, both of you.

They get up.

BABA TAILOR: I cannot take him back.

ALICE: Ah, Baba!

BABA TAILOR: My son was brought up by his mother (*Waves the telegram.*) yet he is a responsible man.

ALICE: (*Kneels, brings out money from within the folds of her wrapper.*) This will cover part of the arrears.

BABA TAILOR: I don't want your money.

ALICE: No, Baba. I will pay what I owe.

BABA TAILOR: David didn't tell you. He called me a thief.

19   Prostrate!

ALICE: David, is this true? Ehn? Baba, please.

BABA TAILOR: I'm sorry but your son is not worth the trouble. *(Goes inside.)*

ALICE: *(Pushes DAVID in the head.)* See what you've done? You allowed that pompous fool to call me a bad parent.

DAVID: It is not my fault/

ALICE: Shut up! When will you learn? What do I do with you now, *n'tori Olorun.*[20]

DAVID: I will find a way, *Maa'mi.* It's time I became the man of the house.

SCENE TWO

DAVID cutting grass. The sound of a tennis match offstage. CHIKE dashes in.

DAVID: *(Points to his watch.)* Chike.

CHIKE: Sorry, Yankee. I got delayed at the port. I went to see off my friend Ade/

DAVID: I beg cut grass!

They cut the lawn. DAVID keeps looking at the tennis players.

DAVID: Man, this is real *akushe*[21] work.

A tennis ball rolls past DAVID.

CHIKE: If you know any better work for grammar school drop outs, let me know.

VOICE: Boy! Ball!

DAVID ignores them. CHIKE throws back the ball. DAVID stops working to look at the tennis players.

DAVID: Look at them enjoying life in our country.

CHIKE: I didn't get you this job to get us fired. Bend down.

DAVID reluctantly continues cutting.

CHIKE: You know who I met at the port? Sanusi. He's working there as a clerk.

DAVID: Sanusi?

CHIKE: His uncle is a supervisor there.

20 for God's sake
21   worthless toil

DAVID: Why should I struggle when a dullard can walk into any job because of his family connections?

CHIKE: That is his luck, Yankee. Me, I'm biding my time. Once I save enough money I'm off to the UK.

DAVID: Ngh-ngh! Chike! Are you going to swim there?

CHIKE: Only an idiot will buy a ticket. My friend bribed Sanusi to let him get on a ship.

The ball rolls past them.

VOICE: Boy! Ball!

CHIKE throws back the ball.

DAVID: Who do you know in UK?

CHIKE: My landlord's son, Kayode. He's been there for three years now.

DAVID: Are there good jobs there?

CHIKE: *Boku*[22]. Kayode started work the very day he arrived. *Oyinbo* doesn't do man know man. They put the right person in the right job.

DAVID: Ehn?

CHIKE: You can study part-time for a certificate. When you return to Lagos they will make you a manager straightaway.

DAVID: But the UK, *loun-loun.*[23]

CHIKE: Yankee is talking of long journey! First you are at Yaba, next you are at Obalende.

DAVID: It's not like travelling overseas.

CHIKE: Think about it. You can be sexing all those white women that you see in your films.

The ball rolls across the stage.

VOICE: Boy! Ball!

ADE enters, despondent. He is wearing a suit and with his suitcase. He throws the ball back.

CHIKE: Ade! What happened?

---

22 Plenty.
23 so far away. Colloquially, 'far, far'.

ADE: This one-eyed sailor caught me just before the ship left the harbour. Ah! I nearly made it.

DAVID: This is the guy you were talking about?

CHIKE: Yes. Ade, this is David.

ADE is too distressed to acknowledge DAVID.

CHIKE: I'll meet you at your place.

ADE: And let the whole neighbourhood see me? I will stay here until nightfall.

CHIKE: The members will complain. I'll take you to my place. David, I'll be back soon.

ADE: I was like Moses seeing the Promised Land. I have to try again, man. I have to try again…

CHIKE leads ADE away. DAVID looks after them. The ball rolls across the stage.

VOICE: Boy! Ball!

PERKINS enters. He picks up the ball and throws it back.

DAVID: In history they taught us about the British Empire. You Empire Boys were our heroes. You civilised us. And for that it was your right to eat the best of my country because that was how you lived in the UK, like kings. And I believed it. I could be a man of my own making. I could live like a king. Then I came here. I saw poor white people. When I think of how I struggled to get here, the family and friends I left behind… (*Yawns.*)

PERKINS extracts a photograph form his wallet. He shows it to DAVID.

PERKINS: That's Mrs Perkins. That's my daughter.

DAVID smiles at the photograph. He hands it back to PERKINS.

DAVID: You miss them, don't you?

PERKINS: Tell me more about your life in Nigeria.

DAVID: *(Tired.)* Another time.

PERKINS: Another time, then.

SCENE THREE

August 1968. The Bridal House doorway. DAVID lies down. He covers himself with his newspapers and falls asleep.

KITCHING and ELLERKER enter.

ELLERKER: Park van round corner.

JONES: *(Off.)* Yes, sir.

KITCHING: Tell Roberts to stick me in for oh one hundred hours. I'll come check on him when I can.

JONES: *(Off.)* Yes, Sarge.

KITCHING's radio goes off. He fiddles with it. ELLERKER points to the right switch. KITCHING switches on the receiver.

KITCHING: *(Into the radio.)* What! … Kitching receiving. Over.

RADIO: What's your current location? Over.

KITCHING: I'm on Headrow. Over.

RADIO: All right. Over and out.

KITCHING fiddles with the radio. ELLERKER points to the right switch. KITCHING switches off the receiver and puts it away.

ELLERKER: You'll soon get the hang of it.

KITCHING: Spying on us. What's the world coming to when police can't trust their own?

ELLERKER: Not a dosser in sight. We keep this up and who knows what will come out of it.

KITCHING: Hope yer get yer promotion. I'm fed up hearing yer going on.

ELLERKER: You'd miss me.

KITCHING: Not bloody likely.

ELLERKER: You should be more like me, Kitching.

KITCHING: I can think of better places to be than up Chief Superintendent's arse.

ELLERKER: I'm a working class lad, too. There's nowt wrong with being ambitious.

KITCHING: S'why yer got such a complex.

ELLERKER: I have not.

KITCHING: You're not used to heights. Come back down to earth like the rest of us.

ELLERKER: Rubbish. Why should only the ponces sit at the high table? You ever ask yourself that?

KITCHING: No, and I don't care to know.

ELLERKER: It's all about power, Kitching. It's all about the big picture.

KITCHING: I said I don't want to hear it.

ELLERKER: My first day at grammar school, I'd never seen my father so proud. His son was going onto higher things. He hated people saying, 'he's done well for himself, considering'. 'Considering what?' He'd ask. 'Get your education,' he told me, 'Get your education and you'll have no excuses. The only moaner is an envious moaner.'

KITCHING: I am not envious. And I'm certainly not a moaner.

ELLERKER: No. You're just happy to be the king of your little castle. Millgarth's a stepping stone far as I'm concerned. Chasing vagrants and gypos isn't what I intend to spend my career doing.

KITCHING: *(Sees DAVID.)* Bloody hell. *(Nudges DAVID violently with his boot.)* Didn't I arrest yer last month?

DAVID: Uh?

KITCHING: Get up! *(Hauls DAVID up.)*

DAVID: I'm only having a nap.

ELLERKER: What's he saying?

KITCHING: What did I tell yer?

DAVID: You said I should keep away from the shopping area.

KITCHING: What the fuck are yer doing here then?

DAVID: I don't have anywhere else to go.

ELLERKER: What?

DAVID: I said I don't have anywhere else to go.

KITCHING: Stop swaying.

DAVID: I was sleeping. You woke me up/

KITCHING: Slap yerself.

DAVID: What?

ELLERKER: Sergeant.

KITCHING: Are you deaf? I said slap yerself.

   DAVID taps his cheek.

KITCHING: I'll do it for yer.

   DAVID slaps himself.

KITCHING: Harder.

   DAVID slaps himself harder.

KITCHING: Now, pack yer rubbish and shove off.

DAVID: This is my skip.

KITCHING: You what?

DAVID: This is my skip.

KITCHING: Jones!

   JONES enters.

KITCHING: Bring van round. I'll show yer where yer skip is.

   PERKINS and JONES.

JONES: *(To PERKINS.)* That night I drove them to Bramhope, six miles out from Leeds. Along the way Kitching made David bang his head on the floor of the van. Ellerker wasn't keen on it at first.

PERKINS: At first?

JONES: Sergeant Kitching asked Inspector Ellerker to join in. David started effing and blinding. Sergeant told David to shut up but he wouldn't. Sergeant punched him. Then the inspector hit him too.

PERKINS: So it was both Kitching and Ellerker who assaulted David? You're sure of this?

JONES: Yes sir.

PERKINS: What happened when you got to Bramhope?

JONES: We chucked him out then drove back to Leeds. Thought they'd seen the last of him. They were right capped to see David a few days later in doorway of Bridal House.

PERKINS: What did they do when they saw him?

JONES: Sergeant Kitching laid into him. Inspector Ellerker joined in from the start.

Inside the police car. JONES is driving. ELLERKER is in the front seat. KITCHING is in the back seat with DAVID.

DAVID: Where are you taking me?

ELLERKER: How about Middleton Woods this time?

KITCHING: Feel right at home there.

DAVID: Home?

ELLERKER: Yes. We're taking you home.

ELLERKER and KITCHING smirk at each other.

KITCHING: We'll just about make the last ship.

ELLERKER: See, we're not so bad.

KITCHING: You'll see your Mam again. Still alive, is she?

DAVID: *Maa'mi*? Yes. She's still alive.

ELLERKER: Been a while, though. She'll have forgotten what you look like. When we get to ship, first we'll get you cleaned up.

KITCHING: And you'll get some food down you. You must be starving.

DAVID: Yes, yes. Thank you.

KITCHING: Bet you can smell your home cooking already.

DAVID: I'm going home.

KITCHING: Yes you are.

DAVID: I'm going home. I'm going home. *(Looks out of the window.)*

JONES: We're here.

DAVID: *(Peers out of the window.)* This isn't the port.

JONES stops. ELLERKER and KITCHING get out.

DAVID: You said you were taking me to the port.

KITCHING: Out.

DAVID: *(Holds on.)* Please, you said you wouldn't do this to me again.

KITCHING: Get out!

DAVID: No! Take me back.

ELLERKER and KITCHING drag DAVID out of the car. They shove him to the ground. KITCHING throws the briefcase on the ground and stamps on it.

ELLERKER: This will keep happening to you if you don't keep away from the city centre.

DAVID: *(Stands up.)* You bastards! Why do you keep doing this to me?

KITCHING: Shut up.

DAVID: What have I done to you?

KITCHING: I said shut up! *(Shoves him violently.)*

DAVID falls to the ground. He springs back up.

DAVID: You bastards! You fucking bastards!

KITCHING approaches. ELLERKER holds him back.

KITCHING: One for the road.

ELLERKER shrugs. KITCHING punches DAVID. DAVID crumples to the ground.

KITCHING: Make sure you don't come back this time.

ELLERKER and KITCHING exit. JONES looks helplessly at DAVID. He exits.

DAVID checks his briefcase. It is broken. He sees a duffel bag. He transfers his belongings from the briefcase into it.

DAVID: I made my way back to the city centre to my usual spot.

PERKINS: Why? You know they'd only find you there.

DAVID: I had to sleep somewhere.

PERKINS: A sensible person would have/

DAVID: I walked six miles back from the middle of nowhere. I couldn't ask for directions because people stared at me as if I was some kind of animal. Who should have been afraid – them or me? So don't tell me about what a sensible person would have done.

PERKINS: Forget what I said.

DAVID: Yes. You're just like the rest of them.

PERKINS: *(Grabs DAVID by the lapel.)* Since I started this case I haven't set eyes on my family. I get dirty stares from people on the street just because they recognise me from my photograph in the papers. Don't get me started on the grief I get from the force. And I'm 'like the rest of them'?

DAVID bites PERKINS.

PERKINS: Ah! What did you do that for? (*Rubs his hand.*)

DAVID: When they saw me back in town they beat me up so badly. I was crying like a baby. They wouldn't stop so I bit Ellerker's hand and held on. Kitching came at me. I got a piece of him too. I did enough damage to stop them from hitting me until the Panda car arrived. I didn't bite you that hard.

PERKINS: *(Stops rubbing his hand.)* So you got your own back.

DAVID: But it wasn't enough. I was so angry. I had to put a stop to it.

SCENE FOUR

Citizens Advice Bureau. DAVID walks in wearily. He sits down in front of CASE OFFICER. She has pen and paper at the ready.

DAVID: I want to make a complaint.

CASE OFFICER: I'm only preparing you for your case.

DAVID: The two officers are the ones I want to report.

CASE OFFICER: David, you're up on charges for assaulting them.

DAVID: I was defending myself. *(Shows her his wounds.)* See what they did to me.

CASE OFFICER: So you don't deny that you bit them.

DAVID: They wanted to carry me back to Robin Hood Forest.

CASE OFFICER: Where?

DAVID: Robin Hood Forest, now! What for? The Bridal House does not belong to them. Why should they keep forcing me to move?

CASE OFFICER: Vagrancy is an offense, David.

DAVID: The owner does not complain. He greets me 'Morning, George'.

CASE OFFICER: Who's George?

DAVID: I'm George!

CASE OFFICER: All right.

DAVID: He left me a blanket. The police burned it. That is vandalism.

CASE OFFICER: It's nearly impossible to make a case of harassment against the police, especially a man with your record. Magistrates don't look kindly on people who assault a police officer. You've always pleaded guilty every time you've been charged. Why is this time any different?

DAVID: They took me away against my will to Robin Hood Forest.

CASE OFFICER: This Forest. I advise you not to mention it in court. Even I haven't a clue what you're on about. And without proof you have no case.

DAVID: Two times they carried me away. Two times!

CASE OFFICER: They needed medical treatment.

DAVID: I was in hospital, too.

CASE OFFICER: They claim you were violent, that they used reasonable force to restrain you.

DAVID: You are on their side. You are defending them.

CASE OFFICER: I'm preparing you for your court appearance, David.

DAVID: Yes, and I will have my day in court. You will see.

SCENE FIVE

Millgarth. The mess room. KITCHING and ELLERKER holding court. The officers laugh.

KITCHING: … You should have seen him when he took stand. Magistrate didn't have a clue what he were on about. I nearly shit myself when he said we took him to Robin Hood Forest.

ELLERKER: Kept banging on. Magistrate had to tell him to shut it or he'd be held in contempt.

HARWOOD: Uggy could have had you there.

ELLERKER: Not a chance. Even his brief didn't understand him. It were a right farce.

ELLERKER gestures to HARWOOD. HARWOOD searches through the files.

HARWOOD: How long's he down for this time?

KITCHING: Twelve week.

HARWOOD: Got no one to play with now.

KITCHING: When he's out, spread word to shift: anyone sees him, report to Inspector Ellerker or to me. Don't arrest him. Don't move him on. You got that?

HARWOOD: *(Looks to ELLERKER. ELLERKER nods. Uneasily.)* Aye.

ELLERKER: Looks like you'll be getting used to those radios after all.

JONES enters. The officers cheer.

ELLERKER: Congratulations Police Constable Jones. Feel like a real officer of Leeds City Police now?

JONES: I'm still in a daze.

ELLERKER: You've a bright future ahead of you if you play your cards right.

JONES: You think so sir?

HARWOOD hands ELLERKER some files.

ELLERKER: Absolutely. *(Exits.)*

HARWOOD: *(Takes the rest of the files.)* Your boy's a man, now, Kitching. *(Exits after ELLERKER.)*

KITCHING: Keep your head down and do what's expected of you.

JONES: Yes, Sarge. Sarge?

KITCHING: Yes PC Jones.

JONES: Over at head office, I heard talk of a West Yorkshire force. Something about us being merged with Bradford and West Riding/

KITCHING: Hearsay. Pay no notice.

JONES: Sounded serious.

KITCHING: Think anyone in their right mind would want to have anything to do with those donkey wallopers?

JONES: No Sarge. Sarge.

KITCHING: What now, Jones?

JONES: Thanks Sarge.

> *KITCHING smiles at JONES.*

SCENE SIX

KAYODE standing outside, having a cigarette break. DAVID limps by.
KAYODE is shocked by his appearance.

KAYODE: David!

DAVID: Kayode!

KAYODE: David… How are you?

DAVID: My man, I'm fine. What of you?

KAYODE: I'm OK. Ah, David.

DAVID: Kayode! What's been happening?

KAYODE: My wife and I have just bought a house in
Chapeltown.

DAVID: Congrats. An Englishman's house is his castle, not so?

KAYODE: Come inside for a few minutes.

DAVID: *(Stays where he is.)* Kayus-Daddy! What of Chike? And
Ade? How are my guys doing?

KAYODE: I've lost touch with Ade. Chike's not speaking to me
any more.

DAVID: Ah, why now?

KAYODE: The war.

DAVID: War? Which war?

KAYODE: Biafra now, David. Where have you been?

> *PC JONES enters.*

DAVID: *(Sees him, cowers.)* They have come, oh!

KAYODE: Who has come?

DAVID: Don't let him see me. He will carry me to forest and
beat me.

KAYODE: David.

> *JONES sees DAVID.*

JONES: Hello Uggy. You on your best behaviour?

KAYODE: He's fine, officer.

JONES reluctantly gets on his radio as he exits.

KAYODE: Why did you run from him, David?

DAVID: You don't know them, Kayode.

KAYODE: He's a police officer.

DAVID: I say you don't know them!

KAYODE: OK, OK. Have a cup of tea. Don't you want to hear about the girls?

DAVID: *(Lights up.)* How are they?

KAYODE: They grow so fast. Tinu is taller than you now.

DAVID: They have become women! Don't let any cheeky boys near them.

KAYODE: Especially boys with Yankee-style trousers, eh?

DAVID: You called me by my name! Yankee Doodle, man. See my trousers. Two back pockets…

KAYODE: That's you, man.

DAVID: Yankee Doodle. I can still jive. (*Dances.*) Eh? Eh?

Bell rings.

KAYODE: Will I see you tomorrow?

DAVID: You owe me a cup of tea.

KAYODE: Take care, David. *(Exits.)*

DAVID: *(Dances.)* Yankee Doodle.

JONES enters with KITCHING and ELLERKER. KITCHING pats JONES on the back.

SCENE SEVEN

PERKINS and WPC MEG HARRIS. She is heavily pregnant.

PERKINS: I hear congratulations are in order.

MEG: Thank you.

PERKINS: Never mind what they say about boys. Girls are the most trouble.

MEG: I should hope not.

PERKINS: How's life outside the force?

MEG: Grand. Wouldn't dream of going back.

PERKINS: Thank you for coming forward. I'm interested in the period after David Oluwale bit Kitching and Ellerker. You were present when they brought him in the next time they met him.

MEG: I weren't the only one there.

PERKINS: You're not being charged with anything.

MEG: I know. I'm sorry I didn't mean to/

PERKINS: That's all right. I just want your recollections of what happened that day.

MEG: Sergeant Kitching and Inspector Ellerker used to brag openly about how they had David's number, how they knew where to find him because he kept going back to the same places to sleep every night.

PERKINS: Go on.

Millgarth station. A loud bang. DAVID tumbles head first into the station followed by ELLERKER and KITCHING. ELLERKER kicks DAVID in the groin. DAVID clutches his groin, screaming in agony. KITCHING and ELLERKER lift him up and slam him face down on the counter.

ELLERKER: *(His face in DAVID's face.)* Bite me again. Bite me again.

KITCHING: *(Drags DAVID up by the rosary beads.)* As a Catholic you should know all about penance. *(Bangs DAVID's head on the counter repeatedly.)* You should know never to bite an officer of the law because there are consequences if you do that. You will pay penance.

ELLERKER notices the other officers looking away.

KITCHING: *(Bangs DAVID's head on the counter.)* Going to bite me now, yer black bastard? Going to bite me now?

ELLERKER: Sergeant…

KITCHING keeps banging DAVID's head on the counter.

KITCHING: Come on, let's see those fangs of yours.

ELLERKER: Sergeant!

ELLERKER pushes KITCHING off DAVID.

ELLERKER: Not here.

They drag DAVID off. His crying can still be heard.

MEG: I never saw a grown man cry so much. Normally he'd fight back. He were always defiant which would rile them up some more. But that day he gave up. Like there were nothing left in him.

PERKINS: Was David treated like this every time he was brought in to Millgarth?

MEG: He were treated in the usual manner when other officers brought him in. It were only when Kitching and Ellerker were on duty that he had it bad.

PERKINS: How many other officers were on duty at the time of this assault?

MEG hesitates.

PERKINS: You don't have to cover up for your former colleagues.

MEG: There were always officers around when they brought David in. That day were no different. Some nights I can still hear his screams. There were times when I made myself believe it were his fault. He should have left city centre. The initiatives were meant to stop things like that happening. But it were the same old Millgarth. See all, hear all, say nowt. *(Exits.)*

DAVID enters.

PERKINS: Why didn't you appeal to the other officers?

DAVID: Does the corn complain to the hen about the cock? You're still thinking it.

PERKINS: I'm not thinking anything.

DAVID: Back in London when you finish work you go home, right? Your children welcome you. Your wife kisses you hello, has your meal ready. You feel safe. The Bridal House was my home.

PERKINS: So what made you move away from it in the end?

DAVID: I remembered my mother's advice. Pick your battles. Maybe that was why I was being punished.

PERKINS: They had no right to touch you.

DAVID: A child who forgets his parents loses his way.

PERKINS: You're the victim here. Never forget that.

DAVID: Moving changed nothing. It was as if they knew my every move. Wherever I slept, within seconds they'd arrive.

PERKINS: They had their officers watching out for you, David.

DAVID: I never wrote home. Not even to say that I had arrived safely. There was always a reason. I never made enough money. I hadn't settled down.

PERKINS: Wherever your mother is I'm sure she's forgiven you.

DAVID: I forgot her, Perkins.

PERKINS: My father had a compass. It was the last thing Grandfather gave him before he passed away. He put it up on the mantelpiece next to Grandfather's picture and warned me never to touch it. I never knew my grandfather. I thought if I held the compass and said some magic word his picture would come to life. So I get a chair and climb up to reach it. Just as it's in my hand, father walks in. Next thing I knew the compass was in pieces all over the floor. He looked at me for a minute while I stood there petrified. Without a word he bent down and picked up all the pieces and put it back next to Grandfather's picture. He touched my head and said, 'don't worry, son. I won't leave you before my time.'

DAVID: To fathers who understand their children's greatest fears.

PERKINS: And to mothers who forgive their children everything.

DAVID: To mothers.

PERKINS: So.

DAVID: I had to get away from them. I could only do that by getting off the streets.

PROBATION OFFICER enters and sits down. DAVID sits down opposite her.

PROBATION OFFICER: It can't help your case if you keep getting yourself arrested.

DAVID: It's the police. They keep arresting me.

PROBATION OFFICER: I'm busy, David. Keep it short.

DAVID: I need accommodation. But every house I go they say, 'no vacancy'.

PROBATION OFFICER: Have you tried the hostels?

DAVID: I tried all of them. They say I cannot stay with them.

PROBATION OFFICER: I'll look into it for you. Anything else?

DAVID: The magistrate has taken all my money.

PROBATION OFFICER: Just serve the sentence instead when next you're in trouble.

DAVID: I said I didn't cause any trouble. Why should they lock me up?

PROBATION OFFICER: I can't help you if you keep going on like that.

DAVID: Give me a pound.

PROBATION OFFICER: I'll try to find you a hostel.

DAVID: OK, ten shillings for food. Ten shillings.

PROBATION OFFICER: I'm not the dole office, David.

DAVID: In my country we don't treat you people like this. If *oyinbo* is in the queue we escort you to the front. We carry your bags. We welcome you into our homes.

PROBATION OFFICER: Have you thought of returning home?

DAVID: Am I going to swim there?

PROBATION OFFICER: There is a scheme, if you're interested. I can get you the application to fill in.

DAVID: I go to police station, I fill paper. I go to court, I fill paper. What is the result?

PROBATION OFFICER: There'll be someone there to help you fill in the form.

DAVID: Like as you are helping me now? *(Leaves. Mutters to himself.)* Fill form, fill form, go here, go there…

PROBATION OFFICER exits.

DAVID and PERKINS stand outside John Peters' Furniture shop. It has a deep doorway.

PERKINS: You went back to the city centre?

DAVID: Yes. *(Goes to the John Peters doorway.)* But not to just any shop. *(Taps his head, presents the shop doorway to PERKINS.)* See?

PERKINS: It's a shop doorway, David.

DAVID: No one can see me unless they come right inside. I'll be safe here. *(Goes into the doorway, out of sight of the audience.)*

JONES enters, patrolling the streets. He walks into the doorway and sees DAVID. He makes to radio but doesn't. The radio goes on. The voice of another PC. He makes to walk away.

KITCHING enters.

KITCHING: Why is it I heard about David from PC Short?

JONES looks away.

ELLERKER enters.

ELLERKER: I'm not too late, am I?

KITCHING: *(Points to the doorway.)* He's smart. I'll give him that.

ELLERKER: *(To JONES.)* Give us your staff. Quickly! You'll get it back.

JONES hands over his truncheon. KITCHING draws his truncheon.

KITCHING: *(To JONES.)* I'll deal with you later.

ELLERKER and KITCHING go into the doorway.

KITCHING: Hello Playmate.

They beat DAVID. DAVID screams.

JONES shudders. He agonises whether to go into the doorway. He exits.

DAVID runs out of the doorway clutching his head.

KITCHING and ELLERKER chase after him.

Darkness. The sound of waves lapping against the shore. Then a loud splash.

SCENE EIGHT

1949. DAVID at home.

DAVID packing his things. ALICE comes in with a load of yam tubers.

DAVID: *Maa'mi*! I cannot carry all that!

ALICE: The *gari* won't be enough for the journey.

DAVID: *(Puts the yams down.)* I cannot cook the yam on the ship.

ALICE: Won't you eat when you reach the UK? *(Goes through his bags.)*

DAVID: Oh Lord! I will miss the ship.

ALICE: You remember what I told you? *(Gives him rosary beads.)*

DAVID: Yes, *Maa'mi* – Don't wander about. Don't do anything that will bring disgrace to our family. Don't put myself in harm's way.

ALICE takes out money from her wrapper and hands it over to DAVID.

DAVID: *Maa'mi*!

ALICE: Take!

DAVID: *(Takes the money.)* I will send you my first salary. I don't care if I starve.

ALICE: You will not starve! Let us pray. *Ni oruko Jesu.²⁴*

DAVID: *Ami*! *(In between the prayer, DAVID responds appropriately with Ami,²⁵ Ase,²⁶ and Ami ni oruko Jesu²⁷.)*

ALICE: The most heartfelt prayer of all is a mother's prayer for her child. No woman bears a child to lose him to the world. David Oluwadamisi Oluwole, you will go safely and return to me safely. It shall be well with you. Your path will be straight. You will not miss your way. A thousand may fall right beside you and ten thousand at your right hand. David, you shall not fall. The sun shall not smite you by day, nor the moon by night. *Ori buruku aisan koni pade 'e.²⁸* You will not fall ill. You will not go mad. You will not be disabled. The wicked shall look for you but they shall not

---

24 In Jesus' name.
25 Amen
26 Amen
27 Amen, in Jesus' name
28 You won't fall ill.

266

find you. Your head shall be raised above your enemies. You will find favour in the UK. You will find success in the King's Country. You will come back to me. David you will come back to me safe and sound, in Jesus' name I pray. Amen.

DAVID: *Ami, ami, ami o, Jesu.*

ALICE: Go well, my son.

SCENE NINE

1969. Millgarth. The Parade. KITCHING addressing the officers, including JONES.

KITCHING: Keep an eye out on Boar Lane. There's been recurring incidence of vandalism. I'm posting extra men in and around Elland Road after the game. I don't want a repeat of last Saturday… And our dear playmate Uggy's body was fished out of River Aire yesterday afternoon.

POLICEMAN 1: Have to find another playmate now.

POLICEMAN 2: *(Joking.)* You didn't by any chance push him in, Sarge?

KITCHING: I'm going to miss the filthy bugger.

POLICEMAN 3: That's not a teardrop is it, Sarge?

KITCHING: Those on duty for Saturday's game: Jones, Frederick, Henry, Smith …

Fade out on KITCHING and the other officers.

PC JONES stands to one side. ELLERKER enters, gives JONES his truncheon, pats him on the back and exits. JONES inspects his truncheon. He hands the truncheon to PERKINS. PERKINS inspects the truncheon and hands it back to JONES. JONES exits.

DAVID: I shared a pauper's grave, my misspelt name on the tombstone. Abandoned in death in a land I called home for twenty years, longing for Lagos that was really no more than a memory. Then you came along.

PERKIN: It was PC Jones who reported the matter. He'd just completed his probation. He wasn't quite part of the team.

DAVID: A bit like you. I still don't understand. Why risk everything for me?

PERKINS: The job gets you. The more you work a case the more you get to know all the characters involved. You replay scenarios over and over until you can see it as clearly as if you were there when it happened. Emotion shouldn't come into it but it does. You feel what's right and what's not, who's guilty and who's innocent. You realise it isn't about justice being impartial. Emotion, instinct, it's all you've got to go on to cut through the fog.

SCENE TEN

1970. PERKINS interviews KITCHING.

KITCHING: I treated David Oluwale no different from how I treated all the other dossers in town.

PERKINS: Did you ever beat him?

KITCHING: Yes.

PERKINS: Just once or on several occasions?

KITCHING: You had to be on your guard around him. He was violent and a repeat offender. You can't deal with his kind any other way.

PERKINS: According to the records you and Ellerker encountered him quite a bit.

KITCHING: Stands to reason. He were always causing trouble on our patch.

PERKINS: So you must have given it to him every time you met him.

KITCHING: I'd tickle him with me boot.

PERKINS: What do you mean, tickle?

KITCHING: I'd nudge him with me boot to get him moving. Not every time I met him. Only when necessary but I never battered him.

PERKINS: You told the other officers that any time they saw Oluwale they were to inform you and Inspector Ellerker.

KITCHING: I didn't want to endanger me officers. He were a special case.

PERKINS: So you took a special interest in him.

KITCHING: I just wanted him off me patch.

PERKINS: Is it normal for an inspector to spend so much time with one sergeant during a shift?

KITCHING: You'll have to ask Inspector Ellerker.

PERKINS: All right so you wanted him out of the city centre. Is that the reason why you and Inspector Ellerker took him out of Leeds on two separate occasions?

KITCHING: We had to make it clear to him that we didn't want him on our patch.

PERKINS: And you were manning your patch in the early hours of 18 April 1969. You were on Call Lane.

KITCHING: I were nowhere near the place.

PERKINS: So you didn't see David Oluwale that night in the John Peters' doorway?

KITCHING: No.

PERKINS: You and Ellerker didn't chase him down towards the river?

KITCHING: No.

PERKINS: You're saying you were not the last person to see David alive?

KITCHING: You think I pushed him in. I touched that animal only if I 'ad ter. He bit me and he bit Inspector Ellerker. You could smell 'im a mile away. He were always covered in shit and piss. You think I wanted to spend me shift running after 'im? I saved a man! Pulled him out of that same river at risk to me own life. I got a medal for it. That's the kind of officer I am.

PERKINS: I'll ask you again. Where were you on the morning of eighteen April nineteen sixty-nine between the hours of 4.30 a.m. and 5.30 a.m.?

KITCHING: I don't remember.

PERKINS: You don't remember. Your fellow officers seem to remember a lot.

KITCHING: You'll have to be more specific, sir.

PERKINS: About that night. About several other occasions when you weren't that kind of officer.

KITCHING: I don't suffer fools. Many of them don't like it that I run a tight ship.

PERKINS: So you deny ever being drunk on duty?

KITCHING: I do not recall ever being drunk on duty.

PERKINS: You've never been drunk with Inspector Ellerker?

KITCHING: Inspector Ellerker and I have had a drink together, yes. You don't refuse a drink with your inspector.

PERKINS: So why is it that the whole of your Group confirm that on one occasion you were so plastered that you were laid out in the market?

KITCHING: That is not true. They are out to get me. They hate it that I refuse to accept slovenly behaviour.

PERKINS: They're turning on you because you're a hypocrite. A thuggish hypocrite.

KITCHING: Where do you get off?

PERKIN: No. Where do you get off/

KITCHING: Coming up 'ere like a knight in shining armour/

PERKINS: What gives you the right to treat a man like an animal/

KITCHING: Thinking yer better than me/

PERKINS: What gives you the right! What gives you the right!

KITCHING: I've nothing more to say.

PERKINS: We'll be seeing each other again, Sergeant Kitching.

KITCHING exits.

DAVID: He confessed! He confessed to beating me!

ELLERKER enters.

DAVID: His colleague has confessed. He will confess too.

PERKINS: Inspector Ellerker, where were you on the night of 18 April 1969?

DAVID: Answer him, now.

PERKINS: Were you and Sergeant Kitching not by the doorway of John Peters Furniture Shop between the hours of 4.30 a.m. and 5.30 a.m.? Inspector Ellerker/

ELLERKER: Your investigation is the result of rumour and speculation against me. That is why I am not prepared to answer your questions.

PERKINS: Suit yourself. You'll have your day in court.

DAVID: Rumour and speculation. *(Shows him a bruise on his face.)* Does this look like rumour and speculation? *(Pulls up his shirt to reveal bruises.)*

PERKINS drags DAVID away.

DAVID: He must confess! Let him confess!

PERKINS: It's all right, David.

DAVID: Bramhope, Middleton Woods, Millgarth, the Bridal House, John Peters!

PERKINS: I've got this David! Two witnesses are willing to testify that they saw you being chased down Call Lane towards the river. We've got them David. We've got them.

DAVID: Penance. Make them do penance.

SCENE ELEVEN

January 1971. London. PERKINS and the DIRECTOR OF PUBLIC PROSECUTIONS.

PERKINS: *(Reads from a file.)* After concluding the investigation I have no doubt that David Oluwale was hounded by Inspector Geoffrey Ellerker and Sergeant Ken Kitching. This campaign of violence culminated in the assault on David Oluwale around 3 a.m. on 18 April 1969. David Oluwale fled from the scene holding his head. This was the last sighting of David Oluwale alive. Sergeant Kitching had made false entries into his duty-book for the crucial hour between 4.30 a.m. and 5.30 a.m. Inspector Ellerker claimed to have lost his duty-book. In my opinion there is evidence to suggest that Inspector Ellerker and Sergeant Kitching had continued their pursuit of David Oluwale down to Warehouse Hill and as a result David Oluwale had jumped or had been forced to jump into the river. These despicable individuals had little or no regard for Oluwale as a human being and as such they actively desired to get him out of Leeds. My investigation has also led me to a systematic failure by the social service to aid a vulnerable person/

DPP: What are we looking at?

PERKINS: Murder.

DPP: We have no hard evidence that they killed Oluwale. We only have staffroom gossip from a group of officers who stood by and watched the poor bugger get beaten up time and again. God knows how they'll stand up as witnesses in court.

PERKINS: My two witnesses who saw them chasing David on the night/

DPP: They couldn't identify the officers as Kitching and Ellerker, or whether the person they were chasing was coloured. Manslaughter.

PERKINS: They hounded the man. They were the only ones in that area on that night who would have wanted him dead.

DPP: No jury will convict for murder, not on the evidence we've got. Manslaughter, assault occasioning actual bodily harm and assault occasioning grievous bodily harm.

PERKINS is crestfallen.

DPP: Chin up, Perkins. You did a great job. After this is over, take some leave. It couldn't have been easy, what you did. Oluwale was no angel. Defence will have a field day with the character testimonies.

PERKINS: He's not the one going on trial.

DPP: I know. But he could have made himself more agreeable as a person. Certainly would make my job easier.

PERKINS: I don't think that was the utmost thing on his mind, sir.

DPP: No, I suppose not. Thankfully this should be a quick trial.

PERKINS: You will do your best, sir?

DPP: You should know not to bring your emotions into a case. What you have in common with Oluwale beats me. Take a break, Perkins. Be with your family.

SCENE TWELVE

November 1971. Courtroom. KITCHING and ELLERKER stand before the jury. DAVID stands in between them. PERKINS stands to one side. Above a projection of the Leeds coat of arms.

JUDGE: I will direct the jury to return a verdict of 'not guilty' to the charge of manslaughter pertaining to the eighteenth of April 1969. On the other charges have you reached a verdict?

FOREPERSON: We have your honour. As to the charge of assault on 7 August 1968 we find the defendants guilty. As to the charge of assault on 4 September 1968 and 26 January 1969 we find the defendants guilty. As to the charge of assault on 10 February 1969 we find the defendant Geoff Ellerker guilty. As to the charge of Actual Bodily Harm on 18 April 1969 we find the defendants not guilty.

JUDGE: This has to be one of the sorriest cases I've presided over. No doubt David Oluwale was an undesirable character. He was filthy, violent and a repeat offender, beyond the pale of civilized society. He was the type of person you'd cross the street to avoid. But as officers of the law he was entitled to your protection. By your wicked misbehaviour you have brought disgrace to our noble force. You have given ammunition to those who are critical of the police. While you serve your sentences I hope you will dwell on your actions.

KITCHING and ELLERKER exit.

PERKINS: They got off lightly.

DAVID: Half bread is better than none.

PERKINS: There must be something I missed. Some piece of evidence I overlooked.

DAVID: They are going to prison. They will have time to repent of their sins.

PERKINS: Don't tell me you forgive them. Because if you say you forgive them then all this was for nothing.

DAVID: I cannot forgive a person who does not ask for forgiveness. That is like sharing wisdom with a fool. He will always repeat his mistakes. You've got a verdict. No one can erase it from the records. *(Extends his hand.)* Let's shake on a future without fools.

PERKINS extends his hand. Light fades on him before their hands touch. DAVID looks at his hand. He sighs.

SCENE THIRTEEN

City Centre. ALDERMAN looks around with pride. He wears both rosettes.

ALDERMAN: Close your eyes. No, you're not in Paris. You're not in Amsterdam or Rome. You're in Leeds. No car horns blaring. No foul and abusive language from rowdy youths, no streets awash with puke. And no rough sleepers. It's all down to the work of our proud police force. *(Exits.)*

A park bench in Leeds City Centre. DAVID is sitting by himself. ALICE enters.

DAVID: *Maa'mi*! *(Stands up.)*

ALICE: You wandered off again.

DAVID: I was right here. Now you are with me I will get us a beautiful house with a garden. I'm going to the labour exchange tomorrow. They say there is tailoring work. I will sew Yankee trousers. People will say, is that not Alice's son looking like John Wayne?

ALICE looks at him. DAVID feels uneasy.

I wanted to write you, *Maa'mi*. I wanted to send you money. The Queen's country is not easy. I couldn't let you to know how bad things were. Please don't look at me like that. I tried my best. But I've had enough, *Maa'mi*. I'm fed up with this country. *Ilu yi ti su mi.*[29] I want to go home.

He places his head in her chest. She cradles him.

DAVID: *Mo fe lo 'le.*[30] I want to go home. I want to go home. I want to go home…

The End.

---

29   I've had it with this country.
30   I want to go home.

IYALE (THE FIRST WIFE)
The Prequel to *The Estate*

Iyale is the prequel to *The Estate*. It was commissioned and produced by Tiata Fahodzi. The first performance was at Soho Theatre on Thursday 14 May 2009, with the following cast:

HELEN	Estella Daniels
LOMI PAKIMI	Javone Prince
CHIEF OLANREWAJU ADEYEMI	Jude Akuwudike
MRS TOYIN ADEYEMI	Antonia Okonma
SOLDIER	Chucky Venn
AFOLABI	Nick Oshikanlu
MRS OKOMILE	Marcy Oni
SOJI ADEYEMI	Tobi Bakare
YINKA ADEYEMI	Babatundé Aléshé
ARCHBISHOP BILLY ROBERTSON	Chucky Venn
ONIJUJU	Marcy Oni
K K FOLARIN	Chucky Venn

All other roles played by members of the company

Director/Choreographer, Femi Elufowoju Jr
Designer, ULTZ
Lighting Designer, Trevor Wallace
Costume Designer, Moji Bamtefa
Soundscape Designer/Composer, Simon McCorry
Fight Director, Tom Lucy
Choral Consultant, Ayo-Dele Edwards
Casting, Nadine Rennie
Assistant Director, Kolawole Oluwole
Assistant Designer, Milja Amita Kilumanga

Characters

CHIEF LANRE ADEYEMI
late fifties aka Baba Yinka (Yinka's father)

TOYIN ADEYEMI
50

YINKA ADEYEMI
mid-teens

SOJI ADEYEMI
mid-teens

PAKIMI
mid-20s

HELEN
18

AFOLABI
late 30s

SOLDIER

MRS OKOMILE
Governor's Wife

ARCHBISHOP BILLY ROBERTSON

K.K. FOLARIN

ONIJUJU

PARTY GUESTS

DOMESTIC ASSISTANTS

The play is set in 1989, Lagos, Nigeria.

Note
A / indicates an interruption.

ACT ONE

SCENE ONE

Saturday, before 9 a.m. The sitting room of the Adeyemi Mansion. In a corner there is a box of party stuff: paper plates, plastic cutlery, decorations etc. HELEN, the house-girl is in a corner on her knees with her arms raised, as a form of punishment. PAKIMI, terrified, dashes in. SOLDIER, horsewhip in hand, chases after him. HELEN runs into the kitchen, screaming. LANRE comes downstairs.

LANRE: Who is that?

PAKIMI: Chief, oh!

LANRE: Officer!

SOLDIER ignores LANRE. He continues pursuing PAKIMI.

LANRE: Officer, I'm talking to you!

SOLDIER catches PAKIMI and is about to whip him.

PAKIMI: Chief! I don die, oh!

LANRE: Touch him and I will report you to your Commanding Officer! How dare you barge into my house?

SOLDIER pauses, hatred in his eyes.

LANRE: Get out!

SOLDIER, eyeballing LANRE, exits. HELEN peeps through the kitchen door.

LANRE: I told you get the car ready. What were you doing on the street?

PAKIMI: Ess sah, he's the one/

HELEN returns to her punishment.

LANRE: Shut up! *Oloshi.*[1] Helen! Get up.

HELEN: E' sah, Madam/

LANRE: Get up!

HELEN gets up.

LANRE: Help Afolabi to clean the front yard.

HELEN curtseys. LANRE exits upstairs.

---

1   Miscreant.

HELEN: *Lomi*! You wan' die? You no fit wait make nine o'clock reach?

PAKIMI: It's because of you.

HELEN: No be me say make you comot before environmental[2] finish. You lucky say Chief dey house. Dat soldier for pieces you.

PAKIMI: I have watched Shaolin Temple. I would have given that beast of no nation. *(Makes kung fu poses and Bruce Lee exclamations).*

> *HELEN is unimpressed by PAKIMI's antics. She rubs her shoulders.*

PAKIMI: Hey, you're not grateful that I do like Amitabh Bachchan and risk my life for you, my lover. *(Sings a Bollywood love song, dances over to her and massages her shoulders.)*

HELEN: If you no disappoint me you for no need to massage me.

PAKIMI: *Nitori Olorun*,[3] Helen.

HELEN: I beg no talk *n'gbati-n'gbati* for me! You say we no go spend New Year for dis house. New Year reach, 'Oh, we go comot before Madam birthday.' Her birthday don reach, we still dey here.

PAKIMI: Once I collect my money from Benjamin we are on our way.

HELEN: Before or after Madam structurally adjust my back?

PAKIMI: *Shebi*[4] you were there when Alhaji Mukaila increased the deposit.

HELEN: When you hear say dem go increase workers salary you suppose to know say na so 'im go do.

PAKIMI: I'm not Archbishop Billy Robertson. If I could predict the future I too would be riding in Benz.

HELEN: All this your talk, 'e dey enter dis ear comot for my *nyash*[5]. All I know be say if Madam birthday meet us for here, all talk of marriage will be suspended until further

---

2   Environmental Sanitation: general cleaning that takes place once a month.
3   For the love of God
4   But
5   bottom

notice by military decree with immediate effect and automatic alacrity. You hear?

PAKIMI: Pack your load! After I leave Benjamin, straight to Alhaji Mukaila. We are moving into that flat today-today. I promise. I will not disappoint you again.

HELEN: Swear.

PAKIMI: I swear on my father's grave.

HELEN: Ah, your papa don die?

PAKIMI: On my mother's grave.

HELEN: Lomi…

PAKIMI: On my grand… On my great-great-great… Allah.

HELEN: You, eh.

They embrace. HELEN pulls PAKIMI down on the sofa.

PAKIMI: Helen!

HELEN: You too dey fear. You suppose to say one day na so we too go live. I wan' be woman of my own house like dis. You hear me?

PAKIMI: *(Anxious, eyes on the stairs.)* I hear you.

HELEN: I wan' my own duplex with swimming pool and garden.

PAKIMI: Ehen, ehen. Swimming pool and garden.

HELEN: I wan' car and driver.

PAKIMI: Car and driver. Batteries included.

HELEN: As our Mama and Papa dey pray, our children go better pass us. My parents struggle no go be in vain. I no go pass from poor to poverty.

PAKIMI: Poor to poverty. I will get it for you.

HELEN: Lomi!

PAKIMI: Sorry! In fact, I will not wait for the year 2000 before I eradicate poverty from our lives…

The sound of a police escort, followed by footsteps descending the stairs. PAKIMI dashes out through the front door. HELEN runs into the kitchen.

TOYIN and LANRE enter onto the landing. They come downstairs.

TOYIN: A soldier entering my house? You must get him sacked.

LANRE: Tell Mrs Okomile. *(Sniggers, lays Yoruba stress on the name to give it a different meaning.)* 'Oko mii lè'.[6] *(Heads for the door.)*

TOYIN: Lanre! Don't be lousy. *(Looks at the time worriedly. Follows him.)*

LANRE: What?

TOYIN: I'm coming with you.

LANRE: What about your guest?

TOYIN: My son is my priority.

LANRE: If I have gone down in your eyes, the rest of society still holds me in high regard.

TOYIN: *(Looks around for HELEN.)* Ah, this girl has released herself.

LANRE: I told her to help Afolabi clean up.

TOYIN: I punished her. She is my house-girl.

> *AFOLABI enters with MRS OKOMILE, the state governor's wife. She has a birthday card in her hand. MRS OKOMILE is in awe of being in the presence of the Adeyemis.*

AFOLABI: Mrs Okomile, Ma.

LANRE: Thank you, Afolabi.

> *AFOLABI exits.*

LANRE: Mrs Okomile, welcome.

MRS OKOMILE: Good morning Chief.

LANRE: How are you?

MRS OKOMILE: Fine Chief.

LANRE: How is the Colonel?

MRS OKOMILE: He is fine sir. He sends his greetings.

LANRE: Tell your husband he's the best governor this state has ever had. Tell him I said that.

MRS OKOMILE: I will tell him, sir.

LANRE: When I saw him standing to attention during Independence Day parade, I said, this is the hard man that

6   I have a hard on.

Lagos needs. He is no soft banana. This cocksure man will penetrate hardened criminals like Shina Rambo and have them screaming for mercy.

TOYIN cringes.

MRS OKOMILE: He is working overtime to crush the armed robbers, sir.

LANRE: Very good. Even an area like ours is no longer safe. Our neighbours the Smiths have hired Kolly Bolly[7].

MRS OKOMILE: When my husband finishes with those animals, you will not need to hire private security.

LANRE: Hm! At the rate he is going we won't want the civilians back.

MRS OKOMILE: Ah, Chief, oh! There is no going back on the transition to civil rule. The military knows its place.

LANRE: Their place is to clean up once we bloody civilians make a mess, eh.

TOYIN: Ahem.

MRS OKOMILE: Ah, good morning Ma! Many happy returns. *(Gives TOYIN the birthday card.)*

TOYIN: Thank you. Please have a seat.

MRS OKOMILE: Thank you, Ma.

They sit down.

LANRE: I am surprised though. When the General changed his title from Head of State to President I thought: this man is not going anywhere.

TOYIN: *Oya*, Baba Yinka.

MRS OKOMILE: You are on your way out, sir?

LANRE: I'm waiting for nine o' clock. Unlike you we do not have special dispensation to break the curfew.

MS OKOMILE: It's my mission, sir. It is of the utmost importance.

LANRE: It must be of the utmost importance for you to break the curfew.

TOYIN: That is what she said.

---

7   Private uniformed security firm.

LANRE: *(Testily.)* I'm emphasizing it. Like a faithful, loyal and honest citizen I will wait for nine o' clock.

TOYIN: It's time.

LANRE: It isn't! Ah, you want Mrs Okomile to tell her husband to restart the War Against Indiscipline? Come to think of it, WAI sounds like a soldier whipping a civilian: 'Wai! Wai! Wai!'

TOYIN picks up her handbag and stands up.

LANRE: Sit down. *(Heads for the door.)* See you, Mrs *Oko mii…*

TOYIN: Lanre!

LANRE: *(Pretend coughs.)* Mrs Okomile. *(Exits.)*

TOYIN: Helen!

HELEN: *(Off.)* Ma!

TOYIN: What can I offer you?

MRS OKOMILE: Tea, ma. Thank you, Ma. I hope no problem? *(Points to the departing LANRE.)*

TOYIN: It's a personal matter. So, what is this important mission you need to see me for?

HELEN enters.

TOYIN: Where were you?

HELEN: I dey for backyard, Ma.

TOYIN: Did you wash your hands?

HELEN: Yes Ma.

TOYIN: Make tea for Mrs Okomile.

HELEN: Yes Ma. *(To MRS OKOMILE.)* Lipton or Bournvita, Ma?

TOYIN: What do we call tea in this house? Bring the wrong one, you will see yourself.

HELEN exits to kitchen.

MRS OKOMILE: First let me assure you, Ma, that the Association of Governors' Wives will be here in full force to celebrate your fifty years on this earth.

LANRE enters.

LANRE: I forgot my briefcase. *(Goes upstairs.)*

TOYIN: Couldn't you tell Pakimi to get it for you?

LANRE: *(Looks about on the landing.)* I can't remember where I left it.

TOYIN: You didn't leave it there.

LANRE: It must be in my room. *(Exits upstairs.)*

MRS OKOMILE: I don't know if you remember me, Ma. I was your student. What a great principal you were. I wept the day you retired. Those sermons you gave during morning assembly inspired me to make something of myself. You taught us that it wasn't a man's world. We girls could make something of our lives.

TOYIN: I was just doing my job.

MRS OKOMILE: If not for you I would not be where I am today. I am helping our country wean itself off its insatiable appetite for foreign goods which is a drain on our foreign exchange reserves thus indebting us to foreign banks. Meanwhile our locally made products are perceived with the same contempt reserved for goods made in China. I assure you, the government is making all effort to ensure that by the year 2000 you will see the label 'Made in Nigeria' as a mark of quality.

TOYIN: We shall be here in 2000.

MRS OKOMILE: Amen, Ma.

LANRE: *(Off.) Ogbele, oh.* Is it in your room?

TOYIN: How can it be in my room? Did you check inside your study?

HELEN enters with the tea.

LANRE comes downstairs.

LANRE: Yes, now. Helen. Is my briefcase in the kitchen?

HELEN: No sah.

LANRE: Maybe I left it in the toilet. *(Enters the toilet. Shuts the door.)*

MRS OKOMILE: Yes Ma/

TOYIN cuts her off with a wave. They wait. HELEN stops, thinking TOYIN's gesture is for her. TOYIN waves impatiently to HELEN to put down the tea. She inspects it.

TOYIN: *Olorun yo e.*[8] *(Cocks her head in the direction of the toilet.)*

MRS OKOMILE: Yes Ma/

TOYIN gestures to MRS OKOMILE to hold on. At last, LANRE comes out.

LANRE: It's not there.

TOYIN: Were you searching inside the cistern?

LANRE: I had to relieve myself. Helen did not pound that yam very well.

TOYIN: You didn't complain yesterday night.

LANRE: It's pounded yam now. It has delayed effect. *(To HELEN.)* Check the kitchen, maybe I left it there.

TOYIN: *(Goes to LANRE. Whispers.)* You didn't flush.

LANRE: Ah, look at me. *(Goes back and flushes the toilet.)*

MRS OKOMILE: The First Lady is/

LANRE: *(Inside the toilet.)* Na wa, oh! You would have thought that Andre the Giant shit this shit. Or is it shat this shit?

TOYIN: Get out of there!

LANRE: *(Comes out.)* Take it easy now.

HELEN: I no see am for kitchen, sah.

LANRE: I will look for it later. Give the toilet one more flush. *(Dithers.)* Don't mind me. Continue with your conversation.

HELEN goes into the toilet. She comes out.

HELEN: Essa, nothing/

LANRE: Flush it!

HELEN shrugs. She goes back inside the toilet and flushes, leaving the door open.

LANRE waits. TOYIN glares at him.

LANRE: Well, then, er, I'd better be going. *(Exits.)*

TOYIN: *(To MRS OKOMILE, apologetic.)* Please…

HELEN shuts the toilet door and comes downstairs.

MRS OKOMILE: It's all right, Ma. As I was saying/

---

8   God saved you.

TOYIN: *(To HELEN.)* You are in your cave, that is why you did not shut the door before you flushed. Because that toilet looks like *shalanga*[9] to you, *abi*? Get out!

HELEN exits quickly.

TOYIN: *Ojare...*

MRS OKOMILE: It's all right, Ma. If not that the First Lady is on official trip to Dubai she would have met with you personally. Her initiative, the Better Life for Rural Women continues to grow, providing women in our rural areas the opportunity to fully maximise their profits in their given trades which allows them to sustain a better standard of living thus leading to/

TOYIN: Mrs Okomile. I know all about Better Life. What has it got to do with me? I'm not a rural woman.

MRS OKOMILE: Yes Ma. I mean, no Ma. Er, due to her numerous commitments the First Lady has decided to step down. To this effect, we are seeking a new chairwoman, one whose standing among women is beyond comparison, one who can build upon the solid foundation laid by our First Lady. Without too much thinking you were the only person we thought worthy of the job.

TOYIN: I see. Thank you for considering me without too much thinking.

MRS OKOMILE: We knew that, as a mother of the nation, you would answer the call of duty to ensure that our country continues to grow spiritually and economically/

TOYIN: I am the secretary of the National Council for Women Society.

MRS OKOMILE: And we appreciate the efforts of the Society in representing women of high status. By heading our association you will bridge the gap between the National Council members and those women who are less fortunate. You will answer directly to the First Lady which is an honour in itself.

TOYIN: I cannot rush into a decision on a matter as important as this.

---

9   pit latrine

MRS OKOMILE: Ah. Em, how soon will I get a reply from you, Ma?

TOYIN: I can't say.

MRS OKOMILE: It's only that I would like to know before the First Lady's birthday next month.

TOYIN: I see. I will get back to you. *(Stands up. Feels pain in her back. Tries not to let it show.)*

MRS OKOMILE: *(Stands up.)* Ah, OK, Ma. Thank you for your time.

TOYIN: Ehen. Bye-bye.

MRS OKOMILE exits.

TOYIN: Áriífín *buruku.*[10] *(Feels her back. Yells.)* Helen!

HELEN enters.

TOYIN: Get me water. *(Takes a box of tablets from her handbag.)*

HELEN dashes back into the kitchen and returns with a glass of water. TOYIN swallows two tablets. HELEN clears the table.

SCENE TWO

Later that morning. The sitting room. AFOLABI and HELEN are exiting and entering, bringing more party things into the sitting room. TOYIN looks anxiously through the window and at her wrist watch. AFOLABI enters and puts down a box. HELEN urges him to approach TOYIN. He is reluctant to do so. The phone rings. TOYIN answers it. AFOLABI and HELEN exit.

TOYIN: Hello? Oh, 'Bidemi. Yes? Ah, you've spent last month's allowance already? Quiet! Did your useless husband impregnate me or you? Find your way to the family planning clinic instead of dumping your responsibilities on me. *(Hangs up.)* It's only when you need money that you remember I'm your sister. *(Resumes her vigil by the window.)*

AFOLABI and HELEN enter with boxes. HELEN shoves AFOLABI forward and exits.

AFOLABI: Ess, Ma. You say I should tell you when the cow people arrive.

---

10   Bloody cheek.

TOYIN: Ehen, thank you, Afolabi.

AFOLABI: Chief say I should keep it secret, but if you see how I redecorate the garden for your birthday party, ah, is very fine, Ma…

TOYIN does not respond.

AFOLABI: Em, ess' Ma. About Ikililu. The doctor say his condition is not change at all and the medicine is too cost.

TOYIN: Did Chief say he would branch at the Ministry of Petroleum?

AFOLABI: No, Ma.

TOYIN sighs. She picks up her handbag. As she is about to leave with AFOLABI…

LANRE: *(Off.)* I should have packed you off to join your brother in the hostel. *(As they enter. LANRE whacks SOJI's head.)* Get inside! Idiot.

TOYIN: Baba Yinka! The soldiers did not kill him, you want to finish him off. *(Hugs SOJI. Checks him all over.)*

SOJI: I'm fine, Mum.

LANRE: He is not fine. He is sick in the head!

TOYIN: Don't talk about my son like that.

LANRE: I'm supposed to see General Abubakar this morning. Instead I've spent the whole day saving this miscreant's life.

TOYIN: Soji, when will you stop this Folarin business?

SOJI: K. K. Folarin speaks the truth! This military government is an illegal occupier. We must get them out.

LANRE: Were you deaf when they announced their transition to civil rule?

SOJI: They are not going anywhere. They are using the transition programme as another chance to loot.

TOYIN: And that is what possessed you to stage a protest in front of Dodan Barracks?[11] Soji! You want to get yourself killed? *(Feels her back. Takes pills out of her handbag.)*

AFOLABI exits to kitchen.

SOJI: Someone has to stand up/

11   Official residence and headquarters of the President.

TOYIN: Shut up!

AFOLABI returns with a glass of water.

LANRE: You see? You don't want your mother to see 50. This foolishness ends today.

SOJI: We cannot stop our protests until they release K. K. Folarin from detention. He is our only hope for the people's revolution. *(To AFOLABI.)* Isn't that so, Afolabi?

Afolabi: *(Caught off guard.)* Ehn?

SOJI: You said you would stand shoulder to shoulder with me at the barricade/

AFOLABI: *(Pretends to answer someone offstage.)* Yes! I'm coming oh! *(Runs out.)*

LANRE: You see? No one with half a brain will join your stupid revolution.

SOJI: If you could have felt the rush I felt when I stood with my comrades before the soldiers' guns singing 'Zombie' you would understand.

TOYIN: Was it not one of your comrades who told the security agents where to find Folarin?

SOJI: That's a lie! Government propaganda. K. K. Folarin says emancipation can only come when the poor understand their condition/

LANRE: Does K. K. Folarin pay your school fees?

SOJI: He is fighting for my future.

TOYIN: Soji…

LANRE: And what have I spent my whole life working for if not to secure your future? Next time I will leave you to rot in detention with your 'comrades'. *(Approaches SOJI.)*

TOYIN stands in between them.

LANRE: Or you don't know it is my name that saved you from being tortured? Talk to your son. Talk to your son! *(Glares at SOJI as he walks past him to the front door.)* Ungrateful bastard. *(Exits.)*

TOYIN: *(To LANRE.)* Baba Yinka. Baba Yinka! *(Turns to SOJI.)* Why can't you be like your mates? At least wait until you

get into university before you start playing Mr Student
Union.

SOJI: I'm not playing.

TOYIN: Are you not prepared for your exams?

SOJI: I didn't protest because of my exams, Mum!

TOYIN: You're trying to impress your girlfriend.

SOJI: Jesus Christ, Mum!

TOYIN: What did I tell you about swearing?

SOJI: You can't tell me you don't see those kids searching
through our dustbins every morning.

TOYIN: What is my business with them?

SOJI: We're one of the biggest oil exporters yet everywhere
I look I see people suffering. I see the poor turning on
each other. Yesterday by my school a mob stoned a man
because he stole an orange. Mum, an orange!

TOYIN: That is one less armed robber to worry about.

SOJI: He stole it because he was hungry.

TOYIN: There will always be rich and poor. You behave like an
atheist. That is why you refuse to accept that fact of life.

SOJI: And what about my comrades locked up for demanding
our human rights? Should I accept that as a fact of life?

TOYIN: If K. K. Folarin chooses to spend his life in jail that is
his business. He should not drag you into it.

SOJI: He opened my eyes.

TOYIN: Still so gullible. You cannot change the world.

SOJI: I can't accept the unacceptable.

TOYIN: You can demonstrate till the cows come home, they
won't release him.

SOJI: Then I will keep on demonstrating.

TOYIN: This man that you have never even met, you show
more love for him than you do for your father.

SOJI: I respect him. He uses his position to help others.

TOYIN: You know how many people your Father has
sponsored their education? Folarin is not a god. We knew
him when we were students in London. Even back then he

was a self-righteous nuisance. Making us feel guilty for not
joining the Pan-African movement. Your father's nickname
for him was nose-picker.

SOJI: He can wipe his anus with his hand, I would shake it.

TOYIN: You know why your Father called you ungrateful?
Because you behave as if the golden spoon in your mouth
is made of plastic.

SOJI: What is wrong in making our country a better place for
all of us?

TOYIN: *Ọmọdé nṣe e*.[12] What life have you lived that you think
you can solve Nigeria's problems? The hungry are in their
houses. You are on the streets risking your life.

SOJI: I'm a future leader. I have a responsibility.

TOYIN: Your responsibility is to yourself! Mrs Eborie's son, in
his final year, what did he die for? So that the riffraff could
loot! You want me to feel her pain? Give thanks to God
that you are born into this family.

SOJI: Soyinka was right. Yours is the wasted generation.

TOYIN: My joy is that you are safe and sound. Don't you ever
repeat that statement to me or to your father if you want to
stay under this roof. Do you hear me?

SOJI: Yes, Mum.

TOYIN: Now, let's get you something to eat. Helen!

HELEN: *(Off.)* Ma!

TOYIN: What are you getting me for my birthday, eh?

SOJI: *(Sullen.)* It's a surprise.

HELEN: *(Enters. Her hands are dirty.)* Ma.

TOYIN: *(Sees her hands.)* Where have you been?

HELEN: The sink block, Ma.

TOYIN: And you brought those dirty hands into my kitchen?
(Rummages under the sofa.)

SOJI: Mum/

HELEN: *(Knows what is coming.)* I be wan' wash am, Ma. Di
water don go, Ma! Di water don go!

---

12   So childish.

TOYIN brings out a koboko – horsewhip. She thrashes HELEN.

SOJI: Mum!

TOYIN: Wash your hands, serve my son his breakfast and after you will clean the whole kitchen. Let me see one smudge, *wa gba Olorun l'oga.*[13] Animal.

HELEN exits.

TOYIN: That is the riffraff you want to risk your life for. They will kill you first with their backwardness. *(Puts the horsewhip back under the sofa.)*

SOJI: Try treating her like a human being.

TOYIN: If you're not hungry tell her not to bother.

SOJI: It won't kill you to/

TOYIN: Your foolish revolution stays outside. You do not tell me how to run my house. Or you want to marry her? Tell me so that I can flush both of you down the toilet this instant. *(Storms into the kitchen.)*

SOJI waits for a beat then follows after her.

SCENE THREE

The sitting room. Later that day. HELEN rubs ointment on TOYIN's back. TOYIN is going through a box of photographs. The box of paracetamol is in front of her. She puts it into her handbag. HELEN sneakily rubs her own back with the ointment. AFOLABI enters, with LANRE's briefcase. TOYIN waves to HELEN to stop rubbing her back. HELEN closes the ointment and puts it on the table. LANRE enters and slumps onto his chair. AFOLABI exits.

LANRE: *(To HELEN.)* Get me a beer.

HELEN curtseys and exits to kitchen.

LANRE: What's that?

TOYIN: I need a photograph for the programme cover. I'm thinking the one I took last year in Paris.

LANRE: Good.

TOYIN: Kunle called. He says hello… I said/

LANRE: *(Testily.)* I heard you.

---

13   You will accept God as your lord.

TOYIN: I said we'd visit him after church on Sunday. It's been too long since the boys have seen their uncle.

LANRE hisses.

HELEN enters with the beer and a glass. She opens the beer and pours it. She puts it on a coaster on the table. She curtseys and returns to TOYIN. She helps in sorting out the photographs.

TOYIN: How was work?

LANRE: Same-same. What did Mrs Okomile want?

TOYIN: She's looking for a new Better Life chairwoman. Bloody cheek, she needed an answer before the First Lady's birthday. She wants to present me to her in wrapping paper. As if that wasn't enough she invited herself and her cohorts to my birthday.

LANRE: You could have invited her.

TOYIN: Why would I invite former goodtime girls to my birthday?

LANRE: She's the governor's wife.

TOYIN: A soldier's wife.

LANRE: It doesn't matter what you think about them. They are in government.

TOYIN: And that gives them the license to misbehave? Dr Otolorin was made to kneel in engine oil. What was his crime?

LANRE: Otolorin[14] by name, Otolorin by nature. Challenging a man with a gun. I don't know how he's managed to stay alive under military rule.

TOYIN: You wouldn't find it funny if it had been you.

LANRE: They know who I am.

TOYIN: Hoh! Did a recruit not trample through our living room with impunity this morning?

LANRE: And I sent him packing.

TOYIN: What about the animals that beat up Basorun Abiona? Did they not know who he is? They won't catch armed robbers, it is to go and beat up innocent people in their homes.

---

14   Otolorin – one who walks a different path, a contrarian.

LANRE: It is talk like this that encourages Soji.

TOYIN: I suppose Yinka is my fault too.

LANRE: You said it.

TOYIN: No one could have foreseen General Abubakar becoming the new petroleum minister.

LANRE: Only you could not have foreseen it.

TOYIN: I don't know why you're so worried. He has to honour your contract.

LANRE: What did you tell Mrs Okomile?

TOYIN: Why are you interested?

LANRE: Why shouldn't I be interested in my wife's affairs? *(Takes a swig of the beer.)*

TOYIN: I should record this moment for posterity.

LANRE: Why can't you answer a simple question without bringing up all kinds of irrelevancies? *(Puts the beer on the table but not on the coaster.)*

TOYIN: So I'm irrelevant. *(Snaps her fingers at HELEN.)*

LANRE: Did I say you were irrelevant?

HELEN goes and puts LANRE's beer on the coaster.

LANRE: *N'gbo,* Helen, you heard me call Madam irrelevant?

TOYIN: You are bringing Helen into my matter?

LANRE: Sorry Ma.

TOYIN: *You are bringing Helen into my matter*!

LANRE: I said sorry, oh!

TOYIN: You continue to amaze me, after how many years of marriage. Maybe you sent Mrs Okomile to talk to me.

LANRE: It was only when you told me that I knew she was coming.

TOYIN: And yet you were so interested in our conversation.

LANRE: It was the pounded yam.

TOYIN: Don't lie to me!

LANRE: Forget it. *(Gets up. Heads for the door.)*

TOYIN: *(Stands up. Goes to LANRE.)* Where are you going?

LANRE: I have a business appointment.

TOYIN: Which other appointment again?

HELEN quickly dips her hand into TOYIN's handbag and pockets the paracetamol.

TOYIN: I said I would think about it.

LANRE: *(Stops.)* And?

TOYIN: I'm still thinking.

LANRE: *(Goes to her. Embraces her.)* Toyin. It will be another feather in the Adeyemi cap. It's your rightful place to be the mother of the nation. Show that fool son of yours that you can serve your country without trying to overthrow everybody.

TOYIN: *(Wants to stay in his arms, but…)* I cannot be your wife only when you need something from me.

LANRE: *(Lets go of TOYIN.)* I'd better go.

TOYIN: Oh. When are you back?

LANRE: After I see General Abubakar I need to change money. Four naira to one pound. Can you imagine?

TOYIN: Let Helen get Pakimi for you.

LANRE: I'll drive myself. You will need him to run errands.

TOYIN: Lanre…

LANRE: What is it now?

TOYIN: … When you return.

LANRE exits.

TOYIN looks forlornly after him. She turns round.

TOYIN: You want me to tell you before you clear the table?

HELEN clears the table.

TOYIN: God knows your time is coming.

HELEN pulls faces behind TOYIN's back and exits into kitchen.

SCENE FOUR

The boys' quarters, later that day. HELEN is in her room packing her things into a bundle. She stops to take two tablets of paracetamol then resumes packing. AFOLABI is outside listening to a comedy show on the radio. There are coolers nearby.

AFOLABI: *(Roars with laughter.)* Chief Zebrudaya[15] *ma ferin pa mi o*[16]! Are you not going to wash those coolers before Madam *bulala*[17] you?

HELEN: If she see me to beat.

AFOLABI: Is how she treat Maria before you, and Comfort before Maria, and/

HELEN: I beg, I no ask you for book of Chronicles.

AFOLABI: Now that you know her ways, you have to monitor yourself. Everything in life is patience. Patience and understanding. *(Roars with laughter.)*

HELEN: Dat one no concern me anymore. I sure say di woman na witch.

AFOLABI: Na you get your mouth.

HELEN: If you hear as she dey abuse Chief. 'You dis 'irresigancy', you dis 'konkobility', you dis second-hand machine gun'... If she no be witch how woman go abuse her husband he no go slap her face?

AFOLABI roars with laughter.

HELEN: Anyway, me I thank God. I no go do servant for sixteen years.

AFOLABI: Hey. I am not servant. I am gardener.

HELEN: But sixteen years! You don become Adeyemi. Once you tell Madam say your pikin no well, she suppose to put hand for pocket one time.

AFOLABI: Is her money. She can give whoever she like.

HELEN: My star no fit shine for dis house. I no surprise say Maria tief Madam bracelet.

AFOLABI: And that is why they call police for her.

---

15 Nigerian comedian
16 don't make me laugh
17 whips

HELEN: So, if you wan' help person and di only way na to tief, you no go do am?

AFOLABI: Allah forbid.

HELEN: *(Slowly brings out the paracetamol.)* If na to save person life, *nko*?

AFOLABI: You see all the *mola*[18] with one hand wey dey beg for road? That is what happen to person who tief.

HELEN throws the paracetamol to AFOLABI.

AFOLABI: Helen! If Madam catch you/

HELEN: *(Extends her hand.)* If you no want am…

AFOLABI: Thank you.

HELEN: How Ikililu body?

AFOLABI: His matter has pass panadol. I am praying people will spray us at Madam party so I can buy the rest medicine.

HELEN: Na you on your own be dat. *(Comes out with the bundle.)* Me and Lomi, we dey check out like 'Andrew' today-today.

AFOLABI: Helen, are you serious?

HELEN: I go invite you make you come see our flat. Two bedroom for Aguda.

AFOLABI: You want to rely on his *jibiti*[19] to feed you?

HELEN: If you know any rich man wey wan' marry me, make you tell me.

AFOLABI: My friend Alhaji is looking for fourth wife.

HELEN: God forbid.

AFOLABI: I know Christian who is having more than one wife.

HELEN: Me I no fit do second wife for any man. Dat is like harlot. And na so, so quarrel with di first wife. She go come put juju for my head. No, oh.

AFOLABI: If you work hard you can be rich for yourself.

HELEN: Then you for don become millionaire. If to say I be rogue, no be only panadol I for tief from Madam/

---

18   Mallam/s
19   fraudulence

AFOLABI: But you are not rogue so why are you following Pakimi…

PAKIMI enters as the advert for Forum Bank comes on.

RADIO: Forty percent interest upfront on any deposit guaranteed. *(Jingle.)* 'Forum Bank, the bank for future millionaires'.

HELEN: Hey! My husband. I don ready.

PAKIMI: Em. Afolabi, excuse us.

AFOLABI: You be soldier?

PAKIMI: Excuse us, now.

HELEN: Afolabi know. *Oya.* Help me put my load for my head.

PAKIMI: I didn't see Benjamin.

HELEN: Wetin you mean?

PAKIMI: He did not turn up.

HELEN: Maybe he meet go-slow for road. You for wait/

PAKIMI: I went to his house. The landlord said there is nobody by that name living there.

HELEN: Na wrong house you go.

PAKIMI: He has run away with my money, Helen.

AFOLABI: Benjamin *ti gba e loju.*[20]

HELEN: But you say Benjamin is honest guy.

AFOLABI: *(Laughs.)* Benjamin dat is professional *jibiti.*

PAKIMI: Give me until after Madam party. I will have the deposit.

HELEN: No. No! I cannot stay here! I cannot stay here.

AFOLABI: Make you wash the cooler quick-quick. You are not going anywhere.

HELEN: *(To AFOLABI.)* Di panadol.

AFOLABI: What of Ikililu?

HELEN and AFOLABI struggle over the tablets. PAKIMI intervenes. HELEN beats him.

SOJI enters.

SOJI: Hey! Hey.

---

20   Benjamin has conned you.

They stop fighting.

SOJI: You should be united in your suffering so that you can overthrow the oppressor.

AFOLABI: Ah, you nearly put me for *wahala* today with that talk. You too, causing trouble for yourself when your exams are so close.

SOJI: How can I think of my exams when there's a war on?

AFOLABI: War? *Hepa*!

PAKIMI: Soji is talking catastrophically.

SOJI: You mean metaphorically.

AFOLABI snorts in derision.

SOJI: Helen, are you leaving us?

HELEN: I bin clean my room. I no wan' make dust enter my cloth.

AFOLABI: Which war are you talking?

SOJI: The war between soldiers and civilians.

AFOLABI: But the soldiers are going. Tradition to civil rule.

PAKIMI: Hey! Afolabi *ta bon*![21] *Transition* not tradition. Thank God I wear my bulletproof.

AFOLABI: I can speak English better than you.

SOJI: Guys, guys. Only one division matters: that between rich and poor.

PAKIMI: What is your own with poor people's problem, sef?

SOJI: Rich, poor, we must all struggle together. According to K. K. Folarin/

PAKIMI: K. K. Folarin will drop his *Aluta Continua* once they flash government post in his face.

SOJI: *Lailai*![22] Anybody who accepts an appointment from this government is a traitor. Who said that?

PAKIMI: The man is using you. He knows the system. He protests against the government, they make him a minister.

AFOLABI: Don't mind Pakimi, Soji. Everybody is crook like him.

---

21 gun shot – slang for making a grammatical error in English.
22 Never!

SOJI: You think he has endured all the detentions and the beatings to become part of them?

PAKIMI: *Wo*[23], this world is all about *kudi, owo, ego*[24]. Even for woman to look at you, you must land naira first. *(More to HELEN.)* And if you disappoint her before she forgives you, you must discharge again. No romance without finance.

SOJI: Not everything is about money.

PAKIMI: Because you have money.

SOJI brings out money from his pocket and gives it to AFOLABI.

AFOLABI: Ah! Brother Soji.

SOJI: For your son.

AFOLABI: I can't.

SOJI shoves the money into AFOLABI's hand. AFOLABI does little to stop him.

AFOLABI: Thank you, Brother Soji. May Allah replenish your pocket.

PAKIMI: My child is sick.

SOJI: You don't have a child.

PAKIMI: In future.

SOJI: In the future none of you will beg for crumbs from the master's table. There won't be a master.

PAKIMI: New table, same master.

SOJI: You are too cynical, man!

PAKIMI: Your mother is going to become chairwoman of Better Life.

SOJI: Mister Pakimi!

PAKIMI: I heard Chief talking to Mrs Okomile.

SOJI: Mum hates the military. There's no way on earth/

YINKA enters with a bag. He walks with a gangsta swagger, holds his crotch.

YINKA: Still talking about a revolution, eh?

SOJI: Hostel boy! When did you land?

YINKA: Just now.

---

23   Look.
24   *Kudi, owo, ego*: money in Hausa, Yoruba and Igbo.

AFOLABI: Yinka! Welcome.

YINKA: Mr Afolabi! How body?

AFOLABI: Body dey inside cloth.

PAKIMI: *Ogbologbo*[25]! The hard man. *(Play-boxes with YINKA.)* Which one, now? *She,* you dey oppress all those fine hostel babes?

YINKA: I'm Oppressor *Numero Uno,* accept. Are you Helen?

HELEN: Yes.

YINKA: Mum wants the coolers. *(Eyes her.)*

HELEN: Yeh!

> *HELEN washes the coolers quickly. PAKIMI tries to help her. She pushes him away. AFOLABI laughs.*

PAKIMI: I will spoil your garden. *(Exits.)*

AFOLABI: If you try it, eh! *(Goes after him.)*

SOJI: Remember! Save the fight for the revolution! *(To YINKA.)* Does Mum know you're here?

YINKA: I want to surprise her.

SOJI: Hostel Boy! Your old mates keep asking after you. You'll jam them at the party.

YINKA: Cool.

SOJI: *(Grabs YINKA's bag. Brings out a video cassette.)* What's this? 'Thunder in Heaven, parts one and two'. *(Unimpressed.)* It's homemade.

YINKA: Guys are saying this is going to be the latest craze.

SOJI: Yeah? This your bounce, eh. You've become *ogbologbo* true, true.

YINKA: You have to be or guys will chance you. Everybody must know their level, you get what I'm saying? You should see what we get up to after lights out. Man, I've been living a sheltered life. *(Keeps getting distracted by HELEN.)*

SOJI: Have you thought of a present for Mum?

YINKA: Not yet. It will be something expensive.

SOJI: I'm short on card.

---

25   Hard man!

YINKA: What crap are you telling me?

SOJI: Easy, ah. I'll rustle up my half, don't worry.

YINKA: I'm starving. What are we eating?

SOJI: There are people who go oh-oh-one[26] every day.

YINKA: Turn off that tap. K. K. Folarin's been released.

SOJI: Na lie.

YINKA: It was on the news a minute ago. I thought you knew/

SOJI: *(Jumps with delight.)* Yeah! People power, man! The revolution will be televised. You'd better join up now before the people rise up.

YINKA: *Oya,* go and celebrate on your own. *(Pretends to beat SOJI.) Oya*!

SOJI exits singing.

YINKA turns to HELEN.

YINKA: Hi there…

Gunshots. Shouts of 'ole', 'thief' and 'armed robber'. YINKA and HELEN run off.

SCENE FIVE

That night. TOYIN and YINKA at the dining table.

AFOLABI: The Smiths, they are all fine.

TOYIN: Thank God.

AFOLABI: Is their motor that they carry.

TOYIN: It's just a car.

AFOLABI: And their TV and stereo system.

TOYIN: They can be replaced.

AFOLABI: And all Madam's jewellery. And all the money/

TOYIN: So they robbed them of everything.

AFOLABI: Eh, yes Ma.

TOYIN: Thank God no one got hurt.

AFOLABI: They shoot the security guard in the leg.

TOYIN: Tell them I will come round with Chief this evening.

AFOLABI: Yes Ma. *(Exits.)*

26   one meal a day.

YINKA: Soji! Where are you?

TOYIN: Yinka! What did I say about shouting in the house? If it was Soji I would understand. You still haven't explained what possessed you to take public transport.

SOJI comes downstairs, dressed in khaki shirt and shorts. He goes to the stereo and plays Fela Kuti's 'Army Arrangement' before sitting at the table. HELEN enters with food and puts it on the table. She exits. YINKA watches her.

YINKA: I wanted to surprise you.

TOYIN: Never again. You tell us you're coming and we send Pakimi to pick you. OK? Nowhere is safe. God knows who you were sitting next to on that filthy bus.

YINKA: It was *Ikene dili Chukwu*.[27]

TOYIN: So what? I hope you chartered a taxi from the motor park. I said I hope you chartered a taxi.

YINKA: I took a Molue.[28]

SOJI bursts out laughing.

TOYIN: Which story did you want me to hear? That you got stabbed or that the molue tipped over Eko Bridge? Try that again you will see my bad side. *(To SOJI.)* Is this amusing you? You think this is a fancy dress ball?

SOJI: I'm celebrating the release of K. K/

TOYIN: Shut up!

YINKA: *(Serves himself.)* You're lucky he wasn't dressing like Fela. He'd be in his underwear.

YINKA digs in. TOYIN glares at him. He puts down his fork.

TOYIN: *(To HELEN.)* Turn off that music.

HELEN turns off the music. They bow their heads in prayer.

TOYIN: *(Prays.)* Father, for that with which you have blessed us, open our eyes to show our gratitude. Amen.

YINKA: Amen.

TOYIN: Soji.

SOJI: *(Reluctantly.)* Amen.

---

27   Luxurious bus
28   Bus. Needs to be seen to be believed.

They eat. YINKA wolfs down his food. He shields his plate with his arm.

SOJI: Yinka, the armed robbers have gone.

YINKA: I'm hungry.

TOYIN: No talking at table. Yinka, you're not in your hostel.

YINKA: I'm hungry!

TOYIN: Are you shouting at me? Is this what they teach you in Odogbolu? Remove your arm!

YINKA removes his arm from around his plate.

HELEN enters with a jug of water. YINKA's eyes trail her as she goes into the kitchen.

YINKA: You'll go through all the house helps in Lagos until no one will want to work for you.

TOYIN: Maria was useless. And a thief.

SOJI: You don't know for sure she stole that bracelet.

TOYIN: Who did?

YINKA: Maybe Soji stole it to fund his revolution.

SOJI: Shut up.

TOYIN: Language!

SOJI: He called me a thief!

YINKA: Where did you get her from?

TOYIN: The usual broker.

YINKA: How old is she?

TOYIN: Why do you want to know?

SOJI: Is it true that you are going to become Chairwoman of Better Life?

TOYIN: Where did you hear that from?

YINKA: You should go for it. You can throw all those fat contracts Dad's way.

TOYIN: We do not need that kind of money.

SOJI: Exactly.

YINKA: Everyone who can is getting contracts from this government.

TOYIN: We are not everyone.

YINKA: It might help you with Dad.

SOJI puts his head down.

TOYIN: What do you mean by that Yinka?

AFOLABI enters with LANRE's briefcase. LANRE enters, weary. YINKA and SOJI stand up. AFOLABI puts down the briefcase and exits.

YINKA: Welcome Dad.

SOJI: Welcome Dad.

LANRE: *(To SOJI.)* Immediately you finish eating, get those rags off, or I'll burn them while you're still in them. Did you pray before eating?

TOYIN: I made sure he did.

LANRE sits down at the table.

LANRE: *(Scoops food into a plate.)* Why aren't you in your dorm?

YINKA: I've come home early for Mum's birthday.

LANRE: Don't you ever come back to Lagos without my permission.

SOJI and YINKA sit down. They continue eating their food.

TOYIN: You heard about the Smiths?

LANRE: Yes.

TOYIN: You have to hire security for the house.

LANRE: It didn't do the Smiths any good.

TOYIN: It's better than nothing.

LANRE: I'll see to it.

TOYIN: How was your appointment?

LANRE: General Abubakar said he would reconsider renewing my licence.

TOYIN: You spent the whole time with General Abubakar?

LANRE: You should have seen the waiting room. Filled with a who's who of Nigeria. I had to wait my turn. Even that televangelist Billy Robertson was there.

SOJI: He's a charlatan.

LANRE glares at SOJI. SOJI faces his food.

TOYIN: These Pentecostals are springing up everywhere. What does he want a license for?

LANRE: Maybe NEPA supplies power to Heaven. God needs diesel for his generator. *(Gives TOYIN a business card.)* He's building a cathedral. He was thinking I could supply him with materials.

TOYIN: *(Looks at the card with disdain.)* He's looking for you to join his church. He will use you to advertise for fellow VIPs. Helen!

HELEN: *(Off.)* Ma!

LANRE: I knew that was his intention.

TOYIN: Then you should have told him you're not interested.

LANRE: I couldn't refuse his card, could I?

HELEN: *(Enters.)* Ma?

TOYIN: *(Gives the card to HELEN.)* Throw it in the bin.

HELEN throws the card in the bin. She exits.

SOJI: Religion is the opiate of the people.

LANRE: If you don't take time, I will thrash your atheism out of you.

YINKA: Some big people have started to attend his church. Jerry Ike's father got his promotion to MD soon after he saw Robertson.

LANRE: *(Looks at YINKA.)* Maybe divine intervention is what it takes to replace an oil license these days.

YINKA averts Chief's gaze.

TOYIN: General Abubakar said he was reconsidering it. That doesn't mean he is cancelling it.

LANRE: I don't know what anything means any more.

TOYIN: You will feel better when he gets back to you. He knows who we are.

LANRE: *(At YINKA.)* When everything is given to you, you've no need to consider the consequences of your actions.

YINKA: I was telling Mum to take the Better Life job so you don't have to keep coming up to Shagamu all the time.

LANRE glares at YINKA.

TOYIN: What do you mean, 'all the time'?

LANRE: It's nothing.

TOYIN: So why didn't you tell me you've been going to Shagamu?

LANRE: Because it was nothing!

TOYIN: *(To YINKA and SOJI.)* Go upstairs.

They go upstairs. There is a smirk on YINKA's face.

LANRE: There was a great business opportunity.

TOYIN: A business opportunity or just an opportunity?

LANRE: This is why I didn't want to tell you.

TOYIN: If your word means nothing anymore at least have respect for me. Have respect for your son's feelings.

LANRE: Did Yinka complain that I hurt his feelings?

TOYIN: Of all the federal government colleges why Odogbolu?

LANRE: You think I would jeopardise my son's future? That I would transfer him to a school in his final year to suit my own purposes? It was either he got transferred or he would have been expelled. In fact you caused the whole problem.

TOYIN: Me?

LANRE: Yes, you! If you weren't always showing contempt for the soldiers he would never have slapped General Abubakar's son.

TOYIN: The boy was rude to him. Juniors should respect their seniors.

LANRE: Yes but his father is now the Minister for Petroleum so there!

TOYIN: You think he won't renew your license just because of that?

LANRE: You don't know these people. *(Stands up.)*

TOYIN: This business in Shagamu, what was it about?

LANRE: Nothing came of it.

TOYIN: You have no shame.

LANRE: How far is Shagamu to Odogbolu that I shouldn't drop by to see my son?

TOYIN: You used to be a man of honour.

LANRE: And what am I now?

TOYIN: You tell me.

LANRE: *(Sits down. His face almost in hers.)* No, Toyin. You tell me. In fact what does honour buy? Does it pay for your clothes? Does it maintain this house? Does it pay for the food? *(Grabs her arm.)*

TOYIN: Let go of me!

HELEN enters. LANRE lets go. HELEN exits.

LANRE: Or does it stop your son being transferred to another school on account of a small altercation? What does it pay for, Toyin? You act like a queen but I'm the one who has to mind the business when the government launches a scheme today and closes it tomorrow. I have to spend forever coming and going from one office to another to get my money back. Then they bring out a similar scheme only it goes by a different name. I sign a contract in the morning with a minister. In the afternoon his replacement tears it up. Tell me if I can afford to be honourable so that I do not offend you. Tell me when I can have support in my own house for being pulled here and there by boys half my age! *(Heads for the stairs.)*

TOYIN: Did you see her?

LANRE: I only saw our son. So what if I did?

TOYIN: From now until after my birthday no more evening appointments.

LANRE: You must be joking.

TOYIN: You will no longer work weekends.

LANRE: I will not be a prisoner of this marriage!

TOYIN: That makes the two of us.

LANRE: What?

TOYIN: Either you agree or I turn down the Better Life job.

LANRE: …And you will take the job?

TOYIN: I keep to my word.

LANRE: *(Holds her.)* This morning. You wanted to tell me something.

TOYIN: *(Shrugs him off.)* Don't forget we are visiting my brother tomorrow after church. Helen!

LANRE is surprised by the rebuff. His face grows dark.

HELEN: *(Off)* Ma! *(Enters and clears the dishes.)*

TOYIN exits upstairs. LANRE waits a while to calm down. He goes upstairs.

HELEN goes back into the kitchen with some of the plates.

PAKIMI enters through the front door. He puts the car keys on the table.

HELEN enters.

PAKIMI: I just need more time. Please.

HELEN continues clearing the table.

PAKIMI: *Haba*, why are you doing me like this? Because of money?

HELEN: *(Sings.)* No romance without finance.

PAKIMI: I will get the deposit. It is only time it will take. Just until after the party. You will see. I will…

HELEN heads for the kitchen.

PAKIMI: Helen! *(Exits back out the front door.)*

YINKA appears on the landing. He comes downstairs, fondling his crotch. He makes sure PAKIMI is gone.

HELEN enters. She steps back in surprise at seeing YINKA.

YINKA: Hi.

HELEN: Good evening, Brother, Brother…

YINKA: Yinka.

HELEN: Brother Yinka.

YINKA: Just Yinka. How do you find it working for my mother?

HELEN: Very good. She is good madam.

YINKA: *(Laughs.)* Oh yeah?

HELEN: I bin wan' ask you before.

YINKA: *(Eagerly.)* Yeah?

HELEN: *(Points at his crotch.)* You get craw-craw[29]?

YINKA stops fondling himself. HELEN goes to the table. YINKA touches her bottom.

HELEN: Brother Yinka!

YINKA: What?

---

29 scabies

HELEN walks past him. YINKA touches her bottom again.

HELEN: Hey! I no be harlot.

YINKA: I'm sorry.

HELEN: Small boy like you come dey…

YINKA: I'm not a small boy! Don't you ever call me that.

HELEN: Wetin make I call you?

YINKA: *(Brings out money.)* You want a guy who can support you in these hard times. Who will you take your chances with: the heir to a fortune or a common driver? Going, going…

HELEN grabs at the money. YINKA holds it out of her reach. HELEN puts on the radio. Music: Fela Kuti's 'Lady'. She dances. She backs into him. YINKA is knocked off balance. She puts his hand on her breast. He rubs her body crudely.

HELEN: No sandpaper me now! You be carpenter?

HELEN gently guides his hand up and down her body. YINKA gets more aroused. He throws her onto the sofa and is about to jump on top of her.

HELEN: Ah! I no be swimming pool! Easy. Like this.

YINKA tries to take her clothes off while he is on top of her. Her dress gets stuck over her head.

HELEN: *(Her dress over her head.)* Comot am!

YINKA: Sorry!

YINKA yanks the dress off her. They fall off the sofa.

SOJI by the foot of the stairs, tired. He sees them and hides.

HELEN: Ah!

YINKA: I'm sorry. *(Gives her the money.)* Please don't tell anyone. *(Heads upstairs.)*

HELEN: Soji dey your room?

YINKA: No he's gone to bed. Why?

HELEN secures the money in her blouse. She takes YINKA by the hand and leads him upstairs.

SOJI comes out of hiding and looks in their direction.

SCENE SIX

The following morning. Offstage, from the kitchen we hear AFOLABI and PAKIMI stacking crates of drinks.

PAKIMI: *(Sings.)* 'Money good, oh. Money good oh.'

AFOLABI: Your *wayo*[30] never do you?

PAKIMI: This is not fraud.

AFOLABI: Bank that is giving you forty per cent interest up front. That is wonder bank.

PAKIMI: They are genuine! Two of their board members are generals.

AFOLABI: All your money is *wayo*.

PAKIMI: Those boys driving V-boot and building duplex in Lekki how did they get their money?

AFOLABI: Not everybody is like you.

PAKIMI: Everybody is a hustler except you. When I visit Chief in my Frontera, you will open the gate for me.

AFOLABI: *Aiye re ko ni da.*[31]

PAKIMI: Jealousy. *(Sings)* 'If you get money, make you *laugh* the people wey no get'.

AFOLABI: Shut up and carry, *jo*! Is Helen I feel sorry for. You will disappointment her again.

PAKIMI: Ah! Afolabi *ro ra pelu oyinbo*![32] I'm not wearing my bulletproof.

HELEN dashes downstairs, fixing her hair. Frantically she clears the dishes from the night before. PAKIMI enters.

PAKIMI: Helen? Ah, no be last night's dinner be dis?

HELEN shoves dishes into PAKIMI's hands.

HELEN: Help me. Quick! Before Madam come down!

---

30   Fraud, fraudulent activity.
31   You will never do well in life.
32   Take it easy with your English.

PAKIMI: I told you I would find a way.

HELEN: Put the plate for kitchen!

PAKIMI shows her a wad of cash. HELEN stops.

PAKIMI: I withdrew all my money and put it in Forum Bank. This is forty per cent interest upfront. By end of the week I will get half the deposit.

HELEN hugs him, overjoyed.

PAKIMI: I told you. I will do anything for you.

HELEN: *(Brings out money from her blouse.)* Put this for your account.

PAKIMI: Where did you get this from?

HELEN: Na my life saving.

PAKIMI: I can do this by myself.

HELEN: I no wan' make Madam party meet us for here. She will not beat me again.

PAKIMI takes the money. They hug. He exits. HELEN looks after him with a mixture of pride and love. A noise from upstairs. HELEN frantically clears up. TOYIN come downstairs dressed for church.

TOYIN: Ah, are these the dishes from last night?

HELEN: Sorry Ma.

YINKA and SOJI come downstairs dressed for church. YINKA waits for SOJI to intervene. SOJI looks away.

TOYIN: I haven't given you anything to feel sorry for yet. *(Points to the sofa.)*

HELEN brings out the koboko and hands it to TOYIN. She keeps her distance.

HELEN: Please ma. Please ma.

YINKA: Mum! Please.

TOYIN: *(To HELEN.)* I will deal with you later.

HELEN exits to the kitchen.

YINKA takes the koboko from TOYIN and puts it back under sofa.

LANRE enters.

LANRE: After service I have a meeting at the club.

TOYIN: Baba Yinka…

LANRE: I will come straight home. I promise.

TOYIN: Is it because we are visiting my brother after service?

LANRE: Is he not coming to your birthday? I will see him then.

TOYIN: *Oya*, let's go. You know what the traffic in Breadfruit is like.

SOJI: What about breakfast?

TOYIN: You'll eat at your uncle's house.

LANRE: One second. I need to call the security company.
(Goes to the phone, picks it up.)

TOYIN, YINKA and SOJI exit.

LANRE: *(Puts the phone down.)* Afolabi!

AFOLABI: *(Off.)* Sah! *(Enters.)*

LANRE: Did you get her?

AFOLABI: She is in the backyard, sah.

LANRE hands him some money.

AFOLABI: Ess sah, about Ikililu.

LANRE: When I return. Open the gate. Make sure she is gone by the time we're back.

They exit.

HELEN enters. She cleans up.

AFOLABI enters with ONIJUJU. ONIJUJU surveys the house. She shakes her whisk at the four corners of the room and makes incantations.

HELEN: Mr Afolabi, who be dis?

AFOLABI: Sh!

ONIJUJU: *(Finishes her incantations, gives AFOLABI a packet.)* Every night, you scatter this powder around the house. No armed robber will enter.

HELEN: What if they have juju of entry to house which have juju?

ONIJUJU: This juju will counteract their counteraction. They will jump up and crow like cock.

HELEN: No be *magun*[33] be dat?

ONIJUJU: This juju is two in one. I hope none of you has cheated on your partner?

---

33   Charm used to punish an unfaithful partner.

314

HELEN takes a step back. AFOLABI carefully returns the packet to ONIJUJU.

HELEN: Ah, Mister Afolabi, you too?

AFOLABI: Shut up!

ONIJUJU: It's OK. *(Gives AFOLABI another packet.)* This one is juju *olorin.* If armed robber step your door, he will drop his gun and begin to dance. He will sing every Sunny Ade song, side A and side B.

HELEN: What if he doesn't hear Sunny?

ONIJUJU: He will sing Barrister.[34] Go and scatter it around the house.

AFOLABI exits.

ONIJUJU: What of you? Can I help you with anything?

HELEN: No, oh.

ONIJUJU: I have love medicine, powder. Rub on your face. Order any man, he will obey you. I have used it myself four times.

HELEN: I don't need your love medicine. My man already love me.

ONIJUJU: Really?

HELEN: Yes, oh. He is ready to die for me.

ONIJUJU: You are a witch! *(Brings out a snail shell.)*

HELEN: No! I no be witch oh!

ONIJUJU: You marry *oyinbo*?[35]

HELEN: My man is hundred per cent Nigerian.

ONIJUJU: They are like that at first. They will do 'love one-tin-tin.' Give them one month.

HELEN: Not my man.

ONIJUJU: You didn't hear me say I've travelled that road four times? Husband number five is starting his own nonsense… You need anybody you want to poison? Everybody get enemy.

HELEN looks at TOYIN's picture. ONIJUJU clocks this.

---

34   Fuji musician
35   the white man?

ONIJUJU: *(Brings out a packet.)* Put this in the food. By tomorrow morning the person will *pafuka*[36].

HELEN: …I no want.

ONIJUJU: *(Clocks HELEN's hesitance. Gives HELEN her card.)* In case of incasity. *(Exits.)*

> *HELEN puts the card in the bin and heads for the kitchen. She turns round and retrieves the card.*

SCENE SEVEN

That evening. An exclusive members club. LANRE with Reverend BILLY ROBERTSON. He is dressed in expensive robes and speaks in a faux American accent, pronouncing 'God' as 'Gad'. A waiter puts drinks in front of them and exits. LANRE banters with a club member who is offstage.

LANRE: So if I ask you for only two million, you can't give me? Ijebu![37] *(Laughs.)*

ROBERTSON: Ah, is that not Chief Ogunbanjo of Ogunbanjo Enterprises?

LANRE: Yes. *(To another member.)* Major Orkar! Nice to see you. I hope you are not plotting coup. You say? *(Roars with laughter.)*

ROBERTSON: Thank you for letting us meet in your club. It is not every day that I sit with a luminary in the midst of luminaries.

LANRE: That's all right.

ROBERTSON: Chief. Nigeria will always be a land of opportunity even for the humble. Why because Gad has ordained it.

LANRE: The meek shall inherit the earth.

ROBERTSON: Exactly! I was a jungle boy living off the streets of Benin. My parents could not feed me. They could not control me. Ah, Chief, I've not told anybody this. I was one of Lawrence Anini's[38] gang. Yes! I was there when he shot off the police commissioner's nose. One of his nostrils

---

36 die, finish.
37 Subdivision of the Yoruba. Stereotyped as being stingy.
38 Notorious armed robber

landed in my lap. But look at me today. Look at me by the grace of Gad – Almighty, El Shaddai, Yours be the glory. Chief! You cannot change your life except you let the Holy Spirit kidnap you.

LANRE: I suppose being an ex-armed robber you would know.

They share an uneasy laugh.

ROBERTSON: Chief, I must tell you that your Anglican church is a dead church. I was in London last month. Come and see empty pews.

LANRE: Uh-huh, Uh-huh.

ROBERTSON: My members, they will tell you that Gad resides in my church. They will tell you how Gad has changed their lives. Some of them checked out of Nigeria. Big professors going to UK to clean windows, drive mini cabs and do all other sorts of menial jobs. One doctor had been a carer for so long, she could tell the anus of a Lewisham quadriplegic from that of a Tooting paraplegic by touch alone! But Gad has given me the trumpet to call them back to the Promised Land, back to the land flowing with *moin moin*[39] and *akamu*[40].

LANRE: Yes, *moin moin* and *akamu*.

ROBERTSON: Chief! Faith is the new oil. No! It is better than oil because faith will never dry up! People are always searching for answers. The cathedral that I will build at Mile 12: one thousand capacity. Already I have to include an extension! That is how fast my church is growing and you must be a part of it. The Lord says you must be part of it. You must! Ah!

LANRE: I'm sure my pastor reads from the same bible as you.

ROBERTSON: Let me ask you Chief, if you don't mind: did you get your license renewed?

LANRE: No.

ROBERTSON: I thought as much.

LANRE: Oh. Did you see it in a vision?

---

39   bean cake
40   cornmeal

ROBERTSON: It's just that when you were in the General's office I heard begging and crying.

LANRE: Oh no, that was not me. You must have been possessed by the Holy Spirit.

ROBERTSON: Ah. Did General Abubakar tell you why he did not renew your license?

LANRE: Quota system.

ROBERTSON: Quota system did not stop me from getting a license. And I know six people from Bendel State who got a license. Even my colleague who is from Onitsha but is claiming Auchi, he got a license!

LANRE: *(Incredulous.)* You got a license?

ROBERTSON: The General's PA is my church member. He came to me with a problem no one else could solve and this is how our Father – Almighty, El Shaddai, Yours be the glory – saw it fit to reward me for helping him.

LANRE: About your cathedral. My company can supply you with the best materials at a favourable price. Italian marble, English oak. Pakimi! Bring my briefcase.

ROBERTSON: Chief. You know Dayo Cole? He's my church member. I'm in negotiations with him.

LANRE: He stocks local materials. It doesn't take long for our wood to rot. When you see my catalogue you will understand what I'm talking about. Pakimi!

PAKIMI enters with LANRE's briefcase.

LANRE: How long does it take you? (*Makes to take the briefcase.*)

PAKIMI: You have a phone call, sir.

LANRE: Excuse me, Reverend.

PAKIMI nods to ROBERTSON.

ROBERTSON: Brother. Are you a Christian?

PAKIMI: Sometimes.

ROBERTSON: It's either you are a Christian or you are not.

PAKIMI: 'Cele'.[41]

ROBERTSON: You should come to the real church. Divine revelation awaits you.

41 Slang for Celestial Church of Christ.

PAKIMI: Can your revelations give me forty per cent interest up front?

ROBERTSON: *(Laughs.)* You put your stock in earthly banks when the Lord offers the greatest returns.

LANRE returns. He takes the briefcase from PAKIMI.

LANRE: Sorry, oh. My wife has me on curfew. She thinks I go looking for bush meat.

ROBERTSON: I don't understand.

LANRE: You know, *bush meat.*

PAKIMI: The type toothpick cannot remove.

LANRE: Who is talking to you? Go and wait by the car!

PAKIMI exits, grinning.

ROBERTSON: *(Laughs.)* Oh, I get you, Chief.

LANRE: What I mean is I cannot stay too long but *(Opens his briefcase, brings out a catalogue.)* have a look at these and tell me if they are not fit for the house of the Lord?

Commotion.

LANRE and ROBERTSON dive under their chairs.

PAKIMI enters stricken.

LANRE: Pakimi what is it? Is it a coup?

PAKIMI: Sah, I have to go to *THE* bank, sah, please!

LANRE: Pakimi! Have you gone mad?

PAKIMI: *(Crazed.)* Please sah! *(On his knees, holds LANRE's feet.)* Please, sah! I must go to the bank!

LANRE: Today is Sunday!

PAKIMI: *(Grabs LANRE's briefcase. Drags LANRE along.)* You must help me get my money, sah! Please sah!

LANRE: I'm really sorry, Reverend! You are my guest. Stay for as long as you like.

LANRE and PAKIMI exit.

ROBERTSON sees a club member.

ROBERTSON: Chief Ogunbanjo! How are you, sir? *(Goes to him.)*

SCENE EIGHT

That evening. The Adeyemi sitting room. HELEN and AFOLABI put up birthday decorations. YINKA and SOJI are watching the Nigerian video film. SOJI is unimpressed. YINKA is into it.

VIDEO: To God be the glory. Stay tuned for Part Two. *(Music.)*

SOJI: Jesus Christ. That was crap.

YINKA: It's all right man. *(Changes the video.)*

SOJI: Hey put on *Rambo*.

YINKA: Shush! Part Two is about to start.

SOJI removes the video from the video player.

YINKA: Soji! Leave it in there!

They tussle with each other. They bump into AFOLABI.

AFOLABI: *Oya*! Watch it upstairs and allow us to finish.

YINKA switches off the TV, snatches the Nigerian video from SOJI and races upstairs.

SOJI: I'm not watching it, Yinka! *(Chases after YINKA.)*

HELEN puts on the television.

AFOLABI: Helen!

HELEN: Make we hear news now.

AFOLABI: If Madam catch you!

HELEN: No be the brothers lef am on?

AFOLABI: Kill the television.

HELEN ignores him. AFOLABI heads for the television.

HELEN: I go tell Madam say you touch the television.

AFOLABI: I don't know you are crafty like this.

HELEN: Government say we must be informed. I dey perform my duty as good citizen.

AFOLABI: Is 'Checkmate' you want to watch.

Music for Checkmate.

HELEN: *(Disappointed.)* Oh, e don finish.

AFOLABI: *(Chuckles.)* Is it not news you want to hear as a good citizen?

HELEN resumes decorating.

Music for the news comes on.

NEWSCASTER: Tonight's headline. The Federal Government closes Forum Bank.

HELEN: *(Shaken.)* Ehn?

AFOLABI: Hepa!

NEWSCASTER: …A government spokesman said the bank's dealings are under investigation. The bank's managing director had stolen the deposits prior to the police raid. His whereabouts are unknown…

AFOLABI: You see? I tell your man. He have throw his money away. God has catch him…

HELEN feels faint.

AFOLABI: Helen, are you OK?

A noise at the door. HELEN recovers and switches off the television.

LANRE and PAKIMI enter.

AFOLABI: Welcome sah!

LANRE: *(Wearily.)* Ehen. *(Goes upstairs.)*

AFOLABI: *(Sing.)* 'If you get money make you no laugh the people wey no get'.

PAKIMI: God punish you.

AFOLABI: You that the curse on your head have work, don't curse people, oh, in case the curse on your head still remain.

PAKIMI: *(Picks up the vase.)* I will smash this on your stupid head!

AFOLABI: If you damage that vase!

HELEN comes between them.

HELEN: Una don craze? *(Takes the vase away from Pakimi.)* Mr Afolabi, make you dey go. I go finish the remaining. *Oya*!

AFOLABI: *(Exits, singing.)* 'If you get money, make you no laugh the people wey no get…'

PAKIMI: You heard the news.

HELEN: Any money remain?

PAKIMI: No.

HELEN: At all?

PAKIMI: I promise, before the end of this year… *(Holds her.)*

    HELEN disengages from him.

HELEN: See the time. You no go see transport go your house.

PAKIMI: Helen…

    HELEN ignores him and decorates the house. Tears stream down her face.

    PAKIMI exits.

    YINKA comes downstairs. He grabs HELEN by the waist.

YINKA: Everyone's asleep. *(Tries to kiss her.)* Are you crying?

HELEN: *(Dries her eyes.)* Na pepper.

YINKA: Come. *(Leads her upstairs.)*

HELEN: I get headache.

YINKA: When I hit you with my double barrel/

HELEN: I no dey joke.

YINKA: I see your game. That's cool. *(Brings out money.)*

HELEN: I no be harlot.

YINKA: OK then what do you want?

HELEN: I wan' my freedom. I wan' future.

YINKA: Is that all? *(Offers his hand.)*

    HELEN hesitates.

    She looks guiltily at the door through which PAKIMI has exited.

YINKA: Suit yourself. *(Heads upstairs.)*

HELEN: Wait!

    HELEN puts up the last decoration and goes with YINKA.

SCENE NINE

The following day. The sitting room.

LANRE and TOYIN reading through the birthday cards.

TOYIN: First Mrs Okomile invites herself and now Reverend Robertson?

LANRE: This card's from 'Bidemi: 'To my darling sister. Wishing you another fifty glorious years'. You must have sent her money. A pity she didn't marry someone like me.

TOYIN: Helen!

LANRE: No. We are having breakfast in the garden.

TOYIN: Thanks.

LANRE: For what?

TOYIN: For keeping to your word.

LANRE: If you want to ruin this moment/

TOYIN: *(Passionately.)* You don't know how much it means to me. My husband.

TOYIN leads LANRE out by the hand.

LANRE: *(Points to upstairs.)* We're going the wrong way.

TOYIN hits him playfully.

AFOLABI enters. LANRE gives him money.

AFOLABI: *(Stunned by the amount, salutes.)* Sah!

AFOLABI leads LANRE and TOYIN through the kitchen. TOYIN leaves her handbag behind.

SOJI and YINKA come downstairs.

SOJI: But you said you had money.

YINKA: And now I don't have any.

SOJI: We can't just give her a card and kisses.

YINKA sees TOYIN's handbag. He opens it.

SOJI: Bobo![42]

YINKA: She won't know anything's missing. *(Holds up a wad of cash.)* How much? Quick!

SOJI: You took Mum's bracelet.

YINKA: Maria took it. They found it on her.

SOJI: Then why did she say that you gave it to her?

YINKA: You're the only one who believes her. Shows what a brother you are.

SOJI keeps his gaze on YINKA.

YINKA: What? Mum would have sacked her anyway.

SOJI: Jesus Christ, Yinka! She spent two weeks in a police cell.

YINKA: She got what she deserved. Who the hell is she?

---

42   Mate!

SOJI: Are you going to give Helen a bracelet too? I know about you two.

YINKA: So what if you know? You're going to tell? And stop looking disgusted! You, 'Che Guevara', you wouldn't dream of doing it with Helen.

SOJI: I wouldn't take advantage of her.

YINKA: Half the guys in my dorm lost their cherries to their house-girls. Guys will be hailing me, you stupid virgin.

SOJI: I'll tell your old friends.

YINKA: I don't care about them anymore.

SOJI: What if I tell your hostel mates that you only just became a 'man'?

YINKA shoves SOJI onto the sofa. He holds SOJI by the neck.

Soji: Yinka!

YINKA: Tell and I'll beat you so bad, Mum won't recognise you.

SOJI: I was joking!

YINKA lets go.

SOJI: What is wrong with you, man? You're behaving like a thug.

YINKA: You wouldn't last one second in my dorm. Talk according to your muscle. That's the law. Any guy can chance me out of my dinner because he's bigger than me. Dad can pay their parents' salary but who gives a damn that I'm Chief Adeyemi's son? So I do all I can to become a happening guy. Just as I'm about to be accepted what does your old man do? He impregnates the school cook. The school cook!

SOJI: You told Mum about his visits to Odogbolu on purpose.

YINKA: The last time he visits me I beg him to transfer me to another school. You know what he tells me? 'You shouldn't have slapped General Abubakar's son.'

SOJI: You could have at least waited until after her birthday.

YINKA: What difference has it made? If he's not sleeping around, he's… I don't know how you can stand it. I was glad to leave home until he came and messed me up.

SOJI: Don't lie. You miss being home.

YINKA: He's still doing it, isn't he? And she just takes it to keep face.

SOJI: Not for a while.

YINKA: Only because he wants her to take the Better Life job.

SOJI: That's not true. Since you left he hasn't/

YINKA: I saw Helen rubbing ointment on Mum's back.

SOJI looks away.

YINKA: It will stop. One day when she catches him in the act. Yeah. Then he'll be too ashamed to do anything. I want to be there looking him straight in the eye. I want to be there when she makes him pay.

SOJI: That's not his wallet.

YINKA puts the money back into TOYIN's handbag.

HELEN enters.

HELEN: Madam is calling you. She want her handbag.

YINKA: I've got it, babe.

SOJI looks at YINKA and exits.

YINKA takes some money and pockets it. He smacks HELEN on the bottom as he exits.

HELEN makes sure the coast is clear, brings out ONIJUJU's card and phones.

HELEN: Iya Onijuju… Yes, na me. Helen from Chief Adeyemi's house. About that love medicine…

End of Act One.

ACT TWO

SCENE ONE

The party in full flow. PAKIMI, HELEN and AFOLABI serve the guests. HELEN is sprayed by the rich guests. PAKIMI rushes over to the guests but they ignore him. Even AFOLABI is given a few notes. LANRE and TOYIN dance to Sunny Ade's 'Congratulations (Happy Birthday)'. The music changes to Nico Mbarga's 'Sweet Mother'. LANRE relinquishes TOYIN to YINKA and SOJI. LANRE dances sexily with MRS OKOMILE. TOYIN watches them concernedly as she receives well wishers. HELEN ushers in Reverend BILLY ROBERTSON. ROBERTSON greets TOYIN. HELEN pockets money from a guest. ROBERTSON approaches LANRE. MRS OKOMILE waits. LANRE signals to her that he will catch up with her later.

ROBERTSON: It's a wonderful party Chief.

LANRE: Thank you.

ROBERTSON: As a present to you and Madam, I am awarding you the contract.

LANRE: You're not going with Dayo Cole?

ROBERTSON: The house of God deserves only the best.

LANRE: *(Pumps his hand.)* See you in service, Reverend!

SOJI enters.

ROBERTSON: Bring your sons. I'm sure they will love it.

LANRE: Soji! Have you said hello to Reverend Robertson?

SOJI: Hi.

LANRE: 'Hi'. Is that how to greet?

ROBERTSON: Don't worry Chief. It is how the young people talk.

LANRE: He is a bloody atheist. If you can covert him to Christ I will make sure he joins your church for good.

AFOLABI enters.

AFOLABI: Sah, General Abubakar is here.

LANRE: One moment, Reverend. *(Exits with AFOLABI.)*

ROBERTSON: When you come to my service/

SOJI: We worship at St. Paul's.

ROBERTSON: Try us one Sunday. You'll be surprised what miracle awaits you.

SOJI: You mean your so-called miracles.

ROBERTSON: Excuse me?

SOJI: And your sermons. You preach that poverty is ordained from on high. You tell people that prayer is the only solution. How is that going to save Nigeria?

ROBERTSON: Anyone who places faith in their own strength is doomed to failure. Not by your own might. Only God can save Nigeria.

SOJI: And how long is he going to take? Or are we not a priority for the God of Israel?

ROBERTSON: Life's mysteries can only be revealed through divine revelation. And it is good that a young man like you is asking questions. For it is only if you seek that you will find. Most of our members are young people like you.

SOJI: Oh yeah. I've heard about your 'love feasts' that you use to bribe hungry students. That's your way of catching them young.

ROBERTSON: I do not bribe them. I entice them away from their usual vices.

SOJI: Sounds like a bribe to me.

ROBERTSON: The choice was theirs to join my church. In fact most of them stay with us long after they graduate.

SOJI: I wonder how many of them leave when they see how many times you pass round the collection bucket.

ROBERTSON: God loves a cheerful giver.

SOJI: He has to, to keep you this well-dressed.

ROBERTSON: My God is not a poor God. Would you prefer that I wear sackcloth?

SOJI: And I suppose he spoke to you in a vision that you must own four limousines?

ROBERTSON: Should I reject my Lord's blessings?

SOJI: Why does he choose to reward you so richly when majority of your flock are suffering? You're not blind to the tragedies that pass you on the street. You're no better than the soldiers who keep us in bondage with their guns. You do it with false promises. You're nothing but a 'Brother Jero'.

ROBERTSON: You who have never known poverty, you want to preach to me. I was roaming the streets hungry while your father and his friends were eating the national cake like there was no tomorrow.

SOJI: So you've come for your share.

ROBERTSON: I'm just a man trying to make it in this world like everybody else.

SOJI: By selling your people to a foreign god.

ROBERTSON: *(Grabs SOJI by the neck.)* And how did your father make his money? Was it not on the back of import license? Even candles he brought in. Anyone who made products locally he made sure he ruined that person. My father grew rice but your kind treated it like it was poison. You ate only 'Uncle Ben's'. This house, I bet you not one thing is made in this country and you want to prove to me, you this bloody *aje* butter. *(Throttles SOJI.)* I will…

LANRE enters. ROBERTSON pretends to pray for him.

ROBERTSON: Father, heal my brother of his unbelief!

SOJI: Ah! Dad!

LANRE: Reverend. It will take more than that to convert him.

ROBERTSON: *(Whacks SOJI.)* Believe!

SOJI: Yah!

LANRE: Ehen! That's right!

ROBERTSON: *(Whacks SOJI.)* Believe! BELIEVE!

SOJI: *(Manages to break free.)* Jesus Christ!

LANRE: Reverend! You have saved my son. Thank you. Thank you so much.

ROBERTSON: Thank the Lord of Abraham, Jacob and Isaac. Amen!

LANRE: Amen! Thank you, Reverend.

ROBERTSON: See you on Sunday, Soji.

LANRE: He will be there!

ROBERTSON exits.

LANRE: Have you said hello to General Abubakar?

SOJI looks away.

LANRE: Outside. Now.

LANRE shoves SOJI ahead of him. HELEN passes them by with a tray. She checks to see they are out of sight and that no one else is around. She brings out ONIJUJU's powder. She is about to powder her face when she hears people approaching. She dashes into the toilet.

TOYIN and MRS OKOMILE enter with LANRE.

MRS OKOMILE: Your party has really done our mother proud.

LANRE: What else can we do? My birthday girl has a pleasant surprise for you.

TOYIN: I hope you haven't touched the pounded yam.

LANRE: Actually, I was just about to go before I saw you. *(Pretends to go to the toilet.)*

TOYIN: Baba Yinka…

LANRE: *(Laughs.)* Okay, I'm going. *(Exits to outside.)*

TOYIN: Thank you for your gift.

MRS OKOMILE: Only the best jewellery is good enough for our mother. The First Lady sends her greetings. She is away on official trip to Switzerland along with the other governor's wives. If not we would have all been here in full force. She is getting you the finest damask for your present. That is in addition to a special gift from each of the governor's wives.

TOYIN: This Better Life is giving better life to some of us.

MRS OKOMILE: Once you become chairwoman, you will see how the benefits trickle down to our rural sisters. But most important, you and Chief will get what you want.

TOYIN: Which is?

MRS OKOMILE: Oh come on, Ma. That is like me telling you your business.

TOYIN: No, please, tell me.

MRS OKOMILE: After all it is you civilians who taught the soldiers how to… Don't mind me, Ma. I'm talking rubbish. It's my euphoria at you accepting the post. It is for you to administer the programme as you please. When I present you to the First Lady, it will be the best birthday gift she has ever had.

TOYIN: Did I tell you that I had accepted the post?

MRS OKOMILE: I don't understand you, Ma.

TOYIN: I put it very clearly.

MRS OKOMILE: So what are you saying, Ma?

TOYIN: What do you think I'm saying?

MRS OKOMILE: You'd rather be the secretary of the Women's Society than the Better Life chairperson?

TOYIN: Do you think I would have ever considered otherwise?

MRS OKOMILE: You have put me in a situation with the First Lady! Chief said you would accept the post.

TOYIN: Did he tell you that while you were sleeping with him?

MRS OKOMILE: Ess, Ma!

TOYIN: You walk into my house fooling around with my husband.

MRS OKOMILE: Please Ma, I've never/

TOYIN: Then you tell me that I'm going to be a present to a girl whom I'm old enough to be her mother. Tell her and tell your cohorts that I want nothing to do with you. Now get out of my house.

MRS OKOMILE heads for the door.

TOYIN: *Ashewo.*[43]

MRS OKOMILE: *(Stops. Turns round.)* I remember my first day at school, how you humiliated me in front of morning assembly, all because I did not wear the correct shoes. My parents worked day and night just to sew my uniform. They could not afford the sandals. You held me up as a 'shining example' of '*awon omo*[44] free education', and how we were going to destroy the school with our *alatika*[45]

43   Harlot.
44   the children of
45   common

behaviour. I was not surprised you retired after the last set of your 'true grammerians' passed out. You couldn't stand the sight of us. Now we are in power and you still hold us in contempt.

TOYIN: Afolabi! Pakimi!

MRS OKOMILE: As for Chief: a man lives by the river yet he goes everywhere in search of water to drink.

TOYIN: How dare you! *(Raises her hand.)*

MRS OKOMILE: We are no more in school. If you slap me I will slap you back. I will so disgrace you in your life you will never forget it. Nonsense. *(Exits.)*

LANRE enters, laughing.

LANRE: Mrs Okomile! Has my wife... Mrs Okomile! *(Looks at TOYIN in askance.)*

TOYIN: Remember what today is and behave yourself. I want to dance with my husband. *(Exits.)*

LANRE is bewildered.

TOYIN: Lanre!

LANRE exits after TOYIN.

HELEN enters from toilet, shocked by what she has heard. She has powdered her face white. She picks up her tray and exits.

The music changes to Fela's 'Zombie'.

PAKIMI and AFOLABI. AFOLABI whistles 'Money good oh' as he counts money.

PAKIMI: These useless rich people. They are only spraying women. *(Makes to take some of AFOLABI's money.)*

AFOLABI: *Kai*!

PAKIMI: Just ten naira now.

AFOLABI: Go and find your own.

PAKIMI sees a head-tie and wraps it round his head.

AFOLABI: What nonsense are you doing now?

PAKIMI picks up a wrapper and ties it round his waist.

Afolabi: *Osi.*[46]

PAKIMI enters the toilet. He leaves the door open.

_____
46   Foolishness.

PAKIMI: Ah see. *(Shows AFOLABI the powder.)* Someone left talcum powder here. This is a sign from God. *(Applies the powder.)* I beg check the sitting room, maybe someone dropped lipstick.

AFOLABI: *Wayo* has turn your head because of woman.

PAKIMI: How much is in your hand that you are making noise? Ikililu is there waiting for you to do your job, you dey do *su egbe*[47]. You'd better find how you will get real money before he dies. Correct *ni mo so fun e.*[48]

AFOLABI: Plus the money Chief give me. It will reach.

PAKIMI: Naira is now five to one. That medicine of ten naira is now double. What will you tell Ikililu next week when naira is six to one? Idiot.

AFOLABI: You are idiot to tell me that/

PAKIMI: Go and serve the guests! Servant.

AFOLABI: Who are you calling servant?

They square up to each other. A rich drunk guest enters. PAKIMI saunters up to him and dances, shaking his bottom. The guest sprays PAKIMI with money. PAKIMI bends down to pick up the money. Aroused, the guest grabs PAKIMI's bottom. PAKIMI pushes him away. The guest is insistent, hands all over PAKIMI. He throws PAKIMI onto the sofa and lays on top of him. PAKIMI shrieks. The guest pulls off PAKIMI's head-tie.

GUEST: *(Realises PAKIMI is a man, jumps off PAKIMI.)* Ehn? A lady man! Oh my God! A lady man!

PAKIMI dashes out, chased after by the GUEST. AFOLABI gathers the money and pockets it. He exits.

YINKA shoves SOJI into the room.

SOJI: Don't shove me! Why is everyone treating me like a kid?

YINKA: You think it is funny changing the music? You should have seen the look on General Abubakar's face.

SOJI: I did it for you! He won't give Dad his license back so why is that zombie and his son here?

YINKA: You did it for K. K. Folarin. You heard that he'd arrived.

47   You're behaving like a moron.
48   I'm telling you the right thing.

SOJI: K. K. Folarin is here?

YINKA: Liar.

SOJI: I swear I didn't know.

K.K. FOLARIN enters wearing a lavish agbada. SOJI is struck dumb.

FOLARIN: Please, where is the toilet?

YINKA points to the toilet. SOJI stares at K. K. FOLARIN in shock.

FOLARIN: Thank you. *(Exits to the toilet.)*

YINKA: He's wearing it out of respect for Mum. We've got to wrap up Mum's present.

SOJI: You do it.

YINKA: Come on. *(Pulls him.)*

SOJI: *(Breaks free.)* Let go of me!

K. K. FOLARIN comes out of the toilet.

SOJI: Mr Folarin?

FOLARIN: Yes?

SOJI: I'm sorry. I wasn't sure it was you.

FOLARIN: Oh. *(Holds up his agbada, laughs.)* I suppose you've never seen me out of my khaki and shorts. This is the first time since I was a child that I've worn one. It's certainly the most expensive.

SOJI: But you're wearing it out of respect for our mother.

FOLARIN: Oh, you're Toyin's boys. Lovely to meet you.

FOLARIN shakes YINKA's hand. He offers his hand to SOJI. SOJI does not take his hand.

FOLARIN: It will be announced tomorrow so I might as well. I've been appointed Chairman of the Taskforce for Rice Importation and Distribution.

SOJI: What?

FOLARIN: Quite a mouthful, isn't it?

SOJI: But who is going to fight for the people?

FOLARIN: There are many ways to skin a cat.

SOJI: But you're joining them. The enemy of the people.

FOLARIN: If I didn't accept this post some corrupt bastard would take it. I can be a paradigm of good leadership. I met with Mr President and he spoke sense. He's a very intelligent man. He has great plans for the country. He needs people like me to help initiate them.

SOJI: But they are soldiers! Anyone who colludes with them is a traitor.

FOLARIN: They are human beings like us. Young man, we have a crisis of followership. You know how much I've sacrificed for this country, only to be betrayed by my own people, and for how much? I'm not giving up the struggle. I'm engaging constructively with this government. I say to you, keep up the fight. *Aluta continua. (Forcefully shakes SOJI's hand and raises his arm in a black power salute. He heads for the door, has one look at SOJI, then exits.)*

SOJI's arm falls to his side.

YINKA: Forget him, man. Come on, Mum's bracelet. Before she cuts her cake.

HELEN enters with a tray. She smiles seductively at YINKA.

YINKA: You're in no mood to be wrapping presents. I'll do it myself. *(Pushes SOJI out. To HELEN.)* I'm digging this your powder.

HELEN starts blinking at him.

YINKA: Have you got something in your eyes?

HELEN: Pick di duster, begin dust.

YINKA: What?

HELEN: Pick di duster.

YINKA: Have you gone crazy?

HELEN: You will marry me.

YINKA: *(Bursts out laughing.)* You didn't really believe me, did you?

HELEN: But you talk say you go look after me/

YINKA: You're funny oh. *(Laughs.)*

HELEN: *(Dawns on her that YINKA has strung her along. She tries to compose herself with as much dignity as she can muster.)* Of course I know say you dey joke now. I know my level.

YINKA: Good. *(Waves money at her.)* Dance for me.

HELEN dances unenthusiastically.

YINKA: What is this lady dance? Give me fire dance. Wait.

YINKA turns on the radio to Wasiu Ayinde's 'Bobo No Go Die Unless To Ba D'arugbo'.

YINKA: This is your kind of music, isn't it?

HELEN continues dancing without enthusiasm.

YINKA sprays her with a few notes.

At the sight of the money HELEN picks up the rhythm.

LANRE enters, his face like thunder. He watches HELEN. YINKA sees him and stops dancing. LANRE signals to YINKA to leave. YINKA exits. HELEN oblivious continues dancing. She bumps into LANRE.

HELEN: Ah! Sorry sah. *(Hurriedly picks up her tray.)*

LANRE: Put it down.

HELEN: Sah?

LANRE points to the table. HELEN puts down the tray.

LANRE: Continue.

HELEN: Sah?

LANRE: Dance!

HELEN dances. A noise from outside. LANRE turns round. No one comes in. He takes HELEN by the hand and leads her upstairs. They are on the landing about to enter to the bedrooms. HELEN breaks free of LANRE. They stand underneath TOYIN's portrait.

HELEN: Please, sah. *(Looks at the portrait.)*

LANRE: *(Smiles at HELEN. Looks at Toyin's portrait. Caresses HELEN's hand and leads her into the bedroom offstage.)*

PAKIMI dashes through the house, chased by GUEST.

GUEST: Did you see him? A lady-man! Oh my God.

They exit.

TOYIN, YINKA, and SOJI enter with TOYIN's birthday cake.

Ebenezer Obey's 'Happy Birthday' plays in the background.

TOYIN: Where is your father? *Oya*, somebody find my husband.

PAKIMI dashes in.

TOYIN: Check if Chief is still outside.

PAKIMI: Yes Ma. *(Goes back out, dashes back in and exits in the opposite direction.)*

GUEST: *(Off.)* I saw him here right now. A lady-man!

TOYIN: These candles will go out, ehn? *(To YINKA.)* Go and check if he's upstairs.

YINKA hesitates.

TOYIN: Quick! Or do I have to go up myself.

YINKA goes upstairs. He comes down and heads straight out the door.

TOYIN: Yinka!

TOYIN heads for the bedroom. As she is on the landing LANRE and HELEN come out of the bedroom. HELEN tries to cover up her dishevelled look.

PAKIMI enters.

PAKIMI: Madam, Chief is not outside…

He sees HELEN and LANRE and is stunned.

SCENE TWO

The sitting room. The party is over. The birthday decorations are still in place. YINKA is by the foot of the stairs looking up attentively. SOJI watches.

SOJI: Can you hear anything?

YINKA: Sh! *(Goes up. Hears a noise and scuttles down backstairs. Confidently.)* You will see. She is going to make him pay.

SOJI: Oh yeah. He's going to pay this time. Just like all the other times.

YINKA loses some of his confidence. He picks up the phone.

SOJI: What are you doing? Yinka!

YINKA: *(Dials.)* I'm calling Uncle Kunle.

SOJI: *(Grabs hold of the phone.)* Don't call him! He'll make things worse.

YINKA: He'll make things worse for him. Let go!

They tussle over the phone.

HELEN enters with a broom.

YINKA: You bitch. You're still here?

YINKA lunges at her. SOJI holds him back.

HELEN exits.

YINKA: Come back here, let me kill you!

SOJI: This is what you wanted, isn't it? You wanted Mum to catch him in the act.

YINKA: I'll kill her. I swear to God I'll kill her.

SOJI: You went after her first!

YINKA: You're saying I planned this?

SOJI: Go back to Odogbolu!

YINKA: Shut up!

SOJI: Like father like son!

YINKA: *(Grabs SOJI by the neck.)* You and your stupid revolution! You gave her the wings! Where were you for Mum?

They struggle violently with each other.

TOYIN comes downstairs with a suitcase.

TOYIN: Stop that right now!

They stop fighting. They see her suitcase.

TOYIN: Never lay a finger on each other again. Do you hear me? You must be each other's keeper.

SOJI: You can't leave, Mum.

TOYIN: I'll be at your Uncle Kunle's in Ikeja. You can visit me anytime.

YINKA: *(Grabs her suitcase.)* This is your home! He should go!

TOYIN: Yinka, let go.

YINKA: You can't leave!

TOYIN: You are the best sons I could ever wish for.

SOJI: Then stay. Who should we call to help?

TOYIN: Hasn't your father broadcast my shame enough?

YINKA: You can't let him get away with it. He has to pay.

TOYIN: It's a man's world.

SOJI: You don't believe that, Mum.

TOYIN: Ah, well…

SOJI: You don't believe that!

TOYIN: I brought you up well. You will not turn out to be like your father.

SOJI: You can't leave us here.

YINKA: I'm coming with you.

TOYIN: You think I don't want you to come with me? I know your father. He will bring in another woman. It will be someone respectable. He can keep up appearances with his peers. No woman's child is going to claim their rights over you. This is your house. You must stay.

TOYIN prises her suitcase away from YINKA. SOJI grabs it.

TOYIN: *(Weeps.)* My boys. My boys. *(She hugs them.)*

The brothers weep.

LANRE comes downstairs. He stops when he sees TOYIN.

LANRE: *(To the brothers.)* Go upstairs.

The brothers stay where they are.

LANRE: Are you deaf? I say go upstairs!

The brothers stare at him defiantly. LANRE grabs the horsewhip from under the sofa.

TOYIN: *(Drops her suitcase.)* Touch my sons and both of us will die in this house today.

LANRE lowers the horsewhip.

TOYIN: Go upstairs.

Slowly, showing defiance to their father, the brothers go upstairs.

LANRE: They are the children of their mother.

TOYIN: Thank God for that.

LANRE: I don't want us to fight.

TOYIN: I was on my way.

LANRE: If you hadn't curtailed my movements this would never have happened.

TOYIN: That's your excuse for sleeping with my house girl on our matrimonial bed on my birthday?

LANRE: That bed lost its meaning the day you moved into your own room.

TOYIN: So it is my fault that you have lost all sense of shame.

LANRE: You know the kind of man I am.

TOYIN: You know the kind of woman I am. I let you sleep around behind my back. I let you buy flats and houses for those stray cats. I turned a blind eye after the first harlot. I realised that screaming at you would only give me hypertension. After Odogbolu I sincerely thought you would come to your senses. I asked you to sheath your penis just for a few days. But your shame has no limit when it comes to parading your wrinkly skin in front of girls old enough to be your grand-daughter.

LANRE: Who made my skin wrinkly? Was it not you with your pettiness? We must be the only people in Lagos who go to parties on full stomachs. For some stupid decorum that no one notices. When you are in the midst of dancers does it make sense to stand still?

TOYIN: Only people of integrity quote proverbs.

LANRE: Here we go! Put down after put down. Lanre, don't be bush. Lanre, don't be coarse. Lanre, that is conduct unbecoming of a gentlemen. I'm surprised we still eat *amala* with our fingers.

TOYIN: You really have no regrets for what you did.

LANRE: You said it already. I have no shame.

TOYIN: Indeed. *(Picks up her suitcase. Heads for the door.)*

LANRE: You should have taken the Better Life job.

TOYIN drops her suitcase. She claps her hands in amazement.

LANRE: Yes! I moved heaven and earth to get you that job.

TOYIN: A job you didn't consult me on. You treated me like I was a piece of meat that you could sell to them of all people.

LANRE: I did it for the family! I do a lot of things I do not like but I do it for the family.

TOYIN: I gave up my job for the family! I spared us the indignity of one day catching you sleeping with one of my students.

LANRE: Oh please!

TOYIN: I saw the way you looked at them whenever you came to visit me. Why you insisted on coming to pick me up when you could have sent the driver.

LANRE: I would have never touched those girls and you know it!

TOYIN: Not the daughters of your associates. But those free education girls, those girls were easy meat for you. 'Bush meat', isn't that what you call them? They were much more your taste.

LANRE: These people that you have such contempt for, they are in charge. I say it every day but you live in your own world.

TOYIN: You brought them into my life.

LANRE: They hold the purse strings! They build a factory in their village whether it makes sense or not. They give by who can kiss their feet or bribe them the most. They award themselves contracts through the backdoor. The rest of us are rats fighting for the crumbs that fall from their mouths. I am a beggar like everyone else. The Better Life job was my seat at the table. My name is founded on money. Without it I am nothing.

TOYIN: Your name is founded on money. Mine isn't.

LANRE: How would you afford your precious dignity?

TOYIN: You took away my dignity when you slept with my house girl.

LANRE: That is what hurts you. That I slept with Helen.

TOYIN: You slept with her in my house!

LANRE: We are going in circles. *(Heads for the stairs.)*

TOYIN: *(Goes after him.)* If not for the boys I would not have put up with you for this long!

LANRE: You should have gone! It wouldn't have made any difference.

TOYIN: Kunle said I shouldn't marry a loose and uncouth man like you. He knew that I couldn't tame you.

LANRE: I look like an animal you can tame? That is your family all over. They never respected me.

TOYIN: I should have listened to them.

LANRE: That makes two of us! I overheard your father and brother say that you had married beneath your station, that you would suffer because I would not amount to much. Of course I overheard them. They said it to my face on our wedding day!

TOYIN: Is that why you were always beating me? You were getting your own back on them.

LANRE: Yes! And what could they do about it? Nothing!

TOYIN: If not for the boys I should have dumped you the first time you hit me.

LANRE: I should have dumped you! You stayed because of the boys. I stayed full-stop! It's a wonder they cannot see you for the woman you are. A woman who will do anything for propriety even at the cost of pain to herself. Any woman with self-respect would have left!

TOYIN: I stayed because I loved you!

LANRE: Ha! Did you really love me?

TOYIN: I loved you!

LANRE: Do you really love those boys? I don't see them with you. But of course they must not leave their father's house. It wouldn't be proper.

TOYIN heads for upstairs. LANRE bars her way.

LANRE: Where do you think you are going?

TOYIN tries to push through. LANRE stands his ground.

TOYIN: Yinka! Soji!

LANRE: You are not taking my sons.

TOYIN: If you think I'm leaving them with you, my name is not Toyin Ogundele.

LANRE: They are not Ogundeles. They are Adeyemis.

The boys come downstairs.

TOYIN: Pack your bags.

LANRE: Stay where you are.

TOYIN: I said pack your bags!

LANRE: If you move! *(To TOYIN.)* You had your chance to leave with your head held high. If you don't get out of my house I will throw you out.

TOYIN: I dare you.

YINKA: Mum…

LANRE: Toyin, I will not tell you again!

YINKA and SOJI are in anguish at the scene.

SOJI: Mum, please…

TOYIN: *(Ties her head scarf round her waist.)* What will you do? You useless petty brute!

LANRE: Tell this woman!

TOYIN: What will you do? You will beat me again?

LANRE slaps TOYIN and in an attempt to drag her through the door pulls her jumper off. Her back is a mass of old scars. He drags her out by her hair. He picks up her suitcase and throws it out and rages after her.

YINKA: Mum!

SOJI: Mum!

LANRE enters. He stands by the door.

LANRE: Don't you ever step foot in this house! You or your bloody brother! I will kill you and I will kill him! I am Chief Olanrewaju Adeyemi. There is nothing any of you can do to me! Nothing! I am the man of this house!

The boys look on in horror.

LANRE: Get to your rooms!

They stand still.

LANRE charges at them. The brothers run upstairs and exit. LANRE comes downstairs. AFOLABI enters, shocked, in askance.

LANRE: If she sets foot on my estate you are fired!

AFOLABI tries to appeal.

LANRE: What?

AFOLABI: *(Quietly, almost choking.)* Yes sah.

LANRE: Lock the gate. Then call Helen.

AFOLABI exits.

LANRE puts on the TV. The voice of BILLY ROBERTSON. PAKIMI enters. He puts the keys on the table. As he heads towards the kitchen door he stops and listens.

ROBERTSON: *(Voice only.)* Only God can save Nigeria. Those of you who toil in vain, seeking a way out. Those of you who seek solutions to life's up and downs, there is only one way. There is only one path to prosperity and you can achieve it through Jesus Christ our Lord. It doesn't matter if you are rich or poor. It doesn't matter your circumstances. Call on Jesus, accept him into your life. This is a time of abundance for believers. All you have to do is kneel down and pray to Jesus. Kneel down and accept Jesus into your life. Kneel! Kneel! Kneel!

PAKIMI kneels down and prays fervently.

HELEN enters. She sees PAKIMI and stops. LANRE beckons to her to join him on the sofa. HELEN sits beside LANRE. She is timid at first. Slowly, she eases into the confidence of the lady of the house. She crosses her legs.

HELEN: *(Authoritatively.)* Afolabi!

AFOLABI: *(Off.)* Ma!

The End.

OTHER OLADIPO AGBOLUAJE TITLES

The Estate
9781840026535

Iya-Ile (The First Wife)
9781840029253

The Christ of Coldharbour Lane
9781840027853

The Hounding of David Oluwale
9781840029024

WWW.OBERONBOOKS.COM

Follow us on www.twitter.com/@oberonbooks
& www.facebook.com/oberonbook